Edited by Valerie Mendenhall Cohen

# Woman
## *on the*
# Rocks

## The Mountaineering Letters of Ruth Dyar Mendenhall

INTRODUCTION BY ROYAL ROBBINS

2011 Centennial Celebration

Celebrating the 100th anniversary
of the Angeles Chapter, Sierra Club
www.SpottedDogPress.com

*Ruth Dyar rappelling at Stoney Point, Chatsworth, California, 1930s*

Edited by Valerie Mendenhall Cohen

# Woman
## *on the*
# Rocks

## The Mountaineering Letters
## of Ruth Dyar Mendenhall

INTRODUCTION BY ROYAL ROBBINS

SPOTTED
DOG PRESS.

# Woman on the Rocks
*The Mountaineering Letters of Ruth Dyar Mendenhall*

©2006 Valerie Mendenhall Cohen
All rights reserved.
Published exclusively by Spotted Dog Press, Inc.
Bishop, California
WWW.SPOTTEDDOGPRESS.COM

**SPOTTED DOG PRESS**

To contact us:
Spotted Dog Press, Inc.
PO Box 1721, Bishop CA 93515-1721
Toll-free: 800-417-2790
Email: wbenti@spotteddogpress.com

Spotted Dog Press, Inc.
ISBN 1893343154
First Edition 2007

Library of Congress Cataloging-in-Publication Data

Cohen, Valerie Mendenhall, 1946-
 Woman on the rocks : the mountaineering letters of Ruth Dyar Mendenhall / by Valerie Mendenhall Cohen ; introduction by Royal Robbins. -- 1st ed.
    p. cm
 Includes index.
 ISBN 1-893343-15-4 (alk. paper)
 1. Mendenhall, Ruth. 2. Women mountaineers--United States--Biography. I. Title.

GV199.92.M44C64 2007
796.522092--dc22
[B]

                              2007007562


                                                    CIP

Printed in the United States of America

For Michael

# Epigraph

∞

*East Face Lake, Mount Whitney, September 4, 1938*

It was quite the strangest place I have ever been. It was like some entirely different element, as one's first airplane flight above a sea of clouds. It was much more like one's imagined conception of the bare plains of Tibet, than any place one has ever *been* or thought of being. It was 4:00 o'clock. The sun had disappeared behind the incredibly jagged line of Mt. Whitney and the tremendous pinnacles to its south. The entire skyline was a tremendous circle of gray colorless jack-o-lantern teeth. There was *nothing* but colorless rock. After all the climbing, it was odd to be walking on the level, across a gravelly boulder-strewn mesa, not a growing thing but a few gray tufts of puny grass with a strange black plume. Presently over the edge of the tableland appeared the small green circle of East Face Lake, cold and still and green except for a rind of perpetual snow on three sides, with the rocky land rising quietly and abruptly out of the clear water. I have never been in a place so tremendously quiet—not a single breath or sound or living thing.

*Ruth Dyar*

# Contents

# Acknowledgments

The History Committee of the Angeles Chapter of the Sierra Club, and in particular, late committee member Muir Dawson, provided great encouragement throughout this project. My mother's old friends Glen Dawson and Ellen Wilts cheered me on, as did Malinda Chouinard. Generous financial support for typing and copying expenses came from Nick Clinch, and from the Sierra Club's Friends of the Angeles Chapter Foundation: Robert and Maureen Cates, Glen Dawson, Ellen Wilts, Dick Searle, and David Harris. My big sister, Vivian Mendenhall, and my cousins Renny Russell, Nancy Dyar, and DeDe Mendenhall, shared family lore and records. Scholarly advice was given by Richard White, Cheryll Glotfelty, Joanne O'Hare, Charlotte Dihoff, Lilace Guignard, Ginny Scharff, Dawn Marano, and Susan Wiggins. Don Lauria helped me with the facts. Members of the History Committee of the Angeles Chapter provided historical background information: Robert Cates, Glen Dawson, John G. Ripley, and John W. Robinson. The Alpine Club of Canada, Gary Vallé, Mark Goebel, the Callifornia Ski Library, the Eastern California Museum, the Angeles Chapter Archives and Wynne Benti gave me photographs. Vonnie J. Rosendahl and Vicki Joerz, working from Ruth's desperately illegible carbon copies, typed 900 pages of letters into word-processing files. My husband, the writer Michael P. Cohen, provided professional guidance, fixed my unremitting computer mistakes, and made certain that I went skiing all winter long. –V.M.C.

*Ruth leading at Tahquitz*

# Introduction
## Royal Robbins

Dear Valerie,

Thank you for asking me for an introduction to the book of mountaineering letters by your mother, Ruth Mendenhall. As you know, Ruth and John were both close to my heart. They were there at the beginning, back in 1950, when, in a burst of youthful enthusiasm, I joined the Rock Climbing Section of the Los Angeles Chapter of the Sierra Club. Of course, I was closer to John, having climbed with him at Tahquitz Rock and on other crags. John was my mentor and my hero–I wanted to be just like him. He was, as has been noted in the following pages, a true mountaineer and a true gentleman. And Ruth was always a true lady–feminine, light, a fine climber, and extremely intelligent. And, as this volume makes perfectly clear, she had a gift with words. When I received the manuscript I had intended to scan it in preparation for writing an introduction, but was surprised to find myself devouring every word! Not only of hers, but of yours too! Your writing, like your mother's, is graceful and illuminating. When you are discussing Ruth, you do so in affectionate terms, though you can't be accused of being your mother's toady, referring early in the book to her being "supercilious." I thought her comments (the ones that gave rise to your use of that adjective) about tourists and some of her fellow climbers to be quaint and amusing, but I don't come from your generation, so perhaps

*Royal Robbins, 1971*
*(Photo: Charles Raymond,*
*The La Siesta Press Collection)*

it looks different to me. In any case, I am so glad that you "decided that Ruth's lovely writing deserved to be published."

I always thought Ruth a charming person–kind, thoughtful, generous, and witty. And her mountaineering letters, starting back in the 1930's and continuing well into the 1980's, reflect her as being just that way. Of course I ate up the early stuff. There is so much magic in beginnings. Ruth captured it, nicely, with her keen observations of the mountain scene–the flowers, the downed timber, the rugged trails, the soaring peaks–and of the people involved in that scene. Then, as time went on, the beginnings disappeared, along with such happy coinages as "The scramble down was another fooey," but her writing got even better and more polished while never losing that immediacy which one finds more in letters than in books.

Ruth was a good climber–competent, experienced, and canny–but not a great one in the sense of leaving her mark on posterity through her first ascents. Nevertheless, besides her eloquence, as unquestionably as Half Dome rises above Yosemite Valley, she had the heart of a mountaineer. Only an eloquent lady with the heart of a mountaineer could leave us with such memorable phrases as "I don't know how people get along without climbing mountains." I've never heard it put better.

I hope your book has many and varied readers. Because that is what it deserves.

# A Note to the Reader:
# Editorial Methods

Historical documents reproduced in this book were chosen from among more than 900 pages of letters that Ruth Dyar Mendenhall wrote about her mountaineering experiences, over a span of 50 years. Full-length letters have been shortened from their original forms, by eliminating extraneous family chitchat, repetitions, and detailed descriptions of travel arrangements. The editor has opted for a clear-text edition, employing silent rather than overt techniques of emendation; spellings are regularized, and marginalia repositioned in order to preserve narrative continuity. Due care has been applied to preserving Mendenhall's personal language, punctuation, and syntax, not only in the complete letters, but in the shorter quotations that appear in each Chapter Introduction. All materials appear in chronological order. – V.M.C.

*Ruth Dyar with her skis, South Pasadena, California, 1937*

## Chapter One

# First Season, 1938

*In the meticulous account I kept in the 1930's,*
*I duly noted I came to California with $40 loaned*
*me by relatives and 25 cents of my own cash!*

RUTH DYAR

Ruth Eleanor Dyar, pioneer mountain climber, was born August 16, 1912, in the farming town of Kiesling, Washington, southeast of Spokane. Her family traced its ancestry back to Stephen Hopkins, whose first voyage to the New World aboard the ill-fated Sea Venture ended in shipwreck in Bermuda; the adventures of these castaways inspired Shakespeare's *The Tempest*. Hopkins later sailed on the Mayflower and helped to settle Plymouth Colony.

Ruth Dyar's father, Ralph Emerson Dyar, was an executive for eastern Washington's newspaper, *The Spokesman Review*. He wrote books about journalism, including *News for an Empire*. Ralph Dyar also wrote for stage and radio; his best-known play, "A Voice in the Dark," was produced on Broadway, and made into a silent film by Samuel Goldwyn. An accomplished fly-fisherman, Ralph Dyar spent his vacations fishing on the Little Moyie River in southern British Columbia.

Ruth's mother, Else Kiesling Dyar, was the youngest of twelve children in a German-speaking farming family. Ralph and Else Dyar had five children: Conrad, Ruth, Joan, Alice, and Margaret. The family described itself as "close-knit," although Ruth's long time climbing friend, Ellen Wilts, says, "I think Ruth was extremely intelligent and was reared in a New England environment. She found freedom from these stuffy ways when she moved to Southern California."

Home-schooled until the age of 14, Ruth attended high school in Spokane and graduated *magnum cum laude* in journalism from the University of Washington in 1934. That same year, the university's School of Journalism discontinued its practice of finding jobs for all its graduates and focused on only helping the male graduates break into the working world. Ruth had no choice but to move to Los Angeles, California, where she was hired as a secretary by her cousin's husband, a businessman named Max Lewis. She wrote to a college

*Ruth Dyar at age 4, 1916*
*Dyar family Christmas card with Ruth and her pony, "Pet," circa 1920*

*Ruth Dyar with "Nancy" in the Lucerne Valley, Southern California, 1935;*
*Portrait, early 1930s*

friend that she was homesick and wanted to return to school. Loneliness sometimes swept over her with, as she described, "the most horribly compelling forcefulness."

Although she lived with relatives, she wrote long letters to her parents and siblings in Spokane every week, making four or five carbon copies, a practice she continued until her mother's death in 1981. She saved the carbons of her letters, many of which told the stories of her mountaineering adventures.

Ruth's greatest ambition was to become a writer. She learned to type quickly on an Underwood manual typewriter that she used until the end of her life. "If I told practically anyone that I just sat down and dashed off nine pages, typewritten, single-spaced, of letters to my family, they'd think I was nuts."

Ruth first saw California's Sierra Nevada in April, 1937, before she ever heard of mountain climbing, and wrote, "the first time mountains actually caught my imagination as something besides scenery was when I saw the long East side of the High Sierra glittering under its April snow cover from Independence. I can recall daydreaming about what one might find there, without any actual expectation of going there."

The Sierra Nevada is 400 miles long (twice the length of the Rocky Mountains), 35 to 80 miles wide, and covers an area of 20,000 square miles. Its highest point, Mount Whitney, rises almost 10,000 feet above the Owens Valley. Steve Roper's *The Climber's Guide to the High Sierra* describes California's premier mountain range this way: "Bordered by a great agricultural area on one side and an inhospitable desert on the other, California's Sierra Nevada is the highest mountain range in the contiguous United States, and some say it is the most beautiful." Sierra Club mountaineers climbed most of the important new technical routes in the range, in the years before and after World War II.

Ruth and her cousin Phoebe Russell decided to join the Ski Mountaineers, a group which had formed in Southern California in 1934 and had built the San Antonio Ski Hut on the slopes of Mount Baldy outside Los Angeles. At that time, there were no ski lifts. Skiers had to carry their packs and equipment up the mountains to ski down them. Ruth and Phoebe thought that by joining the Ski Mountaineers, they might have fun and meet new people, so they attended their first meeting for "skiers and would-be skiers."

Skiers far outnumbered rock-climbers in Southern California. Both sports were inexpensive, and therefore attractive during the Great Depression.

Four months after joining the Ski Mountaineers, Ruth and her cousin Phoebe Russell became sole editors of the *Mugelnoos,* the bimonthly newsletter for the group. (The name is an Austrian-accented pun on the Norwegian word *mogul,* a mound of hard snow on a ski slope.) The *Mugelnoos* was the Sierra Club's very first Section or Chapter news sheet. It reported upcoming climbs, accidents, ski hut construction, political frays within the club, and climbing news from around the world, thus creating and maintaining important social links among the mountaineering community. Ruth loved to assemble news by phone and enjoyed the communal nature of the enterprise. "Phoebe had stolen a hymn book from the church because it had a wonderful rock climbing hymn about the 'rock which is higher than I.' They all sat down and sang hymns for hours. It was so lovely and I always have liked hymns. It was cute to see them there, on the floor of the mountaineerish and untidy Mugelnoos office, earnestly singing hymns–Carl with his shining reddish hair and

*Ruth Dyar and pickup truck, Lucerne Valley, 1937;*
*having just earned her American Red Cross life saving emblem, 1934.*

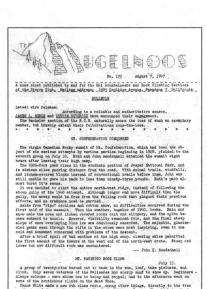

The Mugelnoos, August 7, 1971

deep voice; Elsie, rosy sweet face, beautiful Swedish hair, and lovely high clear voice; Gatesey-lamb following Elsie; Joan and Phoebe. They sang and sang, harmonizing if you know what that is, I am not sure that I do, hymns and Christmas carols."

*Mugelnoos* work wasn't always fun. After editing the newsletter for a while, Ruth wrote, "I have had practice, luckily, in writing mugelcopy and cutting stencils when I was mentally out of the frame of mind. I suppose of the thirty-five or so Mugelnooses I have written, I haven't actually felt like it for more than five or six–I've always been too happy or too unhappy, or utterly exhausted and weary, or so sick I couldn't hold my head up, or there were things I'd so much rather have done, or something. Come to think of it, it is quite a wonder the way every Mugelnoos has come out on time–if I hadn't set myself a deadline and stuck to it, there would be no Mugelnoos now. The Northern Chapter paper, after about four months of publication, laid off for the entire summer." She continued her editorial supervision of the *Mugelnoos* for the next forty years, setting high standards for content, style, and tone.

There is a lot of sandstone and granite in Southern California, if you know where to look. In her first season with the Sierra Club, Ruth joined Ski Mountaineers' practice climbs every weekend at Eagle Rock, Stoney Point, Devil's Gate Dam, and Mount Pacifico. She went to Tahquitz Rock (also called Lily Rock) in the San Jacinto Mountains east of Los Angeles. In 1938, no more than ten routes had been climbed on Tahquitz, though by the 1980s there were more than one hundred.

In 1938, Ruth made her first trip to Yosemite Valley. The same year, she and her companions completed the first ascent of the Swiss Arete route on Mount Sill in the Palisades region of the Sierra Nevada. Though not extremely difficult, this route is still considered one of the classic technical climbs of the High Sierra.

During that summer Ruth made the first of her many climbs up Mount Whitney's precipitous East Face, where the difficulty of backpacking to the base of Mount Whitney impressed her much more than the climb itself. Her accomplishments were quite remarkable considering that only seven years earlier, alpine climbing techniques were introduced for the first time to California climbers by Robert Underhill, a well-known British climber visiting the States. Before that, according to Glen Dawson, rock-climbing with ropes was just not done.

During the snowy months, Ruth learned to ski on unpacked backcountry slopes. The San Antonio Ski Hut that the Ski Mountaineers worked so hard to build on Mount Baldy burned to the ground, barely nine months after its completion. The cause of the fire was never known. Only two months later, using burros to carry materials up the strenuous trail from Baldy Village instead of the backs of their members, the group rebuilt their hut. Ruth ended her first season of climbing with the arduous 9,000-foot ascent of Mount San Jacinto's Snow Creek. Despite all these climbing trips, Ruth held down a full-time job.

*Ruth Dyar, Little Moyie Valley, British Columbia, 1937*

Following Ruth's climb of the Swiss Arete on Mount Sill, Dick Jones wrote to Phoebe Russell, "I know that you will hear all about the Palisade trip from many sources, but would like to add a few remarks. First of all *your chum*, Ruth, is not only an *excellent* rock-climber but a *born mountaineer.* I had the pleasure of having her in my party up Mount Sill (14,100') via a new and difficult route. The mental and physical ease with which she went up the various pitches is really remarkably outstanding–or as Bill Rice would say 'mighty average!' " The climbing party's rope leader claimed that when they had almost returned to camp, Ruth suggested that they *run* into camp, so nobody would think they were tired.

Glen Dawson, antiquarian bookseller, who was a member of Norman Clyde's climbing party on the first ascent of Mount Whitney's East Face, remembers Ruth as being frail and thin, but with great enthusiasm, a fantastic sense of humor, sometimes biting, and an intense drive to participate and excel. After climbing in Yosemite Valley, Ruth wrote, "I think I ought to be a good rock-climber in my time (said she modestly), if I could do that well with only two practice climbs at Eagle Rock to my credit. The great Glen Dawson shook my hand and said 'Congratulations on a good climb!' My, I felt so proud. He congratulated Mary and Sophie, but did not tell them it was a good climb. And when we roped down, they had to be belayed down, they were so tired, and I did not." She was proud to have kept up with the fastest men.

Ruth was indeed competitive, especially towards other women climbers, and supercilious towards flatlanders—this, despite the fact that she considered herself to be a spectacularly poor athlete. Early in her career, she already believed that climbing and skiing were the only two ways to experience the highest points of existence. "How commonplace and insignificant cities seem," she wrote. People who went to the mountains without climbing them were, likewise, commonplace and insignificant. As she described approaching her first climb of Mount Whitney (third ascent of the East Buttress route), she wrote, "A couple of hundred ordinary Sierra Club people were going up the trail about four miles to camp at Ibex; they are awful sissies, even have their food cooked for them and some ride horses, and all let a pack train take in their belongings." Ruth thought Sierra Club members who were not part of the Rock Climbing Section or Ski Mountaineers were not very smart. Describing a Sierra Club banquet, she said, "those Riverside people are SO DUMB. They are no more Mountaineers than [your neighbor] Maizie Albi, even though they are all young and look healthy. They gave the dumbest reports in the utmost detail of simple-minded trips they had made. George said it was like a lady from a country town telling about her thrilling ride on a Los Angeles street-car!"

Ruth's letters, often written on the Monday after a weekend climb, or as soon as an expedition was over, are direct, first-person, and little romanticized. Besides writing thousands of letters, throughout her lifetime Ruth kept journals, small books written in pencil or pen. She carried little lined notebook pages deep into the wilderness, writing down the day's events while sitting in the tent, after a cold and exhausting day, sometimes lapsing into shorthand or speed writing. These pages became the basis for her narratives of long expeditions. However, there are some gaps her record-keeping, during World War II and the decade of expeditions to the Canadian Rockies.

The letters in this book were chosen from among more than nine-hundred pages of typescript. They are some of her most engaging stories, describing a variety of landscapes, with an occasional look into her private domestic life. This is the story of one of America's first women climbers. This is a human story. This is not the story Ruth would have produced for publication.

And so, at the age of twenty-five, Ruth Dyar began a climbing career that would consume her life, bring her fame, and shade the lives of those about her. Ruth believed that mountaineering gave her memories, physical well-being, spiritual strength, exaltation, friends, and fun. After just one year of climbing, she said,

> It suddenly occurred to me that I actually do practically nothing that isn't connected in some way with the mountains. The people I live with, all my friends, all my recreation, all my writing (if any), most of my thoughts, most of the things I read or make or do, are part of climbing or skiing. It hadn't struck me quite so forcibly for some time. Well, I don't know what finer thing one could have as a motivating force behind one's life.

Before leaving for the ascent of Mt. San Jacinto's Snow Creek route, Ruth wrote, "Maybe I'll get some sleep tomorrow night. I'll need it for the Snow Creek trip, which I hope I live through in a way. Still, what Burton Harrison and George Templeton can do, I can do twice over." –V.M.C.

# Mount Baldy

LOS ANGELES, CALIFORNIA

APRIL 19, 1938

*Dear Mother,*

Jonesy invited us to go with him and some other guys to the Ski Hut on Baldy (Mt. San Antonio) Saturday and Sunday, which invitation we hastily accepted. After we got back from the Rock Climbing Section meeting Friday night, we had to pack all our crud into knapsacks or pack boards, including food, etc., and do all the things a man never does till the last night. Therefore we got to bed about 12:00 o'clock and got up before 5:00, and had one of the most terrific and enjoyable weekends that I have ever spent in a long time.

At 6:30 Saturday morning there drove up to our house a strange fleet of three little Model-A Fords, as no one dared take a decent car over the roads repaired since the floods. Hardly any had yet been to the hut—only about six people. As we got arranged, one car, a cream-colored model without a top, contained George Otto Paul Bauwens. He is "No Stemp No Bedt" Bauwens, sort of the housemother of the Ski Mountaineers, and a most remarkable creature. He is a tall angular powerful man of about 50 or 55, with a habit of roaring ferociously at people, a very good kind heart, and a stupendous capacity for work for the Mountaineers. He builds their trails, huts, and so forth virtually single-handed, and is a fine character. In his car also rode

*The summit and bowl of Mount San Antonio or "Baldy," (10,064-ft) the high point
of the San Gabriel Mountains, from Thunder Mountain (Photo: Mark Goebel)*

Wayland Gilbert–a slim gray-haired fellow of about 35, rather quiet in character, who is always doing nice things for a person like filling your canteen without saying anything about it, or lending you his climbing skins. He has been mimeographing the Mugelnoos until we took over.

Phoebe and Marg rode with Bob Brinton and I rode with Jonesy andHoward Koster.  Howard, the chairman of the Rock Climbing Section, is an awfully nice person, a sturdy young architect of about 30, a very hardy-looking soul–rather quiet, but with a twinkle in his eye and a very fine sense of humor. His hair is always straight up on end.

I had never ridden in one of those rattly little Fords with the top down, and had a wonderful time. Every time he stopped, Howard would flit out with a screw-driver and begin to fasten the car together. We darted out of town through a chilly wet fog, and presently got up into the mountains among wild flowers and sunshine. It was a lovely morning. The usual road having been eliminated, we went by a back way none of us had ever been on, a narrow road winding along precipitous mountainsides covered with dark green chaparral and pale blue wild lilac in bloom.

Despite all the terrible tales we had heard, the road was in excellent condition, rather curved and narrow, except for the last couple of miles in the bottom of the canyon, where *everything* had been simply eliminated, and was a mess of granite boulders. The rebuilt road was just darling, and wandered about among trees, yuccas and brooks, up and down and about, and we bounced terrifically. My it was fun. There were such fine little bridges improvised of rocks, logs and boards.

We couldn't drive to the foot of the trail, as formerly, but only to Snow Crest camp about a mile and a half below it. There we parked the car, disembarked, gave each other cookies, and shouldered our loads. We each had a pack weighing between fifteen and twenty pounds, a pair of skis, ten more pounds, and ski poles. Maybe you think that is a delicate little morsel to carry. Skis get in the *way* so when off your feet (and maybe when on them too). The first part of the journey, to the foot of the trail, was mostly along what remained of the road, plus a few piles of first-rate landslide. We soon got strung out, with the Iron Men, Howard, Brinton and Jonesy ahead, and also Mr. Bauwens. The guys had to pack up an awful lot of stuff

*Sierra Club group in front of the Baldy (San Antonio) Ski Hut, c. 1938:*
*Dick Jones (in doorway); in front of Jones is Mary Helen Johnston (later Mrs. Glen Dawson),*
*Bill Wallace far left*

*Baldy Ski Hut, c. 1940 (Credit: Glen Dawson Collection, Sierra Club-Angeles Chapter Archives)*

*(Photo: California Ski Library)*

that Mr. Bauwens made them carry for construction work on the hut. If he wasn't there, no one would ever do any work. Wayland had a terrible box of window-glass, 28 pounds, and no pack-board, so finally Phoebe took that on her pack-board, and Wayland took all his load and Phe's load and Phe's skis–about 50 pounds.

No one waited for anyone else and we all minded our own business. It was a beautiful morning, sunshiney, with a blue sky. The snow was all gone till we got nearly to the hut, so it was quite spring-like. My load felt just awful at first and my legs wouldn't work, but as soon as I became adjusted to the toil and the altitude, I left Marg & Phoebe far behind and had the best time finding the trail all by myself. Though I had been there only once, early in January, everything seemed so nice and familiar. The lower part of the trail was not hurt at all, and I soon passed Mr. Bauwens busily building trail in the first butch with a pickax. The good man toiled that livelong day with pick and shovel, and did the most amazing work on the trail. I am filled with admiration for him. He does it all out of the goodness of his heart, as he gets no pay and little enough thanks.

My friends, you cannot believe, I couldn't have *conceived*, of the utter mess the floods made, not only of the trail, but of the whole mountainside. The trail runs (or ran) up the side of a deep canyon, gaining about 1,500 or 2,000 feet altitude in two and a half miles. The mountainside is very precipitous, and the damage of the waters is truly incredible! It is just one solid mass of loose junk—rocks, mud, earth, ice, snow, boulders, trees, and roots, mixed up together; four feet of dirt on top of six feet of snow. Enormous gullies twenty to thirty feet deep, seventy-five feet across (we call them "butches"), with steep dirt-and-rock-and-root sides, cut the mountainside, where no gullies and even promontories were before. The going was simply foul. You couldn't take one step, not one, without danger of sliding down into a gulch or something. The few patches of snow were icy. Rocks slid. Dirt slid. Everything was so cruddy! And fancy balancing skis and poles over your already pack-laden shoulders while tripping down the sheer and unstable sides of a 20 foot butch. It was such a fine trip—I just enjoyed myself to the utmost. You couldn't get lost, as the hut could be in only one place and eventually you knew you'd get there. After I had been out alone for some long time, I came across Wayland staggering up the trail, so we staggered along more or less together.

Finally we came in sight of the dear little green hut perched on a slight flat place on the canyon-side, and toiled up the last perpendicular cruddy slopes. Howard stuck his head out of the upstairs window and cuckooed like a clock. Jonesy and Brinton were busily waxing their skis. It was 12:15, and we had been coming for 2 3/4 hours. To everyone's astonishment, I had arrived only 15 minutes after the Iron Men, and I hadn't even been trying to keep up with them, as I knew I couldn't and had no idea where they were. Jonesy was astounded at my speed, and confessed he didn't expect us wenches till 3:00 p.m.

I decided not to ski till Marg & Phoebe caught up with me, so sat out on the rocks in the sun yodeling and yelling merrily with the guys. Howard cannot yodel, but can howl in a wondrously fooey way just like a pained cow. They went charging off up the Slalom Hill, and I lay on my back in the sunshine on the rocks, and kept falling asleep, which wasn't healthy as I could fall off quite readily. So I got up and rustled up a sleeping bag to lie on in the sun, and napped for a while, and then had lunch, and as the hours went by I began to *wonder* where Marg and Phe were. *Two hours* after I got there, they dragged their exhausted bodies into the hut. I was most glad I hadn't gone with them. They had a long tale about having got lost in a major butch.

I was rather tired myself, not having had any sleep for nights and nights, but felt it best to ski a little. I had never skied up there and had no very pleasant opinion of the AWFUL hill they have. The snow lies in a sort of perpendicular basin, which ends at the top in a series of rocky pinnacles against the blue sky, and at the bottom in a mess of talus which has fallen from the pinnacle down the canyon. It is a fine place for good skiers, but the slope is pretty awful to a man like me. However, I wasn't going to be afraid to try it, and briskly climbed up the hill, which was covered with perfect corn snow (little round granules of ice), and lovely ascending traverses and swirling descending curlicues made by the fellows' ski tracks. I toiled once up the hill, and came down in a most humiliating manner, as it was so darn steep I couldn't make my turns, and I would fall down and roll straight down the hill. They all thought it was rather funny, and yelled advice at me, and when I complained how *steep* it was, they said with astounded relish: "She thinks it *steep*. She should see Whitney Pass." By that time, I was too fatigued to go up hill again, so just did a few stem turns among the rocks at the foot of the hill, crossed the brook and retired to the hut.

I rested in bed with Marg & Phe for awhile. The toolroom like affair on the first floor has now three bunks built in it for girls, and is called The Harem. The three bunks are one above the other clear to the ceiling. It is a dear little room, and we became fond of it. It even has frilly yellow curtains at the big windows, a mirror and various hooks and shelves.

About 5:00, everyone began to make dinner, so we did too. First we had lamb chops and then split pea soup, cooked in the pressure cooker because of the altitude. Jonesy helped us get our dinner, and we gave him some cookies and pineapple. They were expecting a number of other people that afternoon, and about 7:00, just as darkness was falling, we heard exhausted yodels coming up the canyon, and peered out the windows, yelling at the newcomers.

Homer Fuller, Ren and Tim Wicks, Ingeborg "Inky" Bryan, Glen Dawson and Phil Faulconer were the arrivals. We knew them all but the latter. Homer, Omer-lamb, the Fuller Brushman, is a nondescript harmless guy. Tim Wicks is a horrid little sawed off person who works in a sporting goods store and is a pretty good skier. Ren, his older brother, is a thin gloomy-looking commercial artist, who is wondrously crazy, and goes around talking nonsense in a fine combination of an English accent, French, German, and so forth. Inky is a Hollywood Radio Singer and looks rather like Marlene Dietrich. I don't understand how she comes to be a Ski Mountaineer, as she doesn't seem to fit. However, she is a very good skier. She is married and has a child, and annoys me because she always does every simple thing as if she thought she had an audience's eyes upon her, even to spooning her soup and walking across the room.

Phil Faulconer was the finest ski-character who has come across our horizon for some time. He is a stocky, rosy cheeked yellow-haired boy from San Diego, who is filled with the most lighthearted funny nonsense and sheer bursting of high spirits, of anyone I have seen for a long time. He is constantly doing crazy dances, singing funny songs, yodeling (and he can really yodel), playing an accordion or harmonica, etc. He had heard all about us, apparently, and was most gratified to meet us. I just can't get over our popularity. At one point when he heard me address Phe as "Chum," he turned upon us and cried: "Oh, *you* are the chums!" Apparently he had heard.

They are such a fine noisy bunch. Everyone was through eating early, and sat about the gasoline-lantern-lit hut making a racket. Jonesy, Tim and Phil played mouth organs, Phe and Inky played combs, Renny and Phil yodeled and sang and did dances. Brinton read aloud from a funny English ski book. Howard industriously played phonograph records backwards, especially one horrid record called "Sweet Violets" that they all love, until the Victrola broke. Some had brought up some new phonograph records that were so nasty no one could stand them, so Jonesy casually threw them on the floor. Then they dealt out fragments like cards, spread butter on them, and made phonograph-record sandwiches!

About 8:30 everyone rushed off to bed, ourselves included, just as an impossibly golden moon rose through a gap in the mountains. Next morning about 6:00 we were wakened by some of the Iron Men busily making breakfast and wishing Happy Easter to everyone who came downstairs. We got up before 7:00, had oranges, toast, bacon, coffee and cocoa, and did our dishes in the trough-like dishpan which is just the shape of an overgrown bread-pan.

Everyone was apparently busily rushing off to climb to the top of Baldy, Mt. San Antonio, 10,080 feet in elevation; so we decided we should climb it too. With borrowed canvas climbers on our skis, we set off in the early 9:00 a.m. sunshine, toiled up the Slalom Hill, encircled a rather icy mountainside among wind-twisted Tamarack pines, occasionally meeting a chum or two in the woods, and after two hours of leisurely climbing through the sunshine and quiet, reached the bald snowy summit. It was a hot morning, but on the very top an icy wind swept over the snow. We had a marvelous view, in spite of mists in the mid-distance: Catalina Island and others of the Channel Islands floating in the mist; to the north, a dim snowy line of the Sierra; south and east, the snowy sides of San Gorgonio and San Jacinto rising from lesser mountains. Deserts and valleys. The precipitous canyons of the immediate mountain below us.

No sooner had we arrived than we had to start back, first lunching frugally on a little snow, a little water, and one and a half Lifesavers apiece. Our descent of the mountain was rather ignominious, as we kept falling down and shooting down the slope till we could catch ourselves by jabbing ski poles into the snow—or at least Marg and I did. However, leaving a fine trail of butches behind us, we got safely down. By the time I got to the Slalom Hill I was so tired of rolling down the hill that I just didn't anymore.

We had a hasty lunch and packed our crud. Everyone was leaving the hut about 2:00, so as to make the 4:00 o'clock control on the one-way road out. My pack still weighed 15 pounds, as I took everything Marg and Phoebe wouldn't, but I was used to it by then. We all started down the mountain together. A long line of fifteen skiers, each one with pack and skis and poles, each one in high spirits, yodeling and shouting and yelling happily as they tramped down the cruddy mountainside. One of the funniest sights I ever saw was when the whole line was busily climbing down into and out of the biggest butch–all these skiers clinging, with skis and packs, to the dusty, rooty, unstable sides of the gully, pulling each other out, lowering skis to each other, getting thoroughly dirty in the process. My it was fun!

Toward the lower part of the trail we got spread out again, with the Iron Men in front, I walking down with Phil. It took about an hour and twenty minutes to descend, and my going-down-hill muscles were a bit tired by the time we reached the cars, my shins were a bit bloody, and everything was mah-v'lous.

It was a hot dusty afternoon. A few long respectable cars which had ventured up on that road were creeping along in front of us. They slowed us up so that a lot of the guys leaped out of their cars and went running and cavorting and yodeling along the roadside, springing onto our running board, galloping across the brooks, bounding through the grass, shouting and making noise. It was fine!

Our car was stuck behind Mr. Bauwens' most of the way, and we got coated thickly with filth and dust. About 6:00 we reached home, the hottest afternoon of the year. They all came in to have something cold to drink, though Jonesy was so dirty he washed in the hose, and Mr. Bauwens thought he should spread newspapers on our chairs before he sat down. Jonesy, Koster and I did look rather dismal and gray with dust. Jonesy's hat was a sight–he has a green Tyrolean hat littered with ski medals and other kinds of outdoor-organization-pins till it resembles a Christmas tree, and it was gray with dust. Howard was wearing shorts and a torn shirt and his sunburned face was not precisely clean. For myself, I have quite passed the point of trying to brush my ski pants any more. Marg's were virtually disintegrating. They will never go on another ski trip!

After the guys left, we took baths, put away some of our crud, ate dinner, and finally I believe went to bed. If we didn't we should have. My feet were all blistered along the edges.

Heavens I have been busy the last 3 weeks. I actually have hardly time to eat, and certainly none to sleep. I feel very fine, though, because I've been having so much fun, and I like to be busy. I don't believe I have sat down to read for a month, or even sat down. Monday was an awfully hot day. After getting home, I did a vast washing before dinner. Just when I will iron, I couldn't say. That evening Phe & I started to get out our first Mugelnoos since we became the sole editors. I spent some hours on the phone talking to Mountaineers and getting news–my it's fun. We wrote the copy, talked over the phone to Jonesy for an hour about midnight, went to bed. I got up early the next morning and cut the stencils, and Phe and Marg printed, mailed, and otherwise finished up the job during the day. That evening Max and I worked quite late downtown.

Last night we had the San Gorgonio Ski Hut committee meeting at our hovel. Glen, Wayland Gilbert, Homer and George Bauwens were there from our group, and three long-faced rather passé-looking guys from the Riverside Chapter. It was rather a dull meeting, but we were glad to have them there anyway. Mr. Bauwens, who only a week ago thought we looked too "*frail*," and too much like tenderfeet to go up Baldy, and who was afraid we'd butch the Mugelnoos unless Glen supervised us, complimented us roundly on our mountain climbing and our paper!

tripping over steep slabs of rock arm-in-arm, while
most people -- probably including us a year ago--
would have crept over the slope on their rumps —

Homer and I climbed the White Maiden's Walk Away by the Jensen Variation
(straight up). I had an awfully good time, as it was about the first time I had made
a climb on a fast rope, on an equal basis with the other man. It is a good tough
climb. Homer would lead one pitch and I would lead the next, which worked very neatly, as the man didn't have to change his belay — all we would do was trade the carabiner for the knapsack (the leader never carries anything), and roar on up. The air
was not very cold, and there was little wind, but the sun rarely reaches that part of
the rock, and there was still a little snow in the crannies, and the rock was like
solid ice — our hands got bitterly cold while we were climbing. We had an awfully
lot of fun. Homer is sort of a nice companion and fun to have around.

We got up on top in 2½ hours, and then went down into the sunshine, where others
were, at and divided up my lunch, and chiselled everything else we could. Carl and
Johnny were just finishing the Mechanics Route, and Johnny at least was pretty pooped.
Even Carl was a little subdued. I guess it was rather terrific. They had no lunch,
so I went around begging, borrowing, and downright stealing what I could for them,
as I had already fed half my lunch to Homer. After sitting around for a spell, we
sort of started down the friction route, met some other people half-way, and a mess of
us decided to climb down instead. A couple of ropes climbed down the trough, and Ray,
Carl and I climbed down the Finger Tip Traverse, a little accomplishment often talked
about but never before accomplished. Down below we had an audience of 10 or so people
who had already got down the Friction Route., yelling and yodelling and wise-cracking
at us. Ray & I shook hands in a tearful farewell at the start of the Traverse, but
somehow we all survived. It is wonderful to see Dr. Carl flit over the rock.

When we finally reached the head of the trail, Phe and Joan had fixed a little
Tea for all comers, laid out on pieces of paper, many bits of segmented orange,
raisins, candy, bites of sandwich, lettuce, etc. etc., which we enjoyed. A mess
of us sat around. Finally Doug, Joan and Phe went down, and some of that bunch.
And Walter and Johnny and so on left, all of us sure no one else was up on the rock.
Carl and I started down a couple of minutes after the gang Johnny and Walter. It was
getting twilight, with a rosy sunset, and a blanket of fog piling over the high hills
beyond Suicide Cliff.

We got down the trail and tramped down the road. I felt so good and light and
agile, like one does after a fine weekend of climbing, which certainly introduces a
lightness and flexibility into all the muscles. I carelessly remarked that I felt
as if I could walk on and on for miles — not thinking I was going to have to. Well,
when we got to the parking place, where we thoughtthe Hennies car would be waiting
for us — the skonks were gone. We of course pretended to resent this, but both
thought it was monstrous funny.

There was nothing to do but walk to camp — an indeterminate distance, but
I would judge between 3 and 4 miles, as we walked fast all the way and it took an hour.
It really was nice, though I got pretty footsore, and my legs were pretty weary, long
before we got there. It was a lovely autumn evening, the twilight settling swiftly
through the pines and oaks. The cool air was full of night smells, and dank loamy
smells, and wet leaves and pines and the creak of frogs. The mackerel sky was mottled
and light, even though the moon wasn't up. We tramped along, Carl with a string of
karabiners clanking on his hip, and I with someone's sloppily-coiled rope drooling
over my shoulders, both enjoying the situation to the core. Luckily it was all down hill.

We didn't know the way, and there was a maze of roads, and we made inquiries
at an occasional cabin or dwelling, and went a little out of our way once or twice,
and finally got on to the dirt road which we knew led into camp. There was the
most beautiful moonrise I have ever seen. We had seen the glow on the horizon where
it was coming, and happened to turn around just as the moon was half over the edge.

*Reproduction of Ruth Dyar's letter to her sister Margaret,*
*about climbng at Tahquitz, dated October 10, 1938*

# Yosemite, Washington Column

MARENGO AVENUE

SOUTH PASADENA, LOS ANGELES

JUNE 3, 1938

*Dear Ma and Fa,*

I guess I'd better start to write about our Yosemite trip. We did have so much fun. It should be recorded before I forget everything we did.

Art's car was a weird little ancient Ford with a rumble seat, a huge gas tank holding thirty-three gallons which he had installed in addition to the other tank, and a system of lighting like a General Electric model home. Art himself was as Art Johnson-ish as one could hope for. He wasn't much bigger than Marg–a little on the ape-like side, with hair sticking up in every direction through a green eye shade. He alternated between long silences and strange bursts of humor. We liked him in an impersonal sort of way. When Jim demanded a pun on "isthmus," Art replied, "If you wait long enough, Chr-isthmus will come." We became much more fond of Jim than we had been before. He was awfully nice to camp with, and his character seemed to take a turn for the better. He really loves the woods, is a competent woodsman, and frightfully cute.

Art and Jim took turns driving and riding in the rumble seat, so we took a long time getting anywhere. Had dinner in Fresno at a joint that gave very poor service. We were grumbling that they probably had to send out for all the food, and then found out that they really *did* send clear around the block for everything we ordered!

We went in the back road from Fresno, which is not only the short-
est but the best way now, since the floods demolished the year-round
highway. Got into the valley around midnight, wandering around looking for the Sierra Club campground, number 12, found it, kicked
pine needles into piles for mattresses, and went promptly to bed.

Quantities of people kept arriving all day Saturday. There were
about five hundred Sierra Club people, a hundred and eighty from the
south and the rest from around San Francisco. A lot of them ate in the
central commissary, run by three Negro cooks. We were glad we had
our own grub. A lot of very funny looking people swaggered about in
odd outing costumes with cups on their hips, who were the older Sierra
Club people. However, they didn't hurt us any.

It rained a little that afternoon, and we found Art in camp with all
our gear, under the tarp. Art was in a bad condition, as he had just
got bitten by a rattlesnake! He said he had reached up and didn't see it;
but we found out later (from strangers) that he was fooling around with
it and trying to pick it up.

I had never seen a snake bite victim before, so found it quite interesting. It was a baby snake and got him in the finger with only one fang,
or it might have been far more serious. As it was, his arm swelled all up
clear to the shoulder, and he felt utterly lousy the rest of the trip. He
refused to go and get a shot for it, as he claimed it would cost $10 and
do no good. He spent most of the time lying in a stupor in his sleeping
bag wearing an old dark red stocking cap. The first night he moaned
and groaned for hours.

Sunday was my best day, and my first big rock-climb. I had been
told by any number of good kindly souls that there wouldn't be any
rock-climbing I could do, so when Glen Dawson himself appeared
prepared to take some of us beginners up the Washington Column to

the Lunch Ledge, quite a difficult climb, I was quite eager to go. Jim disapproved to the utmost, and even offered to take me on an easier climb, I guess so I wouldn't feel I couldn't go climbing anywhere. But I resolved to myself that if Mary Van Velzer and Sophie Rice could go, I certainly could. We started out at 8:00 o'clock, I having hastily gathered together a foul little lunch of buttered pumpernickel, rye-crisp, and candy bars.

It was rather a weird expedition, totally different from anything I'd ever done before, and yet it came perfectly natural. There were eight of us going up in all. The Washington Column is a huge perpendicular projection of cliff about 1,200 feet high. The Lunch Ledge was about half-way up. We drove up to the woods at the foot of the cliff; climbed over granite talus for a few minutes through underbrush and swarms of nasty little mosquitoes; and finally roped together for the climb.

Homer Fuller and Sophie Rice went up on one rope. Sophie is a tall, very nice looking girl–one of the few girls who really look well, and at home, in outdoor clothes. Her brother Bill Rice is one of the outstanding rock-climbers. She doesn't know much about it and was rather scared, and I don't think she should have been allowed to go. Some guys, led by little Muir Dawson, went up on the second rope. And Glen, who is a very excellent rock climber, and very matter of fact and nice, led our rope. I was in the middle of the rope, and Mary Van, a little wench of whom I am very fond, on the end. I think there is about 40 feet of rope between each person. It is a very highly developed technique, and with a good leader, there is hardly any danger of getting hurt, as he gives you an "upper belay" and if you fall, you just fall on the rope and go your way. However, for myself, I didn't fall.

I could readily see where experience would help–at first the rope seems to get in the way so, for one thing; the theory of progression is

*Glen Dawson, 1938*

that the leader climbs up first, belays the second man up, who belays the third man up, and on you go. Each stretch which you climb without stopping is a "pitch." The places we *went!* It is just as well that you can't see them. Never had I been in such places, and it was so weird to keep on climbing up and up, hour after hour. Of course it took us much longer than necessary, as we had so many people to wait for. While I was belaying Mary, Glen would usually give me an "anchor" from above, so we couldn't possibly have gotten hurt.

We climbed for about 3 1/2 hours, going up and up; up perpendicular cracks with no handholds, that one mounted merely by sticking the toes of your tennis shoes in the crevice; up one weird place where one toe went in one crack and the other in another; up a sort of "chimney" climbed with back on one wall and knees on the other. I simply loved it! I think I ought to become a good rock climber in my time (said she modestly), if I could do that well with only two practice climbs at

Eagle Rock to my credit. Of course, my whole life has been devoted more or less to that sort of thing. It was *so wonderful* to be way way up on the remote granite cliffs where almost no one ever gets–so far above the valley; it was a marvelous day, neither hot nor cold, sunny, breezy; little shrubs and trees and ferns and succulents grew way up on the cliff. It seemed so peaceful and far away.

About 12:30 we got to the Lunch Ledge, and the great Glen Dawson shook my hand and said "Congratulations on a good climb!" My, I felt so proud. He congratulated Mary and Sophie, but did not tell them it was a good climb. And when we roped down, they had to be belayed down, they were so tired, and I did not. We stayed up there quite a while, eating our lunch and drinking water out of the thimble-sized cap on Glen's canteen. My candy bars were rather in poor condition, as water leaked on them, the pitons cut them up, and they got rather mashed in the knapsack going up the chimney. I forgot to say that in rock-climbing etiquette, the leader doesn't have to carry anything, so Mary Van & I hauled up the knapsacks full of rope, jackets, caribiners, pitons, lunch, water, etc.

Then we roped down. It is the most wonderfully easy way of descending. It is so fine to know you don't have to climb down, as climbing down is harder than going up, as anyone knows. We came down in six or seven long rope-downs, most of them about 100 feet long. One is supposed to have a leather patch on his pants–and you certainly need it! However, those of us who didn't stuffed our jackets or sweaters into our pants, and tied a knapsack over our shoulder for protection. The theory is that with the rope twined just so around your hips and shoulders, the friction lets you down gradually. The rope is fastened double through a piton or a "sling" of rope tied around a tree, and can be pulled down after the last man.

And at the end of the next-to-last rope-down we had the most pleasant surprise! We found a body! All my life I have hankered after finding a corpse, and finally I helped find one. One of the fellows suddenly said, as we were sitting about on a sloping ledge drinking from the brook, "Here is an old shoe with some bones in it!" First we hardly believed it. Yet we looked—and it *was:* a weathered man's shoe, lying upside down, filled with human bones. For some reason, we were all immensely pleased. It didn't seem horrible, as it was so old and mossy and impersonal. We decided we ought not to disturb it, but go and report to the ranger. We felt sure there were more bones under the pile of gravel. Later the head ranger and some of the boys went and dug up the remains. They found more bones, though not the whole body, a camera case, a watch case, and various odds and ends. They do not know who it is, but figure it must be six or seven years since the person died. Probably he was carelessly climbing on the cliff, alone, in the wrong kind of shoes, and fell down. He could have easily remained unfound forever. We thought that was a sprightly close to a rock-climb, and maybe it was as well that we didn't find it before we started.

Monday morning we took a long time for breakfast. About 11:00, we got all the crud lashed in a scientific fashion on half the rumble seat and over the running boards. It was a hot day. In Bakersfield we had dinner. Then I took a turn at the rumble seat going over the ridge. It was windy, and nice and remote, and the sky was full of stars. Finally about 11:00 we got home, felt an earthquake (the first I ever felt) and went to bed.

I have been gosh-awful busy all week. I get busier instead of less so. It is fiendish. Today I have washed clothes and hair. Now I have to wash the dinner dishes.

*Please write soon, and much love.*

# Tahquitz

## THE FIRST DAY OF SUMMER
## MARENGO AVE., SOUTH PASADENA, CALIFORNIA
## JUNE 21, 1938

*Dear Pa, Ma, Eliot and Judpud,*

Someone tried to poison us all last week. Marg spent Wednesday morning having a stomachache of the more violent order; Aunt Alice followed her lead a little later in the morning. I felt rather odd, but laid it to my imagination and went to the office. Max was right surprised when about an hour after lunch I suddenly remarked that I too was sick, and with no warning began to turn rapidly green. I went to the ladies room and lay on the hard slippery leather couch, and felt unhealthy, also popped the cookies, and finally Elizabeth came in and took me home. Thursday we all spent in bed. I got up once and put a leather roping-down patch on my overalls, and went to bed again immediately.

More important than for me to fall in love with one of the Mountaineers, is for one of the more worthy to fall in love with me, you know. I am getting to be quite a little flirt, even in overalls.

Well, I must proceed to tell you about the weekend's rock climb. As usual, it was one of the best weekends I ever spent. I had several secret misgivings about going at all when I was just up from the sick bed, and thought I would use a little sense and not do much strenuous exercise. However, Tahquitz Rock, about 30 miles beyond Riverside in the

*Ruth Dyar on the Lichen Traverse, 1930s*

mountains, is a famous place for the chums to climb, and I had never been there, and everyone was going to be there. Rock-climbing, without question due to the Ski Mountaineers and the Mugelnoos, has become very fashionable.

I went to bed about 8:00 Friday night, but didn't sleep very well. I got up at 5:15 a.m., feeling lousy, dressed in my hiking garb, ate breakfast, and then had to quietly lie down until the chums came for me. I wished I wasn't going, but couldn't think of any manly way to get out of it. About quarter to 7:00, Brinton, Muir, and a young boy, a friend of Muir's, Curtis Whittlesey, arrived. We drove to Riverside, a village I had not been in for some time, through rather damp, mildly raining weather. Then started through fields and farm country, gradually gaining altitude as we climbed up towards San Jacinto (one of the major mountains around here, pronounced Ha-*sin*-to). Finally we broke out of the clouds, and it turned into an exquisitely sunny summer day.

The highway leads in a general way to a Riverside County public camp. There are also a lot of private cabins strewn through the woods. We started up the "Fern Valley" road which is a dirt road winding for a couple of miles between tall evergreens, much like Spokane country, and carpets of ferns, with the stupendous and startlingly huge hunk of granite which is Tahquitz Rock looming up against the blue sky among steep mountainsides of granite. It is a long rectangular thing set on end against the canyon-side, and I just couldn't get over its size–probably 800 feet high from base to summit, the back side blending into the hill but the other three sides distinct and sheer.

Brinton at once wanted to take me up the Fingertip Traverse, but I said I wasn't going to climb. I got tired of explaining about how someone fed us arsenic. However, I decided no matter what I did I wouldn't feel much worse, so I decided to climb up the back side, which is easy and for beginners, with the other novices. There were three ropes of three. Gatesy took up two people, Johnny Mendenhall took up two, and Jim led Curtis and me. Johnny Mendenhall, a rock climber whom I had never met, proved to be a most intriguing character, and I have quite a crush on him at the moment. He liked me too. He is a brawny youth who wrestles in the winter, a construction engineer, who looked quite dashing and rakish in a horrid dirty bright red hat. He started out commending me at great length and with great sincerity upon the Mugelnoos, later upon my rock climbing skill, and before the morning had worn away, was busily planning to throw me off the cliff, so I knew we had become friends; he has one of those nice horrid senses of humor which mean so much when combined with a really nice character. People who can be nasty without meaning it, are so much superior to those who are sticky-sweet without meaning it.

I will say that rock-climbing is all that an invalid needs. As the day went by, I felt better and better, till by evening I was so exhilarated and improved that I felt practically as good as I ever did in my life. I had a nice easy climb on Jim's rope and learned quite a lot. Jim told me admiringly that I was going to be a "darn good rock climber" and I felt pretty good about it. We arrived hours before the others. Maybe you wonder just where we arrived at. By a new route no one had ever climbed before, we arrived at the very summit of the rock, which took about two hours or more. It was right cute up there–pinkish pale granite, beautifully stained with orange, yellow, dark and light green lichens–broad expanses of it strewn with monstrous boulders–dropping down far below to a misty forested valley–looking off to granite-spired mountainsides–far far off toward San Diego to the new observatory buildings on Mount Palomar.

Brinton and others had reached the top by then, and we had lunch. The lunch, I will say, consisted of raw carrots, chocolate bars, water, dried peaches, and fig bars that I didn't eat. Johnny and Jim paid me much attention. It is quite the thing to be the only female among many handsome guys on the top of a rock. I had scraped my arm so badly the blood actually ran out, and they had fun putting on iodine while I acted stoic.

Finally we all roped down the Trough (one of the climbs). My new leather patch on the rump was ideal, and just the thing. I was feeling awfully good by then. At the base of the rock we climbed on a boulder and ate someone's watermelon, and some crackers and cheese. Then we *ran* full speed down the trail in ten minutes in a great cloud of filth and dust which accumulated all over us.

We got to the cars about 6:00 and drove back to the Riverside County camp, where all the rock-climbers were camping at the far end. The place was swarming with chums. I had the best time camping among such a great mass of boys! There were girls about too, of course; Adrienne was there, though she can't climb yet; and blonde roly-poly Mary Adley; Agnes Fair, who had been climbing that day, and who is rather dopey and wears a wicker Japanese hat on all occasions, is jealous of me and is always asking me if I "was the only girl there," a question I would never be so dumb as to ask any other girl.

We had supper with salad, sauerkraut and wieners–which was no invalid's diet but tasted *marvelous*. Then we retired to the campfire built by some good souls, and sang songs. I borrowed Johnny's toothpowder, which he strewed generously on my brush, telling me how it was a special preparation recommended by his dentist–and then screamed with laughter when I found out it was only horridly strong salt-and-soda.

I went gladly to bed, and got waked up by early risers at 4:30 in the morning. I emerged from my sleeping bag sufficiently to sew a patch on my overall rump. I hacked the patch off the bottom of the pant leg with a knife. It was lucky I had brought a needle and thread, as I had to loan it to Johnny for the same purpose. Agnes had also worn out a huge hole in her pants, which were feeble slacks, and which Muir told her coldly were good only for sitting in a chair. The boys even admire my overalls.

After breakfast, we drove up the boulder-strewn "road" again. Brinton, Agnes and I were to go up the Trough, followed by another rope led by Johnny. Jim told me I could "lead to the first piton," so we started out with me first on the rope. And oh my friend, Brinton let me lead clear to the top of the Trough! Leading, going first on the rope, is the most important, because that man does not have an "upper belay"—that is, if you have an upper belay, and fall, you just fall on the taut rope and aren't hurt. A leader will fall way below the second man who is belaying him from below. So they never would have let me if I hadn't been pretty good.

Not to be unduly catty, but the other girl on our rope seemed to me to have the wrong mental attitude; she got up all right, but had to wait for Brinton to tell her practically every move to make with hand or foot.

The climb was steeper than it looks from below, going up several cracks that we climbed by wedging toes in the cracks and using rather smooth handholds, or else getting a grip on sharp edges with our fingers and placing the crepe soles of our tennis shoes on sloping spots.

I *love* rock-climbing so, and all the guys are overwhelmed at my skill. It is the most marvelous feeling to suddenly excel, with no effort, in a wonderful sport, when I have always been, and will always be, a lousy skier, a mediocre swimmer, and not fond of most other sports and unable to even throw a ball.

This week has been customarily hectic. Last night, I rushed home to gobble dinner and, with Jim, get the Mugelnoos ready for printing. Jim is the *best* helper, so efficient, and is so much fun to work with, and is so handsome. He is in awe that I am not afraid of *snakes*—he said, "I never *saw* such a girl; you aren't afraid of *anything!*" He is an architect student at USC, or UCLA; I think he graduated once from Cal Tech. He is going to cut a linoleum block and make us a special Mugelnoos letterhead sometime.

Tonight we mimeograph and mail the thing. I also have to make a down sleeping bag sometime this next week so I can go on the Palisades Fourth of July trip to the High Sierra.

# Mount Sill, Swiss Arete, First Ascent

JULY 5, 1938

*Dear Marg,*

Since you have the greatest interest in it, I do believe I will address my letter about the Palisade trip to you. It was SO WONDERFUL, perfect in every respect. It is remarkable how our trips can go on and on being so marvelous, each in its own way!!

Joe and Jonesy picked me about 7:00 p.m. Friday. We flung my duffle into the back of Joe's car, said goodbye, and raced down the steps and leapt into the car, in a great rush to be gone.

So we started for the Sierra, most glad to be on our way. Jonesy is a lot of fun to go on trips with, he gets so excited like a little boy. We discovered that the back shelf of the coupe, which is a wide one, padded with an air mattress, made an ideal place to ride (lying down), so took turns doing that. I wore Dick's alpine hat, and Jonesy played his mouth organ (a special one with 4 notes which he brought for my benefit in addition to his big one–he wants to know if I ever saw a metal ocarina, as he wants one), and sang songs. He knows a lot of fine songs. And we drove on and on up the road to Owens Valley, which is becoming quite familiar. While I was driving, I inadvertently ran over a little animal, which looked rather like a porcupine, though for the sake of the tires we hoped it wasn't. It made an awful thud. Jonesy immediately began to serenade me with songs about "Blood on the tires, Blood all around."

We drove till about midnight, to just south of Lone Pine. There we explored two or three little side-roads, finally found a good flat gravelly place to lay our sleeping bags. It was out of the flat desert among the sage, with grass-hoppers rustling in the brush. The sky was rather pale blue and very full of stars, and the sage smelled very sweet, and a strong wind rushed over us.

At 4:30 they woke me up. Four hours of sleep isn't much, but I felt as good as ever, or better, all day. We dressed inside our bags, combed our hair a little, omitted washing as we had no water, and

*Dick Jones in the Palisades, July, 1938*

drove on our way. We went as far north as Big Pine, turned to the west toward the Sierra, and drove about 10 miles up a little dirt road which wound up through desert hills toward the mountains. We drove behind Wayland's car part way. They had a vast bundle of luggage on top, rolled in white canvas, and Wayland and Muir got up and rode on top of that, and Brinton stuck his great feet in white wool socks out of the window, and we drove alongside and conversed with them, and it was all rather screwy.

At the end of the road, beside a rushing mountain brook, we parked, cooked bacon and eggs on Joe's gasoline stove, loaded up our packs. Dick and Joe carried all the food, and I took Jonesy's bed roll and the ice axe. I guess my pack weighed about 25 pounds, and theirs seven or eight pounds heavier.

It was a fine wide pale gray trail, about as steep as the Gorgonio one, full of switch backs, following in a general way a rapid rushing brook, skirting barren hillsides, winding across streams and through marshes filled with huge fat shooting stars, wild onions, wild iris, paintbrushes, wild columbines, and all manner of lovely little plants. The hike, about 5 miles I think, took us two hours. At 10:00 in the morning, after skirting along some little lakes–First and Second–we came to Third Lake, our camp.

We were the first ones in–Brinton, Muir, Wayland, Earl and Bill Wallace, Joe, Jonesy, the Mendenhall, and I. It was *such* a lovely little camp. The heart of the High Sierra wasn't quite as I expected–it was more desolate and barren and tremendous. At an elevation of 10,300 feet (higher than the top of Baldy!), Third Lake, deep green in color, lay in a little hollow at the foot of a long ridge of glacial moraine. There was still a great deal of snow–far more than last year at this time. The banks of the lake were ringed in snow. The steep mountainsides were deep with snow, and out of the snow rose those tremendous jagged granite cliffs which towered above us, ragged and imposing, all around 13,000 and 14,000 feet. It was a cold windy morning, and clouds kept blowing across the thin sunshine.

Our camp was on a little rocky point which consisted of a series of little flat shelves, each about big enough for one sleeping bag, and small straight clean Tamarack pines, and hunks of pinky gray granite, and patches of clean white snow, and little inlets of deep green water (it was a tiny lake). Everyone at once flung down their packs and rushed about looking for places to sleep. All the chums were so *good* to me. Dick and Johnny each picked out what they considered as the best spot for me to sleep; I chose the one near the lake, under a tree, with a nice boulder beside it for a table, and they piled logs all around me to keep off the wind. It was the best spot there. Everyone fell to busily "gardening" and hoeing up their beds with ice axes to make them soft. Johnny hoed up mine for me.

About noon, we were wondering just what to do. We didn't want to do much climbing as we had to save our strength for the next day. Three pairs of skis–Muir's, Wayland's and Earl Wallace's–had been carted up. Jonesy rented Wayland's skis by carrying his sleeping bag way up on a ridge for him, as he wanted to sleep there. Dick, Jonesy, Earl and Brinton skied on the steep slope across the lake. The Johnny invited me out for a lesson in "snow and ice work," and Bill Wallace also came.

My costume was rather mixed up. I had on my ski boots, my overalls, my red flannel shirt, and my black fishing lid. That hat, by the way, excited much comment, and everyone loved it. To cross the lake, we had to follow the shore a little while on our side, step over a kind of dam of logs and branches, and pick our way over snow patches and boulders of the long ridge formed by the lateral moraine (Art told us that was what it was, or I wouldn't know) on the other side. Then we reached the long sweep of snow that rose abruptly for 1,500 feet to the ridge against the sky. Johnny, Bill and I climbed up toward a couloir at the base of Temple Crag. A couloir is a long tongue of snow that reaches up into an indentation in the face of a cliff. The snow was soft and mucky, so we weren't really doing any "ice work," but he showed us how to use the ice axe, and told us a lot about mountaineering on snow and ice. An ice axe is a charming little weapon about 3 or 4 feet long, with a spike on one end like a ski pole, and on the other end one pointed edge and one flat edge. Our pants got very wet.

I do believe the Johnny is fond of me. When we were going home about 4:00, I was strolling along feeling right at home with the ice axe, and he told me I always reminded him of a photograph he had seen in an advertisement of a girl all togged out in beautiful fashionable alpine clothes, standing casually on a mountain top (which you knew was in the backyard of the photographic studio), because I always looked so casual about whatever I did. This pleased me no end, because I know it is all right to *be* an athletic woman, but there is not any benefit in looking it too much. It is also odd how they know a wench can charge up a 14,000 foot peak with great stamina, but regard her as unable to fetch a cup of water from the lake two feet away.

We returned to camp and dried our pants by the fire. By that time, more chums had come. There were around thirty in all, though some came late or left early. Agnes Fair, Ray Ingwersen, the Hennies, Hensel Framsted, Koster, Art Johnson, a few people I don't know or don't know very well, Chet and Mrs. Chet (being very Mrs. Chettish–I have decided I like Helen Hennies far better), the Ashcrafts, Bill Davies (very Bill-ish), Jim Smith. When Jim hove into camp in a pair of brief blue shorts, he shook my hand and said, "It is nice to see you in the High Sierra, Editor Dyar."

Jonesy-lamb brought a *marvelous* commissary, and it cost us only 90 cents apiece! I have heard tell of people losing their appetites in the higher altitudes, but for myself, I didn't greatly suffer along that line. We had the most wonderful goulash of noodles, dried pea soup, and canned sausages. We ate an absolutely vast dish of it, of which I ate about half; Jell-O; and a few other items. It was a cold windy night, and I was glad for my hat. About 6:00 we built up a big campfire, and huddled about it, and Dick played his mouth organ. Muir and I

*(From left) John Mendenhall, Joe Momyer, Ruth Dyar, Dick Jones, and Wayland Gilbert, packing into the Palisades, July 4, 1938*

wanted so badly for it to get dark so we could go to sleep, and at 7:00 we could still see sun shining on the higher crags. It was very discouraging, and finally I got mad and went to bed while it was still light, at 7:30. We were to climb the next day, and laid out everything the night before. Jim was sick, popping the cookies several times for no reason he could determine; he was very pale and felt awful. Yet when I went to say goodnight to him, as he lay like a large stiff corpse in his huge sleeping bag under a tree, with a bandanna tied over his eyes, he was able to gasp out a little kindly advice about my next day's climb.

You will be glad to know that my sleeping bag was perfect. It was so lovely and cozy; rolled up so tiny; was perfectly warm that night despite the high wind and the lake freezing over! There are little tricks, such as fluffing it out each time before you get in.

I slept soundly till the chums got up about quarter to four, and Joe brought me a hot bacon and rye-crisp sandwich with Jonesy's compliments. Six of the boys were going to climb North Palisade, the toughest climb–Brinton, Johnny, Walter Hennies, Hensel, Fremstad, Muir and Wayland (who had slept way up on the ridge alone). They started out before 5:00. At 5:20 a.m. our two ropes started–Jonesy, Joe, Spencer Austin, Ray Ingwersen and I. The rest, led by Koster and Jim (who had recovered) were going to hike or fish or climb Temple Crag later.

The climbs were all difficult because of the very deep snows. It was excessively cold. I wore my woolen long underwear, wool shirt, ski jacket and parka hood (for which I was very glad), ski boots (later, on the rocks, changing to tennis shoes), and mittens. It was a long grind up that 1,500 foot icy hill. Fortunately, footsteps from the day before were easy to follow up. About 7:00 we got up on top, and looked across the Palisade Glacier to the crags rising out of it beyond.

It was magnificent. The glacier, this early in the year, is only an enormous bowl-shaped snowfield lying in a semi-circle of granite crags. To our left was the sheer sharp face of Temple Crag, to the right (reading to the left)–Agassiz Needle, Thunderbolt, the North Peak of North Palisade, North Palisade, and Mount Sill–all about 14,000 feet or higher. The skyline was incredibly rugged and jagged against the deep blue sky. Below us we could see First, Second and Third Lakes, strung together like green beads, and higher were Black Lake, and Fourth, Fifth and Sixth Lakes all frozen over and covered with snow.

By now, of course, the glacier being at about 12,000 feet, we were way above timberline. There were no crevasses, but we could see the bergshrund where it tore away from the cliffs. Way off toward North Pal, our six chums moved like six tiny dots across the glacier. The snow was very icy, and we weren't particularly well equipped. Jonesy let me wear his crampons–they are so *wonderful*, the way those iron spikes bite into the crust, and they look so fine on the feet–heavy iron lashed on with rope. Joe had crampons, Spencer had nailed boots, and we had two ice axes. We roped together and started off along the steep and steeper edge of the icy glacier, Spencer first cutting steps with his ice axe (it was SO fine and Alpine), I next, then Ray, then Joe, last Dick.

We plodded on. Dick was a bit dubious about the climb, as the snow was so deep up the regular route. Finally we started up Sill off the regular route–and as it transpired, we made a very difficult First Ascent of the Northeast Ridge of Mt. Sill (elevation 14,100 feet)! Dick said there were no more difficult pitches on the famed East Face of Whitney.

It was such a good climb! I was very gratified to find that high altitudes had no effect on me at all. First we roped up rather easy pitches, stopping occasionally to eat. It got harder and harder. Time flew. It was *cold*. Occasionally a little ledge in the sun, out of the wind, would be warm, but in the main we shook and shivered with cold for hours.

I *love* climbing so. We could occasionally hear the boys yelling from North Pal, though it was too far off to see them. Down below us, Koster and another fellow were starting up Sill by the usual, easy route. Joe and Ray were getting dreadfully tired. I don't believe Joe really likes rock climbing; it scares him, and he gets awfully pooped. For the first time, I understood why Dick and Brinton and Glen gripe so at people who *won't* hurry on the rocks. When you are climbing against time, and are bitterly cold, it is awful to have to wait and wait for someone who won't even start a pitch. We got into some fine difficulties. One long traverse, with virtually nothing to hold on to, was the hardest pitch I have ever done; then we came to a long 120-foot pitch where we had to tie both ropes together and bring up five men and a knapsack separately. I roared cheerily up it, and when Ray got up he was so exhausted he had to lie against the rock shaking with exhaustion, and Spencer had to drag Joe up on the rope. I don't know if you know those guys. Ray is large, chubby, simple. Spencer Austin is kind of sappy, very delicate-looking, with a weasely face and a mustache, but he was filled with admiration for my climbing ability, which warmed me toward him. He said he had heard "a lot about girl mountain-climbers, but I certainly have to take my hat off to you," and admired my stamina, etc.

After the long pitch, and another delicate traverse, we came out on a ledge. By then it was after 3:00, and it was a question of whether we ought to start down without making the top. At that point, the Koster appeared on the summit, and cheered us on. Spencer and I went roaring up on one rope, and poor Jonesy brought up the others eventually. When we all got up, we rushed to the summit and signed the register, at 4:00 p.m.

It was my first 14,000 foot peak, my first *real* mountain–and it was MARVELOUS. Sill has one of the most famous views in the Sierra. You remember the McGee view. This was that view multiplied to an indescribable pitch of beauty. In *every* direction rose those sharp jagged granite peaks, sweeping off into the most exquisite shadings of blue and white, with the loveliest line of billowing clouds just over the peaks, with the blue mists and the snow in the valleys, with the lakes below us, and the snowfields, and exquisite little turquoise lakes lying in the hollows of the snow, and the gray-purple close crags outlined against the dimmer blue crags beyond.

It was only a glimpse of the whole grandeur. It was 4:00 o'clock, and bitterly cold, storm clouds were rolling across the sun, and we had to get off the rocks by dark. We had to climb down the usual route, as there was no place to rope down. Koster showed us where to go, and charged on down, getting to camp an hour before us, bearing tidings of our famous climb. Spencer and I went down on the first rope, and the other three followed far behind. Climbing down the rocks was not especially hard, but it was tricky, and dull, and we were tired. Then when we finally got off Mt. Sill, there was a long trek through snow, first soft, then down steep slopes getting crusty, which we ran down digging in our heels, or slid down on our rumps.

At about 7:30, as dusk was falling, after a fourteen hour grind, we plodded into camp. All those left at Home stood out on the granite point, and yelled remarks about why didn't we pick up our feet. But when we got home, they welcomed us like long-lost travelers. It was so lovely to receive such a warm welcome from a band a chums. They treated me like a little hero because I was the only girl to breeze up the rock. Helen Hennies couldn't get over how I "was the only girl and came in smiling." I had had *such* a swell time. Art Johnson came to me and quietly advised me to put on a lot of coats for an hour, as my vitality was low. I advised that I was already wearing all the "coats" I had, and Jim  gave me the shirt (literally) off his back. Helen and Agnes brought us hot tea, and hot bouillon, and hot pea soup.

We sat by the fire. It got dark. We expected our chums from North Palisade to come home about 9:00. But 9:00 o'clock came, and they didn't come. 10:00 o'clock came and they didn't come. The camp got kind of quiet, as we sat wearily about our big hot fire out on the point, our eyes roving up to the snow notch to the right of Temple Crag, beyond which the weak silver moon was setting. Jonesy and Jim quietly planned to go and look for them in the morning. Finally most of us went to bed.

I didn't sleep very well. I was cold, even though the night was warmer than the one before, and I had on my long underwear over my pajamas–I guess it was because the long chilly day had sapped all my vitality. One could hardly help wondering about the chums that didn't come back. At 4:30 the next morning, Jim, Dick, Spencer Austin and Gatesy–breakfasted by others–prepared knapsacks of hot soup, hot water in canteens, first aid, spy glasses, etc.; arranged a series of signals by flashes of mirrors (twice: okay; three times: help from our camp; four, get a ranger; two series of three, help from below). About 5:30 they started up the long long hill.

The camp was a very subdued one, though no one said much. All of a sudden everyone was very generous and kind and chummy. No one built individual cooking fires any more, but brought their food down to the big fire; everyone ate each other's food out of unidentified and unwashed dishes, and pressed someone else's tid-bits upon each other.

Never before have I been where people did not return. It took so long for the tiny black specks even to disappear over the hill. People offered theories of contrasting hope and despair. I couldn't understand why they weren't back by 8:00, even if they had to spend the night on the rock, nor could I imagine that all six could have been killed or badly hurt. Dean Ashcraft pulled in Eastern Brook after Eastern Brook from our point of rock. Someone remembered that the last thing Johnny said the night before was, "The crags in the moonlight always remind me of monuments to the skiers and rock climbers who didn't come back."

Suddenly, a little after 9:00, someone let out a shout. From the far-off brow of the hill a mirror had flashed in the sunlight. It is a marvelous way of communicating over long distances. We counted the flashes again and again, hardly able to believe our eyes when each time we saw only two–meaning everything was all right. Art, focusing by two rocks lined up, flashed the signal back. Everyone sort of gasped with relief, and how that camp did perk up! One wee black dot started down the hill, very slowly. A second dot also appeared. Eventually the first one developed into Jonesy, who had carried Wayland's skis across the glacier, a tedious hour's trip, and skied back to signal to us in ten minutes time! The second dot finally turned into Brinton. They came down the snowfields, along the ridge, and crossed the stream at the dam. For myself, I rushed along the shore to meet them. I have seldom been so glad to see anyone as I was to see the good Brinton. He plodded into camp, hardly able to lift a foot, but grinning from ear to ear in his gat-toothed way–his fore-head so sunburned he had it tied up in a handkerchief, his nose half raw with sunburn and the rest of it yellow with sun paint. How we showered the man with loving attentions!

I am glad to say that it wasn't our mountaineers' mistake. About halfway up the rock, they met with a party of three boys of about 19, who were screwily climbing with nailed boots, alpine stocks and no rope. They were good fast climbers and were doing very well until they dislodged a loose boulder and had their morale all shot. Our boys didn't know just what to do with them, and finally roped them to the summit. Then they had to rope down, and the newcomers were scared, and didn't know how, and there were nine men on a rope, so each rope-down took an hour. By dark, they had reached the snow chute at the bottom, which they dared not descend in the dark. So, cutting steps in the snow with an ice axe by flashlight, they managed to cross to a sizable ledge, and spent the night. It couldn't have been pleasant. It was below freezing where we were, about 3,000 feet below. At the crack of dawn they started down, but it took a dreadfully long time because the others were so slow and there were so many. The poor *poor* chums.

A long time afterwards, the others poured over the hill. Wayland skied down but couldn't make a single turn, he was so weary. The second into camp was Walter Hennies, grinning, shoulders droop-ing, welcomed by his wife. Next came Johnny, groggy and stumbling, but cheerful, and almost the first thing he did was to pat me on the back and say, "Congratulations on breezing up Sill–you did just as well as I thought you would." (Brinton also congratulated me the instant he saw me.) Then came Hensel, almost blind with weariness his hands bloated with cold. Then Wayland, gaunt and hollow-eyed.

And a long long time later, poor little Muir, who had been ill, and was so tired that he slept between every rope down, and by the time he got down couldn't walk more than twenty feet without lying down to rest. And even Muir was smiling. They were all rosy with sunburn through their beards.

We gathered about them, and fed them tea and fruit, which was all they wanted, and a pan of Jell-O. Koster finally called a little formal meeting out on the point, in the sunshine, with the campfire smoke blowing in our faces, and had Brinton tell the whole story so everyone would have the same tale. Brinton cheerily recommended a bivouac for every rock-climber.

Finally, at about noon, we started out in little groups to tramp down the hot trail. We reached the cars, washed our feet in the stream, started off. At Big Pine, everyone stopped for gas, and to drink milk shakes.

We left Big Pine about 4:00. Joe drove first, while Jonesy and I fell into a deep stupor, and neither of us even looked at the Sierra. I drove from about 6:00 to 8:00. We got home about 10:00–though it felt like midnight.

I seem remarkably fine today. Aside from chapped lips, I am very healthy–haven't even a skinned knuckle or a stiff muscle. I wish I could go to the Sierra every weekend, or at least every other weekend, and climb a few peaks.

# Mount Whitney, East Buttress Route

THIRD ASCENT

HUNT DRIVE,

SOUTH PASADENA, LOS ANGELES

SEPTEMBER 7, 1938

*Dear Mother,*

I must tell you about our perfectly *wonderful* Labor Day Mount Whitney trip. It was certainly the most terrific trip of *my* mountaineering career.

We went in Wayland Gilbert's car, pack-boards and other crud done up in white canvas on top. Two of the passengers were Wayland's Sierra Club friends, Jim Clark and Dick Putzier. They were rather odd simple souls, the kind of people who regard Rock Climbers with uncomprehending awe. Also there was George Templeton, one of the newer rock climbers, a sallow, mildly unhealthy youth who lives near San Bernardino.

We drove north toward Owen's Valley, stopping for food and gas in Mojave, a desert town of a smutty nature, whose main features are switching railroad trains and a perpetual strong wind. It is about a 240 or 250 mile drive to Lone Pine, then west up a dirt road into the mountains. We came to the end of the road about 1:00 a.m., slept for four hours, then started up towards East Face Lake and the big climb. There were eleven rock climbers, nine fellows and two girls. . . .

. . . At 6:30 the next morning, all eleven of us awoke at East Face Lake ready to climb the 1,700 feet more to the highest peak in the U.S. First we climbed up a steep boulder-strewn hillside. About an hour later we roped up, and ascended the Sunshine PeeWee Route, which only two parties have previously climbed. About twenty-five have climbed the old East Face Route since 1931. A year ago the Sunshine PeeWee route up the buttress was pioneered by Glen, Brinton, Koster, Jonesy, and Muir. A few weeks later Art Johnson and Bill Rice climbed it.

I often can't recall a long climb. I also don't deem it best to describe in detail all the pitches, the 1,000-foot sheer drops to snow banks below. It was no harder than many climbs I have been on. It was a fine sunny warm day, not complicated by the cold and uncertainty of Sill on the Fourth of July. East Face Lake dropped and dropped below us, the most exquisite deep blue-green I have ever seen. More and more granite, everywhere. The "peewee" was a monstrous hanging beak of rock near the top.

The end of the climb was incongruous. When we were almost up, we could see a hundred or so Sierra Club members hanging over, training binoculars and cameras on us. It turned our lonely occupation into a spectator sport. They told us we had to go and sign the Sierra Club register–and not a single rock climber would walk 25 feet to sign it. Presently the register, previously described as un-removable, came to us.

We climbed down the Mountaineers Route, a precipitous talus chute just to the north of the utterly sheer East Face. It takes *so long* to get down. We got our packs and continued down to Mirror Lake for the night. Monday was another exquisite sunny pure day. Wayland, George, and I set out for a little 5-hour climb as a bracer before lunch. We climbed up the face of the Misprint, so called by the Rock Climbing Section because its elevation marked on the map is 1,000 feet too high. Afterwards, I started hiking the rest of the way out alone. It gives one the most charming feeling of independence and self-reliance and mobility, simply to slap your pack on your back and go when you are ready. I felt wonderful and able-bodied. Halfway down, a slight bronzed youth came up behind me, and we tramped down the steeper old trail together chatting. He confided that every time he got a new girlfriend he would take her for a mild hike in the mountains, wear her all out, and lose her love. He also confided that he had almost got married two months ago, but the girl decided he liked his sports more than he liked her. I am not sure whether this was an indirect proposal or not, but I didn't take him up on it.

On the way home, I drove for a couple of hours, with Wayland sitting beside me directing my driving technique and making penny bets to keep awake on when 2 miles had passed, or how far to the top of the ridge, or how many cars we would meet in the next 10 miles. I do believe I still owe the man 10 cents.

Eventually, about 10:30, we got home. It was *such* a fine trip. I learned so much about climbing, and mountaineering.

*Good-bye,*

*Your mountaineer daughter*

# Mount San Jacinto, Snow Creek

HUNTINGTON DR.,

SOUTH PASADENA, LOS ANGELES

NOVEMBER 14, 1938

*Dear Mother,*

Before I forget the details, which already seem rather long ago, though scarcely twenty-four hours ago I was hungering for lunch in Idyllwild having had but half a tin of sardines for breakfast, I must write you about the Saga of Snow Creek.

It was one of the funniest trips I have ever made. It began to be funny long before the time for the trip arrived. Snow Creek, in the first place, is notorious as a place where people take awful beatings, and the Rock Climbing Section is filled with vague legends about how long the climb takes–from twelve to twenty-seven hours–how dreadfully tired people get, how Nelson Nies went to sleep on top with a piece of cheese hanging out of his mouth–how cold people get–and all that kind of thing. This particular trip was vague from the start, it never being certain who was going, no one apparently wanting to go very badly, transportation evaporating and appearing again, etc.

Snow Creek is one of the longest climbs in Southern California, considered impregnable by Old Timers and plenty stiff by everyone who ever made it. For myself, though I was rather filled with foreboding, I had a better time, with much less hardship, than I ever expected. San

Jacinto is a 10,805 foot peak in Riverside County, perhaps 120 miles east and south of Los Angeles. Its southern slopes are forested, approached gradually through brush-covered foothills, and the peak can be climbed on this side by a gentle 9-mile trail that begins at Idyllwild, at about 5,500 or 6,000 feet elevation, near the foot of Tahquitz Rock.

The northern side of the mountain drops abruptly to the desert at Palm Springs, elevation about 1,500 feet–almost 9,000 feet of precipitous slopes covered with large hunks of good gray granite. From about 7,000 or 8,000 feet there is good timber. Below that, it is desert-like and brushy. Snow Creek is the main drainage of that side of the mountain, dropping down a sharp granite-walled canyon, over falls and boulders and out into the wide white wash that runs through the desert valley. Directly to the north, across the brown valley, mountains rise in bare, brown eroded slopes to the 11,000 foot peak of San Gorgonio (beyond which are Keller Peak and San Antonio). Snow Creek, one can see from the foot, rises through wild rugged brushy mountains, making one or two sharp well-defined turns, and finally, far and away and high up, spreads out into two or three gray almost perpendicular channels that cut the upper ridges of the peak–all the mountainside very steep and rocky.

Well, to begin at the beginning. Thursday night I made up my simple little pack and went to bed early. A little after 9:00 the next morning, Burton Harrison came for me and we went to Fontana, near Riverside, to get George Templeton. Four people were to make the climb–Burton Harrison is a chubbins indeed, with a doll face, a wondrous English accent, and a merry little giggle. He is married, about 35 I guess though I can't tell, had done quite a few interesting things in his day, and in my opinion isn't much of a climber; he was very nice to me, and seems a good enough fellow, but I just don't like him–he smokes and drinks a lot, and I suspect is utterly selfish. Art Johnson was supposed to take me up the peak, and while Art is a very odd moody creature, I like him, and have great respect for his mountaineering ability. Burton and Art had both climbed Snow Creek a couple of times before, and were meant to be guarding and guiding us two beginners (neophytes). George Templeton is a silent quiet boy–goes to Junior College, has a long sallow face, not much of a sense of humor, but is a very nice lad; rather inexperienced in mountaineering, but a conservative, logical youth; not overly healthy, I fear.

At Fontana, Burton went to do some errands, while I stayed at George's house. Mrs. Templeton is a short fat little lady who worries volubly about her only son. I helped her assemble his commissary, busily assuring her about how Safe our blood-curdling little jaunts are, while George prowled moodily about the home, and Mrs. Templeton wished vocally that he wouldn't *do* these things.

Burton returned for us, and we drove like bats out of hell to Redlands, where we called on Joe Momyer to borrow his 2-pound sleeping bag for George, only Momyer wasn't home and neither was the sleeping bag, so we chatted for a moment with his mother (a slim alive little woman with white bobbed hair and bright black eyes under strong black eye-brows) and his grandmother (a dainty little old tiny lady, with lovely soft white hair, who explained to us why she couldn't go into the mountains much). We then drove out across desert country, and up the road that starts up the Snow Creek wash, to where we were to camp that night. Burton left, to visit his family in Palm Springs a few miles away, and George and I had the afternoon to while away.

We were in an odd state of mind. The elevation was only about

*Doug and Rob Roy McDonald*

2,000 feet and it was in the desert, and rather warm, but we were so filled with the idea of how cold we'd be the next day that we nearly froze. We had done nothing at all that day, but were so tired thinking of the next day that we could hardly move a muscle. There was a strong wind blowing. Snow Creek rose in a gray streak up to the sky. (Burton, Art, and George all definitely *saw* that the canyon was filled with snow. I for one claimed I couldn't see any, and I was pleased because there wasn't any, as it turned out.) George and I ate lunch, climbed a few rocks in a weak way, and wandered aimlessly about getting firewood. The country was covered with dry grass among pink granite boulders. The creek was clear and cold, and smelled good with the brown Sycamore leaves, and the willows and the alders, dropping into the water. Everything was quiet except for the wind. George was an odd companion because he was so quiet. It was almost like being alone with the mountains, except there was somebody there in case you wanted him.

Being so weary, we built ourselves a little fire about 4:00, and put the stew on to heat. About 5:00 we had supper. It was pitch dark a few minutes after 5:00. This shocked me considerably, as I hadn't Realized. Well, it *is* mid-November. We had cups of stew, which was made by George's ma and tasted exactly like our family stew, and milk, and loganberry jelly (of which I ate the whole jarful), and cake. I was so sure I needed a lot of sleep, that I was in my sleeping bag and sound asleep at 6:00 p.m.! Burton came in at 7:00, and I talked to him a few minutes. Art drove in about 10:00, and I felt as if I'd had a full night's sleep, and I talked to him. Then to sleep again. My bed was on a little knoll on the grass, neither soft nor even, in the wind, and I slept like a log. The three men all had mattresses, and lay awake most of the night brooding over the wind.

We were supposed to start at 4:00 a.m., but no one got up till 6:00. George and I had stew and milk for breakfast, and we made up our little packs. Mine consisted of my sleeping bag, canteen, a meager supply of food, and a little cloth sack of personal things, lashed to Adrienne's light pack board—I suppose it weighed 8 or 10 pounds. And then the men began to drop off around us. It was rather disconcerting. First Art said in his quiet almost unnoticeable way that he hadn't done anything for four months, and had a cold and stomach trouble all week, couldn't make the peak, and wasn't going. He said he would go around by trail and meet us on top. I was kind of taken aback, as I didn't want to climb with Burton Harrison, on whose breath one can always smell whiskey and I *knew* he would never get to the top. Art gave me the food he had got for our climb and took me quietly aside and said "Burton is going to fold up on you." I said I knew it—but didn't know it would come quite so soon. We hadn't climbed more than 45 minutes when Burton was quietly sick in the grass. He said he couldn't go on, but we could if we wished, which we did.  As we found out later Burton took a couple of hours to get back to his car–and then when driving back, what should he find but Art, who was supposed to be bringing food and water by trail to the peak for us, quietly and feebly sleeping in his sleeping-bag out in the wash.

Meanwhile, George and I, the two inexperienced little mountain-climbers that we were, with one thing in common–the inner urge to climb Snow Creek (and we also are both unable to carry a tune and don't like raisins)–were forging happily ahead, quietly minding our own business, conversing occasionally but generally enjoying ourselves each in our own inconspicuous way.  I had no great confidence in George's leadership, but on the other hand, I had been on several trips with him–he climbed the East Face of Whitney–and I knew he was sensible and probably would get along all right.  On the other hand, I was tremendously relieved that Burton was not going; knew I *couldn't* get lost; and was confident that *I* could make the climb.  In fact, it was fun sort of sharing the responsibility, helping pick the way, making decisions, and for the first time going on a real tough trip somewhat on my own responsibility, and not cared for by some-one who knew all about it.  One has to learn sometime.

Through the early-morning light we picked our way; the lower part of the canyon was filled with trees, and we climbed up a brushy rocky ridge, which was a flat little mesa on top with a path that led we knew not where.  We followed quietly along it, across the hilltop covered with yellow grass and mesquite and rocks.  After an hour or two, the path turned sharply to the left, and we deserted it, to clam-ber down a rocky canyon-side to Snow Creek.

Then the climb began.  None of it was especially hard–just a grind.  The creek bed was strewn with boulders.  The canyon walls rose in slabby granite to brush-grown rock-strewn rugged mountain country. In about 5 miles, the creek rose almost 2 miles–and you can figure out the angle from that. We climbed easily and steadily over huge boulders–our tennis shoes sticking by friction to their sides. It went up and up and up. The stream dropped over sheer falls which we could climb around the sides of, or occasionally had to climb altogether out of the canyon and do a little strenuous time-wasting bush-whacking to get over the rocks. There wasn't much rock-climbing, in the real sense of the word, except a couple of rather nasty pitches, which we should not have climbed unroped with a pack, except we had no rope and there was nothing else to do!

The air was cold. You could tell by the stiffness of the face, and the way you shivered when you rested. But climbing was a warming exercise. The sun didn't appear till after 8:00, and scarcely got into the canyon at all, since the canyon faces north. It was rather discouraging the way the sun set at 10:00 a.m., appeared again weakly and briefly, and set for the final time at noon! Yet we could see it shining warmly in the valley, and casting beautiful topographic shadows on all the erosion patterns of the opposite range, which dropped and widened and spread in its brownish purple and red hues beneath us.

Gently we climbed up and up with our little packs. George got cramps in his legs, and lagged behind for hours and hours. I wasn't sure he ought to go on, and was rather relieved when by 2:00 o'clock I knew it was easier to go on than turn back. All that time I led the way, silently enjoying the exhilarating air, the exertion, the adventure, and the mountains and rocks and plants about me.

The creek was frozen tight almost all the way up. There were the most wonderful ice formations! Many of them were like Death Valley formations, only in ice. I had never seen anything like it, was fascinated by it. It poured over rocks in sheer ice-falls of 20 or 30 feet, with water dribbling out of it into clear deep black pools in the rock. It flowed over flat square slabs of rock like a fringed table-cloth. It formed sheaves of icicles. It bubbled up in knobby sheets of clear ice, or white bulbs of ice. It made icicles like leaves, icicles like electric light bulbs. There were pools of black ice and white ice, of clean ice and dirty ice. And plenty of ordinary icicles. It formed thin sheets of ice over the rocks, which you had to be very careful not to step on. George thought the ice was warmer than the rock and I that the rock was a little warmer. About 2:00, I stopped to fill my canteen from a pool broken in the ice, and spilled a little water on my jacket. Before I could brush it off, it was frozen to balls of ice–at only 2:00 p.m., thousands of feet below where we slept! There were little purple flowers, and red scarlet buglers, black with cold. And yellowing maiden-hair ferns. And golden willows. And rich beds of ferns under gigantic chock stones. And sheets and slabs and falls of soft gray ice over the gray rocks.

About midafternoon, we came to the place where the creek seemed to rush out of the mountain like a spring, which from Art's description we thought was the last water. Here we filled our canteens, and went on up the more and more abrupt, boulder choked canyon. We hadn't any idea how far it was to the top. We knew, and had known all day, that we couldn't reach the top by night. I was comforted and sustained by the thought of my sleeping bag–almost everyone goes without one.

About 4:30 I got terribly weary. My legs were *so* tired. I wasn't sure I'd ever climb another mountain. By this time, we were climbing up a ridge, just as rocky as the creek bed, among golden-trunked wind-warped Tamarack pines. We were fighting altitude, which takes the breath, as well as weariness and cold and rocks and climbing. I was suddenly quite appalled at where I had gotten myself, entirely by my own energy, and by the fact that nothing but my own energy would ever get me out.

George wanted to climb right on after dark. I was too tired, and anyway I had no intention of risking climbing in the dark over those rocks. Of course, my decision wasn't entirely unbiased, as I had a sleeping bag, but on the other hand, I knew we couldn't be much more comfortable on top than where we were. First I said we had to stop and rest a couple of hours, and then broke the news to him that I wouldn't stir a peg till 3:00 a.m. when the moon was up.

At 5:15 p.m., when I was utterly exhausted, and just as darkness closed swiftly over us, the good George walked into the only camp spot on the whole North face of San Jacinto, as far as I could see–one of the loveliest spots I have ever seen. There were actually flat places, commodious flat places covered deeply with pine needles; huge angular blocks of granite piled about and above us to cut off any wind; tall trees silhouetted against the deep blue, starry night sky; lots of firewood. We built a fire and sat in a stupor before it for an hour or so. I don't know how cold it was. It was cold in such a quiet insidious way that you didn't notice it. Yet the tumultuous creek had been frozen stiff thousands of feet below at midday; the night before, the airlines reported 2 degrees above zero at 11,000 feet near there; the canteen 2 feet from the fire froze stiff, and the tea bag 2 feet from the flames froze solid to the rock!

Finally we got up strength enough to heat water, drink bullion, then sweet tea, and then eat my can of corned beef hash. I then crawled into my sleeping bag and went cozily to sleep. I don't think I can ever make anyone believe how comfortable and happy I was up there, but it was true. I *love* the mountains so. The bed was not quite even, and not long enough, so my toes were wedged under a boulder. But it was soft, and so warm. I was sleeping under a great sloping wedge of rock, with the firelight flickering on the gray granite, and could look up between the huge angles of rock to the stars. Turned on my other side, I could see the soft warm beautiful glow of the campfire, and the trees against the stars beyond. I slept soundly and contentedly, feeling only mildly guilty about George, who sat by the fire wrapped in his blanket, moaning to himself once in a while for company, and occasionally waking me up and telling me we had to be moving, he couldn't stay there. Next morning he confessed that he wasn't really cold–there was no wind, luckily–but merely worried about being cold.

At 2:40 a.m. I got up. What an *hour* to arise, if I might say so. I hurriedly ate the scorched remains of the hash, and a few dried apricots, which I regretted for an hour, as I felt slightly sick at the stummick. We made up our little packs, and put on all our clothes, and started to climb. It was one of the funniest things I have seen. George had a huge red bandanna over his head, and a stocking cap over that, and a long untucked-in shirt on. I had on my ski jacket and parka hood, and mittens. With our little packs, in our tennis shoes, without saying a word, or making a sound as we moved, we moved softly through the woods. The woods were marvelous in the moonlight, bright and shadowy, the rocks gleaming whitely, as we moved confidently by friction over their sloping sides, the stars so brilliant. Beneath us lay the lights of Palm Springs in the valley, and beyond, the mountain ranges in the moonlight, and around us the trees, black and stiff, and the rocks, white and shining. We charted our course by the Great Dipper. It was fiercely cold in such a very dry way that we hardly noticed it. But it was so cold we couldn't breathe deeply, it hurt the lungs too cruelly and made one breathless, so we moved very slowly and gently as to not get winded. And very silently we climbed and climbed through the forest.

We reached the top of the ridge. By moving a short distance across the ridge, we could first see a sheer drop-off to the east–then a panorama of desert and mountains to the north–then an even wider forested panorama of mountains to the south, all laid out in the moonlight. We both felt rather sick, but climbed softly on. We thought we had a good four hours of climbing. Neither of us knew how far the peak was, though we knew it lay to the west. In the moonlight, we scaled a slight hump of smooth slabs of granite heaped up one on the other–we couldn't contour it successfully either to the north or the south. And suddenly, abruptly, at twenty minutes after 4:00, we were on San Jacinto Peak! You know how what you think is the peak, never never is. Yet here, hours before we expected it, unhoped for, even, we were on the top, shouting exultantly over the Sierra Club wrought-iron register on top.

We didn't bother to sign the register. We dropped down to the little plateau below to find the small hut which is there for wayfarers. It was a dirty little stone building with broken windows, and two double-deck wood bunks like on a school sleeping-porch, and a deep stone fireplace. We built a fire in the fireplace, and George was a little sick, and then went to bed on the bunk nearest the fire, and I got into my sleeping bag, and slept soundly and warmly till quarter to 7:00.

The sun was streaming in the eastern window. The dirty floor of the hut was ankle deep in debris and gum paper. There were two cooking dishes, two bottles and a box of tea on the mantle. We had hardly any water so couldn't eat. In spite of everything we'd been through, we suddenly found ourselves sitting before the fire gaily discussing the Santa Susanna Flake climb at Stoney Point. I hadn't washed for two days, but went so far as to comb my hair, and we put on our packs and started on the 9-mile hike down the south side.

It was such a *glorious* morning, there on the peak. The air was so cold, and dry and clear. We were quite ringed with mountains flowing and throbbing with early-morning blue. Way off to the east, in Imperial Valley, lay the Salton Sea, a great flowing mass of gold, so golden that it seemed to float above the blue plain, detached from the landscape and unreal. Far beneath us and to the south lay snow in the forests. To the north were brown-purple desert and hills glowing with blueness in the clear cold morning.

There is an excellent and very pleasant trail on the south side. But still, the 9 miles were rather long. At 8:30 we sat down in the dusty trail and ate a tin of sardines between us. It was all we had except some dried apricots, which I could not bear to eat. I had lost a square of chocolate–a major tragedy. The sardine breakfast was *so good*. A little farther along the trail we found some streams of clear icy water. It was such a beautiful morning. Deer leapt and bounded through the brush. At 8,000 feet and below was snow. It was odd–climbing *up* to timberline and *down* to snow–there had been no precipitation above 8,000 feet. The trail skirted mountainsides–was covered with a mixture of man and deer tracks. Even in tennis shoes, it was so *good* to tramp through an inch of dry creaking snow. The sky was so blue, the sun so golden, the air so clear and fresh. The evergreens were covered with an odd ice-snow formation; chunks of ice having formed on the limbs, were now dropping and rattling off in the sun. The willows were golden, and their little curling leaves fell on the snow. The trail went gently along and down. Mountain meadows and forests and peaks were spread all about us. Granite lay in chunks in the woods. The trail eventually dropped down a cold gloomy canyon-side in abrupt and endless switch backs. My legs were so tired by then. The creek was frozen stiff. Tahquitz Rock jutted out of an adjacent mountainside, from this angle the final jag in an imposing series of rock ribs along a ridge. We met a few clean neat people coming up the trail–they were the first people we had seen in two days, and it was kind of a shock. I guess we looked pretty dirty and frowsy and they regarded us with suspicion.

The trail eventually dropped below the top of Suicide Cliff, which is a familiar landmark across the valley from Tahquitz Rock. The snow thinned a little, and we scuffled along frozen ground and snow mixed up with brown oak leaves, acorns and pine needles. It was so good and home-like to join the Tahquitz trail. And suddenly we found a note in the path from Burton, saying the car was down the road a piece. We were back.

We managed to drag our carcasses down the road to where the car should be, and wasn't at that moment, and laid ourselves down in the sun, under the golden trees, to wait. Suddenly we were terribly hungry. Visions of malted milks, and candy bars, and big triangles of chocolate cake, floated in the air. Some capering, dreadfully clean and energetic people nearby began to lay out a great hamper of picnic lunch, and when one girl remarked in a high-pitched voice, "I forgot the salt! So what!!" we just couldn't bear it. Tired as we were, far as we'd come, we got up, shouldered our packs, and started down the road.

In a few minutes Burton drove up–exceedingly relieved to see us I can tell you–and we to see him–and we drove out of the mountains to Hemet or some little town and gorged on milk-shakes and hamburgers, and ate slabs of cake which were left in our commissary and we'd forgotten about, all the way in. We were tired but felt good. We were all very gay. In Fontana we left George around 3:00, and I was home by about 4:30. Not a scratch; very filthy; smelling like sardines; unkempt; happy. I took a long hot bath, and put on a lot of clothes, because while I wasn'tcold, I felt as if I ought to be. And I called up Art to tell him I'd got to the top and back. The poor fellow was still suffering from his cold, and was much worried that I hadn't had enough to eat.

(Weeks later I found out that the RCS Powers had told Art that *UNDER NO CIRCUMSTANCE* were George and I to go alone. Heh.) Neither Art nor George would let me pay them for the food they provided, so all the trip cost me was $1.50 for gas and 15 cents trail fee. And a slight expenditure of energy of course. Anyway–I have climbed Snow Creek in November. Everyone thinks I must have suffered, which I did not. It was fun.

*Ruth E. Dyar*

# Mount Baldy

HUNTINGTON DR.,

SOUTH PASADENA, LOS ANGELES

DECEMBER 12, 1938

MONDAY

*Dear Mother,*

Well, I seemed to have survived my Christmas Party this weekend.  In this case, Andy proved to be a good date because he didn't bother me much.  Andy is much too dignified for the best enjoyment.  He is kind of nice, just rather chubby and very shy and quiet; Braeme I am actually getting to detest, though I thought I wouldn't mind him when he isn't my date.  He looks so skinned from the back, with his bald spot covered with a silly beret, and his ears sticking out, and I secretly think he is sort of a Social Climber.

I got home Saturday after a busy morning at the office.  I figured I might be a little more civilized for a party, so put on my flannel slacks, freshly pressed (in fact, I can't remember their ever being pressed before), and my green corduroy jacket, which never fails to excite favorable comment.

Braeme, Phoebe, Andy and I left about 3:00.  We had a pleasant time buying 10 cent Christmas gifts at a small-town store en route.  It was a wonderful store, with the cutest things, much more novel than ever seen in a ten cent store in town, and no one in the place but us.

Harwood Lodge is 40 or 50 miles from L.A.–east on the San

Bernardino highway, then up San Antonio Canyon to the north into the mountains. Much of the canyon hadn't been materially improved by the fires, what was left of it after last year's floods.

The Lodge did look Christmassy, with a huge fire blazing in the great stone fireplace, a little lighted tree, and tinsel, boughs, mistletoe, and bells draped about in the accepted manner. All we needed was snow outside, but the crisp mountain air was a delight after the week of torrid weather. The living room was filled with long tables (there were over a hundred to dinner, including many Ski Mountaineers). Our dates had to serve at dinner. It was a good meal—vegetable soup; tea and coffee; rolls; lots of butter; baked spuds; some kind of fish with a dab of juice on top; mince and apple pie; cheese. I was on the dishwashing committee. The sink was quite a sight, filled with a swarm of nasty dish water, and tons of tea leaves mingled tastily with fish bones.

There was a guy there who played the accordion all evening, with quite a blank patient look on his face. I love to dance, and we danced steadily from about 7:30 till 12:30, with only a little while out for Santa Claus to give presents, to sing a few carols and see some home-movies. Guess what I got from Santa Claus: a box of *raisins*. Walter Hennies had received a lady's white lace collar, so we traded. At 12:30 the music stopped, and I went off to bed up the hill, under a Live Oak tree, with the moon shining on the forest on the ridge above me.

I woke up about 7:00, brushed my teeth and washed my face in canteen water, and put on my complexion and combed my hair before putting on overalls and getting out of my sleeping bag. I no sooner got out than my hands got petrified with cold. It was good to get into the Lodge before the fireplace. We had an excellent breakfast of canned peaches, good hot mush, coffee and cocoa, some fancy coffee-cake rolls made by chef Dean Curtis, a chubby man who likes to strut about in his lovely white cook's hat; scrambled eggs, bacon, and plenty of everything.

After a while, we drove up the road to the foot of the Ski Hut Trail. It was a magnificent sunny morning, with the canyon and valley below filled with blue mists, every turn and stone in the part of the trail which I helped build, familiar. An hour and ten minutes brought us to the dear familiar little San Antonio Hut, perched on the precipitous canyon edge among the great pines, the terrifically steep scree (and ski) slope beyond, sweeping upward to the pinnacles against the sky.

We drank water and visited with people already there. Unfortunately, there were far too many people for the tools. Fritz wanted to climb Baldy to look for his watch, which he lost last week, and wanted me to go with him for company. I wasn't in much of a mountain-climbing mood, but finally went because there was nothing else to do anyway.

We started up the little creek of Gold Ridge Canyon about 11:45. The canyon was vaguely reminiscent of Snow Creek, as we climbed steeply over hunks of rock, although they were not water-worn and smoothed, but harsh and angular as they had broken off and rolled down the mountain. The water in the creek bed soon disappeared, and we climbed over talus and slipping scree. After half an hour, we came to a huge log, and decided to have lunch. We sat down on the scree slope with our feet braced on the end of the log. My lunch the Braeme had made the night before, contained some immensely thick, tough, and rather good French bread sandwiches with hamburger and cheese in them. After we had eaten, we were so weak that we rested for nearly two hours in the sun before we could go on.

*Harwood Lodge in the San Bernardino Mountains*
*Typical Harwood revelers in costume, mid-1930s. L to R: Muir Dawson, Sally Olin, unidentified man.*
*(Photographers: unknown; Sierra Club-Angeles Chapter Archives)*

It was so nice lying there in the full blaze of the December sun, out of the wind, the only sound in the great stillness the wind. We saw one bird and two ants. Everything else was stark and barren. Our mountains here are so incredibly *abrupt!* Up that high, Baldy is mostly steep barren gray sweeps of infertile talus and scree–with occasional mottlings of dark green brush, or a wind-twisted Tamarack pine. There was an immense simplicity in the land-scape–gray reaches of talus, far-off trees with conical down-slanted shadows on the gray talus, rocky pinnacles far up against the intense blue of the sky. Down the canyon, which reaches into the valley almost at sea level, wisps of white cloud were floating against oppo-site blue ridges, and there was a flat layer of cloud which from beneath must have been "high fog," from above was like the clouds one sees from an airplane, solid and white, topographical in forma-tion and looking definitely like something tangible that one could walk on and explore. We snoozed, our heads pillowed on the wardrobe Fritz had in his knapsack; soaked in the sun; watched rain-bows between our eyelashes and patterns of light against the inside of our lids; talked; Fritz is a sweet person.

Finally, about 2:00, we figured we'd better climb the mountain. A short scramble up more talus brought us to the trail which leads to Baldy's summit from somewhere near Harwood. Joan and two fel-lows had climbed the ridge and were on the trail a few hundred yards below us, but were too lazy to come on. Another half hour's easy climb brought us to the summit. The trail was merely a slightly flat-tened line along the expanses of broken gray talus that covers the barren ridge and summit. It was rather cold on top, though not very windy, quite different in aspect from the snow-whitened dome last Easter. We put on our jackets, studied Fritz's maps. He didn't find

*Muir Dawson painting exterior wall at San Antonio Ski Hut, circa 1939;*
*(Photo by DeDe Cartwright. Glen Dawson Collection, Sierra Club-Angeles Chapter Archives)*
*Drawing of the Baldy Ski Hut on an old Angeles Chapter outings schedule*
*(Sierra Club-Angeles Chapter Archives)*

his watch, poor lad. The scramble down was rather fooey. I was glad I had on my tattered ski boots instead of the tennis shoes I'd longed for coming up. In the fine scree we could practically glissade as if down a precipitous snow slope, but you know what it's like climbing down abrupt talus slopes. However, it wasn't a very long descent to the creek bed and down to the hut. I felt lean and exhilarated and glad I'd come.

We got there about 4:00, and nearly everyone had left. Glen, Kurt Mosauer and I hiked down the trail watching the soft pink of the sunset through a fog bank which we descended into and got underneath. Back at Harwood, Braeme seemed to be in a suppressed rage at my tardy return, but no one else minded. We were supposed to go to DeDe Cartwright's for dinner, but Braeme claimed he didn't have time now, and dropped Andy and me at Andy's house and we went on in his car. I was quite impressed with his dwelling–a magnificent big home, obviously very expensively furnished, but with practically no furniture–just nice big empty expanses with nice rugs, drapes, a few nice pieces of furniture and a lot of books. His father was a cute dignified old man with a white mustache who was sitting bolt upright reading a book. I think his mother or someone must be an invalid, as I got a glimpse of a sick-room with a Japanese maid. I felt slightly soiled, in my mountain climbing garments and my wind-wild hair.

We then drove to DeDe's, where after supper we played a lot of enjoyably silly games, and had contests racing some large cardboard turtles operated with a string. We then came home a little after 9:00, and I took a bath and to bed.

*Much love,*

*Ruth Dyar at Stoney Point in Chatsworth, 1939*

Chapter Two

# Base Camp, 1939

*John was washing and drying great stacks of dishes,*

*swathed in his grandmother's blue apron.*

*Olga and Glen were cleaning house, but were not only hindered*

*but perturbed by being unable to find the vacuum cleaner.*

RUTH DYAR

"At the end of my first season," Ruth remembered years later, "filled as it was with revelation, ecstasy and learning, I wondered if I could possibly enjoy another year as much. As a matter of fact, the most striking thing about the next spring turned out not to be climbing as such, but the establishment of a coeducational boarding house for climbers and skiers. Nowadays it might be called a commune, but since the term had not been invented in 1939, we had to pick a name of our own. We considered and rejected 'Green Gables,' 'Seven Gables,' and 'Clark Gables,' before we settled on the appropriate name of 'Base Camp.'" Base Camp is the term used by mountaineers for the staging area they establish below a multi-day climb, such as Everest Base Camp.

Base Camp was a large brown stucco house on North Griffin Avenue, a couple of blocks east of the Arroyo Seco Parkway (which became the Pasadena Freeway in 1940, now Route 110). Rent was $60 a month, not a high price. The house came furnished, had a fireplace, piano, and back yard, and immediately became the unofficial headquarters for the Ski Mountaineers and Rock Climbing Sections. At the beginning, the house was shared by three men and three women between the ages of 21 and 30, all with college educations and jobs. Detailed rules and regulations rotated chores among the six tenants, with no regard for each person's actual talents. Each team had one male and one female, none of whom had ever run a household before. Ruth wrote:

> I became busy, as usual ironing a dress before dinner on the Mugelporch while John and Olga cooked, and Howard watered the lawn, and Glen practiced typing on my typewriter–he can type thirty-six words per minute and has to get up to forty-five (which he won't, but I don't tell him so) by Monday so he can pass a Civil

Service exam. However, he was unwisely copying Clarence King's book on the High Sierra, and soon I found him reading the book instead of typing.

Ruth shared a bedroom with her sister Joan. Howard Koster roomed with Glen Warner. Olga Schomberg and John Mendenhall each had their own small room. Base Camp eventually expanded to ten tenants, with personnel changes from time to time.

Though Glen Dawson never lived at Base Camp, he visited often and was in the house on the nights when the *Mugelnoos* was published and prepared for distribution. He recalls that "there was a 'work party' on publication nights which included the final text, proofreading, running the old mimeograph machine, sometimes putting color in by hand, addressing, folding, stapling, and stamping. Plans were made for future trips. There were refreshments." He says that "there was complaining when someone did not do an assigned job (shopping, preparing meals, cleaning up, taking out trash, gardening), or failed to do it properly. However, several successful marriages came out of Base Camp."

Open country lay near the house and the Arroyo Seco ran close by on its way to the Pacific Ocean, from its source high in the San Gabriels. When the grassy hills at the end of the street turned brown in early summer, Ruth was reminded of the wheat fields back home in Eastern Washington. She loved the dark plumes of the eucalyptus trees, and the harsh blue silhouette of the Sierra Madre to the north. "It was a cold cloudy night," she wrote, "with glimmerings of a thin moon through the clouds. I was tired, melancholy, and felt that no one loved me. I started out into the grassy, little-inhabited hills, wearing tennis shoes that nearly fell off because they are so big and I was wearing no socks." Another evening, Ruth "descended the practically perpendicular and very queer cement 'steps' that go down the old river terrace 25 feet from our backyard, then crossed a few streets to the Arroyo Seco, a stream bed which is the (mutter) gutter of gutters. They are building an *immense* cement runway for the stream, virtually on the scale of Coulee Dam—and down the very bottom of this trickles a tiny rivulet of water."

The women at Base Camp took the Number 2, Griffin and Montecito Streetcar to work, which was supposed to come every ten minutes, then every sixteen, and sometimes took thirty-five, making everybody late to work. "Our streetcars are quite hideous, resurrected from some Happy Hunting Ground of broken-down streetcars," Ruth wrote. "They are built in three sections, the front and back compartments open and furnished with conventional wooden seats, middle part furnished with two long benches, running under the windows. One night–you won't believe this but it is the absolute truth–there was a man on the car so bulky he took up one *entire seat* and no one could sit beside him. I sit on the car completely absorbed in *The Romance of Mountaineering,* hardly conscious of the sloppy housewives with their shopping bags, the decaying males, and the hard-eyed business girls, while Saussure climbs Mount Blanc, or four daredevil cragsmen make a fiendish ascent of the Scarlet Crag, Skrlatica, in the Julian Alps. When we get off the car evenings, up the street the clean blue San Gabriels jut craggily against the sky, behind the ripe yellow-brown grass of our warm hills."

In 1939, Ruth was already thinking about writing a book. "Dear Daddy, Your idea for a book on mountain-climbing has great possibilities! I can think of no more pleasant assignment than being sent out to climb all the peaks. As it is, a work of this type should doubtless start out and be kept in order as the peaks fall beneath one's feet–my

Snow Creek trip and the East Face of Whitney being the only ones worth mentioning at the moment. When I read books or articles of other peoples' climbs, I promptly write excellent ones–in my head; which is doubtless a bad habit as it is too easy a substitute for putting it down on paper."

Ruth first met John Mendenhall at Tahquitz in June of 1938. In those days she called him "Johnny," a term of blithe affection that she ceased to use after a few years. John had begun climbing alone in the Sierra Nevada as a teenager, near Mount Morrison and Convict Lake. He studied library books on climbing and taught himself how to belay with a rope. In his book, *Climbing In North America*, climbing historian Chris Jones says that "Mendenhall's staying power was remarkable. In 1930 he was perhaps the first person to consciously belay in the Sierra when he climbed the Northeast Gully of Laurel Mountain."

Members of Base Camp continued to ski and climb that spring and summer, not without occasional minor miseries–scratches, bruises, abrasions, mosquito bites, poison oak, a stiff finger, even a horrible case of flea bites. Ruth continued to learn climbing technique. "Johnny came down behind me giving me many tips on mountaineering," she wrote. "I learn a lot from him, because he loves to give instructions. I still am most fond of him, but I think I like Jim better at the moment. Or at least Jim likes me better, which has some effect. They just brought me along on the climb because they wanted me. It was so cute the way as soon as one got out of sight around a corner of rock, the other would begin to flirt." The following spring, John invited Ruth to go skiing on Mount San Gorgonio, which at 11,502-feet is the highest mountain in Southern California. Ruth and John were engaged to be married by the end of July, 1939;

this marked the beginning of a climbing partnership that would last more than forty years and take them to unexplored regions of the Sierra Nevada and Canadian Rockies.

John Mendenhall was born in 1911 in Burlington Junction, Missouri, and came to Southern California as a child. He graduated *Phi Beta Kappa* from the California Institute of Technology in 1933, one of two "honor men" in his Civil Engineering class. Ruth introduced John to her mother by way of a long letter:

He isn't very tall, about 5'8", but marvelously built–with tremendous broad shoulders, an arm like the Arm & Hammer Soda trademark, strong nice hands, small waist, etc. He isn't particularly handsome, but I like the way he looks. He has brownish hair, that sort of kinky variety, and will be baldish someday. Nice clear complexion, blue eyes, fairly heavy eye-brows, small nose. He is a good, level-headed, straight-thinking, highly intelligent young man, sober and industrious in business and with a will to get on in the world. After Cal Tech he worked for several years with Consolidated Steel as a structural engineer out in the desert, a pretty tough job I imagine, handling construction crews and one thing and another. I imagine he was awfully lonely during those years. At present he is a designing engineer–designs bridges and things, and supervises their construction–for the Pacific Electric Railway. I guess he is a civil engineer, I am not sure. The examination he is studying for is a State examination for some kind of engineering license–usually they don't let men even take the exam who aren't much older and more experienced.

I am very glad we both like to climb. We both know there are other things in life, professions, home, etc., but for us the mountains and the rocks are something extra and wonderful.

Never fear, he will take care of me on the rocks—he admits he will never climb his best with me on the rope as he will be too busy being careful. We have so many of the same ideas, about homes and houses, and how to bring up children, and the mountains, and people, and families. It is all quite remarkable. We know that to be happy people, we have to like and respect and appreciate one another, as well as love one another, and really try to get along. He is so *good* to me (and for me), so thoughtful and considerate. On the surface he is very very polite, but I am glad he isn't really too polite inside. I know you and Fa' will both highly approve of him. I only hope I make as good an impression on his family as he will make on mine. If I provide Johnny as a son for you, I think I will have gotten you about as nice a one as you could ever want! Anyhows, I am sure he's the man for me. It makes me nervous just to think if anything should Happen.

Between Sierra ventures, Ruth and John climbed twelve times at Strawberry Peak to establish new routes. At the head of the Arroyo Seco and far above Pasadena, Strawberry Peak's nearly vertical north face, with its friable rock and lengthy approach, never became popular with rock climbers.

By an odd family coincidence, Ruth's cousin and Phoebe's sister, Elizabeth Russell, hiked to the top of Strawberry Peak eight years earlier, when she was 19 years old, with the intent of committing suicide. Elizabeth wrote in her journal, "How lovely the mountains were, so still, sweet, and waiting, that day as I climbed Strawberry—my 'last meal,' of chocolate and cold water. . . . And oh, how cold, how cold how CO-O-OLD it was up on my jumping-off place! . . . I didn't want that long, icy swoop through the frigid atmosphere to mark my end." The entry concludes with words eerily similar to Ruth's own Strawberry story in this chapter. Elizabeth wrote in her journal, "All through the early night I sped back over the dim, twilight trail, as though I were floating along, spiritually, if not mentally, in utter, utter peace. . . ." Strawberry Peak was completely abandoned as a technical climbing area after Word War II, due to the poor quality of the rock.

There were numerous trips to Tahquitz, during the summer of 1939. "It is always so delightful on the cliffs: the wind and the sun are purer and cleaner and fresher; the little ferns, the delicate wild columbines, the dainty little bushes similar to ninebark, the crisp little yellow violets, that spray out of the crevices, are so clean; the orange and green and black lichens on the gray and pink granite, the good clean solid granite, are so bright and pretty; below are the solid columns of trees rising out of the underbrush, the great hollow valley of forest sweeping down from the rocky peaks, and far off, south and west, the valley, mist-filled, from which rise peaks of the Palomars, other mountains, and Catalina Island.  And the marvelous comradeship and teamwork essential to climbing, as in no other activity." Of the route she climbed that day, the "Piton Pooper," Ruth said, "I guess I was the first girl ever to make it."

Ruth and John also climbed in the Minarets, near Yosemite National Park, and on Labor Day weekend of 1939, just as war was breaking out in Europe, Ruth and John made the first ascent of Mount Whitney's Third Needle.

Ruth wrote to her parents, "we have high flung hopes of climbing in the Cascades and the Olympics, and the Canadian Rockies, not to mention the Alps and the Himalayas before our day is done." –V.M.C.

# Mount Charleston

MUGELNOOS NIGHT AT BUENA VISTA TER.

LOS ANGELES, CALIF.

MARCH 7, 1939

*Dear Daddy,*

I spent the weekend in Nevada with Phoebe, Elizabeth, and Max. (I myself was quite homesick all weekend for the Ski Mountaineers. We miss them so when even a day goes by without seeing a few dozen of them.)

Charleston is a 11,910-foot peak about 350 miles north and east of L.A., good highway all the way–first to San Bernardino, then over Cajon Pass to Victorville, and on across the limitless expanses of San Bernardino County and into Nevada. It was a very long time since I had driven across the desert, and I had quite forgotten those lovely expanses of great empty Space–rolling miles of flatland grown with angular Joshua trees, spicy sage and creosote and manzanita, spiney yuccas, strange cacti, ringed on all horizons with eroded, stern, bare, and richly colored mountains and buttes. All that clean empty space, after the cluttered noise of cities, was wonderfully peaceful. It was a stormy afternoon and evening, with clouds, spurts of rain, a howling driving wind, and actually a snowstorm out in the desert, with cactus and Joshua trees oddly plastered with snow in the light night.

After leaving Las Vegas (impressionable mainly for a lurid array of neon signs advertising fine wide-open gambling dens), the road led off into the gradually rising and encompassing mountains. It was a strange weird night. The moon etched all the bare, snow-scattered hills and ranges in sharp, exquisite contrasts of white snow and black rock and land. Everything was mysterious, silent, enormous, and beautiful.

About 11:00 p.m., we arrived at Charleston Park Resort, where we were expected, and were shown by the caretaker to as lovely a mountain cabin as we ever saw–spacious, commodious, rustic, with a huge fire glowing in a wonderful deep fireplace. There were three enormous bunks, bigger than double beds, complete with bed-springs. We went to bed at once and slept till 8:30 the next morning. I will say it wasn't a very industrious weekend. We were the only guests in the resort, except occasional Las Vegans who dropped in to get drunk at the lodge, and they all thought we were Important or something, and all the employees, hostesses, managers, etc., spent the whole time showering us with such kindnesses and attentions that it was quite debilitating.

It was beautiful mountain country. The resort was situated near the mouth of a great horseshoe shaped canyon which rose up to north and south in towering limestone cliffs and forested ridges. East lay Grand Canyon desert and mountain country. To the west, at the end of the canyon, a good 10-mile trip, was the snowy bare hump of Charleston Peak. The most interesting feature of the landscape was the stratified nature of the limestone, lying in layers and shelves which went to make up great layers of cliffs, snow etching the various shelving strata. I think it would be far better rock-climbing country than ski country. The whole place is too much cliff, flat gully-bottom, and brush, for the best skiing.

In fact, I think skiing is a rather backward condition in Nevada. Fancy your daughter Ruth being the best skier on the entire mountain! Of course no one else was there Saturday, and only four schuss-boom fellows on Sunday.

The snow wasn't very good, being a rather icy crust with little changeable drifts of powder snow blown about on it. The weather, I will say, was magnificent and sunny, the air marvelous, the scenery entrancing. They have one ski run which would be excellent if the snow were decent–you drive up the road, which makes a long circle, ski down the run hacked through white-trunked young alders in a gully, and then someone drives you up the hill again. The hostess at the lodge had us to lunch, and nearly killed us with the good food–yummy chicken soup, light hot homemade rolls, fried chicken, mashed spuds, gravy, punkin pie, tea. We ate so much we could hardly ski come afternoon.

Just before dark, there was a lovely sight with the huge round silver full moon hanging in a pink and blue sky framed with mountain ranges and big trees (the forests were beautiful–Yellow pines, Foxtail pines, spruce). We then all lay about before the fireplace, had dinner, and occasionally dashed outdoors to look at the landscape in the moonlight–the moon was so brilliant that the trees made sharp clear black shadows on the snow, and the huge majestic serene mass of Cathedral Rock towered in a massive triangle 1000 feet above us, one side black in shadow, one side gleaming whitely in the moonlight, with an unearthly snow-silver line etched along its skyline, tall trees framing it, and a bank of white clouds forming a backdrop for it beneath softly glowing stars.

Went to bed very early–around 8:00–and got in eleven or twelve hours of sleep for a change. Next morning after breakfast Elizabeth, Max and I (Phoebe had hurt her ankle mildly and didn't go), set out to climb Cathedral Rock–not by its vertical front side, but around behind where a steep snow gully leads to its top. It was a lovely sunny day, the air crystal, the sun warm. I had fun "leading" the climb, which was about 2 miles I imagine, up a steep forested slope, along the base of the Rock with the alder-choked gully to our left, then traversing back and forth up a ridge, and finally taking off our skis and continuing over rocks and snow-patches to the top, whence we could look directly down upon the resort and trace in maplike detail the road and ski run–and look far off to the blue, violet, and snowy ranges southeast.

We ate our lunch on a dry spot under a pine tree, I huh-ing on the limestone and figuring out that it was shale, in my geologic manner. The snow was nasty skiing down, as it changed its character every two feet through every type of powder snow, various kinds of crust, ice, spring snow and drift. However, we got down alive.

The Manager of the resort belonged to the Desert Ski Club of Las Vegas. I don't know why he wasn't skiing, but anyway he broke down and gave me a membership in their club and one of their swell emblems–a fine felt circle about five inches in diameter, sand-colored with a nice design of crossed skis and poles in brown against a blue cactus, and DESERT SKI CLUB, LAS VEGAS, NEVADA printed on it. I was quite pleased with this trophy.

Finally about 4:00 we started home. About 7:00 we stopped on a crest looking over a glorious sunset behind mountain ranges, to heat up stew for supper. I quickly took a mile or so walk across the desert, in the gathering dusk, straight into a cutting biting wind, with the sunset glowing behind my shoulder, and the quiet fragrant desert all about me. I found a little mine, took a sample from its heap of tailings, peered into the glory hole, and hurried back for a bowl of steaming stew. A very sleepy drive home, whence we arrived about midnight.

*your loving daughter and sister,*

# Fourth Annual Ski Races at Mount Baldy

LOS ANGELES, CALIF.,

MARCH 20, 1939 —TUESDAY

*Dear Maw, Paw, and Chillun,*

This weekend were the Fourth Annual Races at San Antonio–the best weekend since Christmas, I believe. Practically everyone went up Saturday morning, but I worked, dashed home at noon, got dressed in my newly patched and pressed ski pants and clean flannel shirt, ate my lunch.

Finally my transportation arrived around 2:30–Dr. Carl with even a worse patch on his ski pants than mine, made out of blue denim and most conspicuous. Hensel Fremstad, quiet, smiling, with small head and big hands. Louis Turner, tall, slim, long-faced, with a sort of English accent and great charm and delightful wit. And Seth Blakeman, short, dark, stocky, humorous–he flies a Navy plane off the U.S. Ranger, formerly of the U.S.S. Tuscaloosa. (Carl asked Seth what he "did" and Seth didn't answer, so Louis said with great glee that Seth was so modest that he always told people he didn't do anything, and Seth put in modestly and in confusion, "Well, I *don't.*")

We stopped at Harwood Lodge to see if all the central commissary food was carried up yet, which to our great joy it was. Then we drove up the road to the falls, where a huge number of cars was parked, boding a full house at the hut. My skis were already up there, which I was very glad of. The others spent quite a time lashing their skis to their packs–straight up and down, or fancily crossed, and by and by we all started the grind up the trail. It was a hot afternoon. The woods had that lovely piney smell of thoroughly wet warm needles. The trail was dry nearly all the way so the climb took only a little over an hour. An appalling amount of snow had melted off the slalom bowl during the last week, which was very hot–where a week before it had all been white, now great gray rips of rock and talus reached from the pinnacles on the skyline way down into the bowl. And what snow was left was tattle-tale gray, and pitted and scarred and kind of used-looking.

Sometime between 5:00 and 6:00, I forget when, we reached the hut. It was at once apparent that the crowd was gay, the weekend good. The bare space under the pines in front was filled with stacks of skis. Little specks of skiers were moving from the slalom slope toward the hut. In the kitchen Mary Helen and DeDe, Helen Hennies and Walt and Brinton and Aggie were laying slices of pineapple on lettuce for the supper salads. The living room and Harem and upstairs were massed with milling skiers. I dashed upstairs and to my great amazement found one of the rope bunks with a mattress unoccupied, and quickly laid my sleeping bag upon it.

Everyone we knew was there, and others too that we didn't know very well, and some German friends of Phil's from San Diego. Oh it was fun. Phil and another lad played the accordion in shifts, and several of us danced furiously to its music in the dim light of a distant candle. There wasn't room on the dance-floor for more than two couples at a time, if that many. The lockers were crammed with people–everyone likes to sit en masse anyway, so no matter. For some reason I got a lot of Attention this weekend, which of course pleased me.

The table-setters, meanwhile, were getting the very meager supply of tables set for thirty-five people, and presently we all made a dash for the best places, and were crammed together so tight we couldn't move an elbow, which called for much yelling, and pushing, and bad manners. We had a fine dinner, as we always do at ski huts—Swiss steak, peas and carrots, pineapple and cottage cheese salad with trimming, baked spuds with lots of butter, hot rolls, violently strong tea, water, cookies, and absolutely divine Jell-O—nice and quivery, with thick masses of slopping whipped cream in which they had mixed pink ice-cream powder, and chopped nuts. We gobbled it like pigs, and later when Helen Hennies brought in a couple of extra dishes of it we pounced on it like a bunch of chickens leaping on a heap of grain or a twig of alfalfa. Phil Faulconer and I got a dishful between us, and since there were no spoons, gobbled it down on the edge of the cookies.

There is always such a fine Atmosphere at the San Antonio hut—everyone acting insane, and not a single person who doesn't exactly fit. Goodness knows they are all different enough, but they all get along so well. Every person seems to have a distinctive likeable character of his own, yet to fit in with the bunch. After dinner was over, the bodies settled in a great mass upon the lockers. Some people whose job it was did the dishes. Phil played the accordion at my elbow, and Louis played his mouth-organ in the really accomplished way he has, and everyone shrieked and joked.

A bunch got hold of Phil's little notebook of songs, and gathered in a mass around the table. They howled "Row row row your boat" till the hut nearly fell down with the sustained roar, and until some of the people in the room couldn't stand it and sat and screamed at the top of their lungs till they broke it up. They sang with fury until

10:00 o'clock when everyone decided it was time to go to bed. Sleepers were all over the hut, three in the harem, the lockers downstairs covered, Carl curled up in the cellar, and the upstairs full of twenty or twenty-five.

Actually getting to sleep upstairs was quite a process. They all love to act like infants. In the occasional beam of a flashlight a violent eviction went on where someone had annexed a bunk. Much joking, and punning, and kicking the person up above one. Everyone settled down, and then someone started to blow his nose, and Wayland remarked in a deep voice: "All okay on track 7" which sent everyone off into lengthy sieges of giggling. Everyone slept till 7:00 a.m., when simultaneously, they all decided it was time to get up.

The day of the great slalom had come. They couldn't have the Downhills from the top of Baldy due to the shocking shrinkage of snow.

Breakfast of grapefruit, oatmeal, gallons of good hot cocoa, cinnamon buns and toast. My duty of the weekend was the simple process of helping stack and scrape the breakfast dishes, this light task being arranged by some good friend or other. After that Phil and I found a can of something out in the snowdrift, which we didn't know what it was but drank it anyway–it was the pink dregs of the slurp for the last night's Jell-O, and very tasty. Phil once found someone's old bottle of chocolate-milk in a snowbank up there–with 6 baby chipmunks drowned in it.

Everyone was getting ready to ski. The "front yard" was filled with people briskly slapping sticky Klister on their skis, while the jaunty notes of a Bavarian phonograph record, or of the accordion, blasted out the door. The day was warm, but overcast and muggy. The place buzzed with skiers doing dishes, waxing skis inside and out, prowling into their lockers, getting drinks of water, brushing their teeth, standing in line for the gaboon and yodelling heartily at each exit, fussing endlessly with their equipment.

About 9:00 a.m. people began to assemble in the Slalom Bowl with their white cloth numbered bibs tied to their fronts. As there were about forty-five of us by now, the slope was quite covered with skiers. Muir, Brinton and people like that skittered about the hill setting the gay slalom flags. The course was ghastly. It started far up among the pinnacles, on the icy perpendicular slopes at the far right-hand edge of the slalom slope. I toiled halfway up it, and decided I'd rather live than try to run down the thing. DeDe, little RobRoy, and I, a blond boy who broke a ski, and one or two other happily chicken-hearted souls, sat on an outthrusting rib of talus, shivered in the wind, and watched the slaughter with glee. (This was the Press Rocks). There was a long period of people setting flags, toiling up the hill on foot, scuttling down in practice runs, and saying ominously between their teeth: "It looks *tough*."

Everyone had drawn for places–about thirty-five entered the race. Many were disqualified for taking too long or getting off the course. A little knot of officials at the bottom timed the racers with a stop watch. At the top a gyrating, and then descending red flag on a pole marked the start. The whole thing was hair-raising. We were in a fine place to watch the best falls on the upper slopes, which were icy. Only four people made the run without falling. Once one tumbled on the upper slopes, they were so steep that the skier would roll and somersault down the slopes for hundreds of feet. The sky was overcast, the wind rather cold, and occasionally there would be a slight spitting of hail or snow. Sizeable rocks kept shooting off the pinnacles and hurtling down straight at people–Bill Davies was literally chased by one, and had to leap over it as it whistled for him, much to our great amusement.

Brinton started the race, running down like a bat out of hell, much too fast, went head over heels near the foot of the course in the most magnificent spinning windmill of skis and poles and legs and arms that we ever saw–coming out with only a shattered pole (the equipment casualty-rate was very high). Mary Helen gamely entered the race (only two gals finished), rolled down and down the steep slope, and landed in a rock pile. Earl Wallace took honors for the longest slide, and lost all the hide off one arm. Bud Halley spun like a top on his rump. Two skiers crashed together. Someone did a marvelous cartwheeling somersault, rolling onto his skis again and on down the hill. Larry Thackwell crashed headlong into a pile of rocks, leaped up, and tore *on skis* across the strip of talus, and rushed on down the course. People would fall down the hill so far they had to climb up again to get through the flags, losing much time. It was all very entertaining. Fuzz Merritt, slim, pleasant Pomona College football coach, took First place, Louis Turner Second, then Muir, then Bob MacConaghy, then Hensel. Opal took First for the women, and Aggie, being the only other gal who could finish, Second.

About noon it was all over, and we staggered home to the hut, leaving skis on the hill. They served a rather horrid central-commissary lunch, which we all enjoyed mightily. Soup, milk (dried kind mixed with water) and cocoa. Bread and butter and jam. We were all overjoyed to find that some of the bread was mouldy and when you shook it, bugs fell out. DeDe looked wistfully at the slice she had prepared lathered with butter and stacked with jam–shut her eyes and went on eating. Phil played his accordion.

Afterwards, I managed to get back to the ski slopes. But the snow was slushy and I was tired and inadequate, and soon returned again to the hut about 3:00, to rest and eat tid-bits, and read with pleasure "Lunn's High Speed Skiing." Lunn recommended the "Telemark Lunge" which pleased us, but we all felt we needed a book on "Slow Speed Skiing" worse.

Around 4:00, people began to pack up and leave. And so one's days, however good, come to an end. Disorganized bunches of us filtered down the trail. The sky was overcast, the woods sweet-smelling. We had an awfully good time going home in our car. Coming out, not knowing each other very well, we had been rather prim. Going back, Louis, Seth and I settled down in the back seat to one long siege of wrestling, struggling, howling, talking, and screaming like infants with protest and laughter. The others sang intermittently.

At Dick's Place in Azusa, no less than twenty-eight of us, nearly everyone who had been at the hut, crammed themselves at table for dinner—we always have to sit at one table, no matter how many tables we have to push together. I was wedged in between Wayland and Seth, who alternately beat me and I beat them, and we yelled and played with the silver, and ate hot biscuits dripping with honey and melted butter, and complained of the service, and had a mighty fine time. (Then we always wonder why restaurants don't like us.) Then a mass of us pushing out of the door, and several people scattered through Azusa shrieking loudly, "Dyar didn't pay her check" in a shameful fashion, and back into our cars—and home.

All the snow is melting and our minds are already turning to climbing. Everyone I know is going to the High Sierra for a week in April.

# Mount San Gorgonio Ski

BUENA VISTA TER.

LOS ANGELES, CALIF.

MAY 1ST, 1939 — MONDAY

*My Dear Al & Marg,*

I must take a little time to tell you of my weekend, "just another ski trip"–but as lovely as any I've ever had. I think I enjoyed the skiing, and did more of it, than ever before. Oh what *do* people *do* without these high-points of existence, these peaks of exaltation, that one experiences on a mountain?  How commonplace and insignificant cities seem.

Almost the end of the '38-39 ski season.  Johnny, Earl and I went out in Johnny's coupe Saturday afternoon.  It had been a funny, cloudy morning in town, but by the time we got out into the inland flatlands, and then up into the mountains, it was warm and sunny.  It was nice to be driving through those lovely woods again, with the tall mighty Sugar pines and Yellow pines (which I can't tell apart), and the vast tall beautiful Lodgepole pines.  A great deal of snow had melted off San Gorgonio since two weeks before and the tan rocks and talus jutted through all along the ridge above the snowfields and the forests.

We gathered together our packs, and started the 4-mile tramp in to the Meadows.  Johnny rushed ahead to pick out a campsite and start the fire.

I hiked in alone–I like hitting the trail alone; one feels more at one with the mountains and woods. It is such a lovely lovely trail–not very steep after the first mile or so, which is a variation of the original trail, invented by skiers. If one wasn't looking at the craggy, rocky, snow-gashed slopes far above, the woods were like summer. It was warm–and as evening set in, there wasn't that keen bite in the air, which bespoke winter, like two weeks ago, but rather the pressing coolness of a spring night in the mountains. The cedars were sharply green in the late sunshine. The woods were silent except for the distant singing of the brook in the canyon, and the clear calls of birds, and an occasional yodel from a comrade which sounded rather like a bird too. I sometimes think we don't appreciate the sheer loveliness of our trails enough: there are so many things to see–the way the mountains to the south, beyond the trees, are as blue as water; the golden growing tips of the gray willows; the chrome-yellow of the huge log at the avalanche butch; the way the rocks are split from a winter of frost; the funny towsled appearance of the brush after being covered all winter with heavy snow.

A little after 7:00, I came into the Meadows, passed by a couple of campfires, and spoke with the campers: a group of fellows whom I knew by sight; Bob and Luella MacConaghy; Mary Jane Edwards and her new friend, Heinz Krebs, who came out from N.Y. with Renny Wicks, a funny, homely, lean, gat-toothed German, frightfully good skier, formerly of the German Olympic team and quite a famed creature.

Found our camp spot toward the upper end of the Meadows. It was the loveliest night! I know of no more beautiful place that one could camp than the Meadows of a Thousand Springs. Its gentle gray-green-grassy slopes, broken with brooks and big trees, and patches of snow, and the mossy over-hanging banks, and the exquisite ringing of the myriad lovely brooks over the rocks and under their banks. Our campsite was right beside one of the brooks, under tall trees, and it was an enchanted night, with the moonlight lying in lovely silver lights and shadows on the snow patches, and on the shimmering ghostly peak far above us, and on the pines. The sky was clean and blue with a few soft points of stars. The brook rushed by us in a musical incredibly beautiful white motion, the moon lighting the water.

It wasn't very cold. Our glowing campfire in the stone semi-circle was lovely behind our cooking pots. We had one of those marvelous suppers eaten from tin cups, of Klein's soup, and vermicelli goo flavored with tomato paste and chili beans, and pork chops, and lemon drops, and hot tea, and marshmallows, and cookies. We meandered about visiting our neighbors, and they visited us, and we walked out into a clearing and looked at the mountains in the moonlight, so beautiful they almost set one to shaking.

About 9:30 we got into our sleeping bags, spread out on someone's pine bough bed about ten feet square, and it was so lovely in the snow and moonlight, among the brooks and trees, with the fragrances of pine boughs and wet pine needles and brooks and campfire smoke, and starlight and mountains, that we could hardly bear to go to sleep, but lay with our heads on our arms and just looked at the night. But we hadn't really been in bed long before sleep overcame us, and we had a lovely warm night of deep slumber.

We had determined to start out early next morning, and for a great wonder we did it. It was probably the most industrious ski-day of my life. We got up about 5:30, and dressed. I went off across the brooks and meadows to another brookside and sat on a rock and combed my hair and fixed my face. It was quite cold–the towel I had moistened to wash my face froze stiff while I was combing my hair, and the foaming brook rushed and sang past me.

We then had a fine nourishing breakfast of a little fruit, oatmeal and canned milk (I quite love it), and a couple of lemon-drops. Just before 7:00 the sun tipped the eastern ridge and the air grew hot. We started the climb to the Big Draw. The snow was still petrified and it was easier to walk than climb up on skis. As the previous day, Johnny went ahead, then came I, later Earl chaperoning Bill and Al. There were other people about of course–for example the bronzed man from San Diego who appeared in our camp at breakfast, and commented that it was exactly like a group of skiers in the Alps (where he had spent three and a half years). One meets the most cosmopolitan group of varied and interesting people on San Gorgonio–they have been, and come from, simply everywhere, and are lovely souls.

It was a still, sunny morning, not a sound in the woods except the clear call of a bird, that had four notes in his cry, and the scratch of my own boots on the granitic snow. It is quite a long climb to the Edelweiss hut–over one and a half hours. The little low black hut had a fine bare patch of wood-yard in front of it, and there the Edelweissers were sitting about in the sunshine. They are nice, friendly, tough and hardy souls, older than the Ski Mountaineers–mostly around 40–all lean, brown, easy-going creatures. I know quite a few of them by now. Wearing outlandish costumes, white ducks, and purple sweaters, and faded blue sailor pants, and Chinese coolie slippers, all frightfully good skiers and mountaineers, and very experienced, all like something out of a book rather than reality, they fussed around in the sun, joking, talking, cutting wood, waxing skis.

After resting there for a time, Johnny and I put on our skis and climbed on up into the Big Draw. We left our pack at the lunch rocks (a lot of red granite boulders sticking out of the snow), filled the holes in our favorite rock with snow so we could have water at noon, and tramped on up and up.

Three times that day I was to the top of the Big Draw–a good forty minutes' climb up, and about two to five minutes down! The day just flew by. I was on skis, or climbing, from 7:00 till 4:00, plus four miles packing out. San Gorgonio is so beautiful! The purple desert mountains to the southwest, the incredibly deep blue sky, the rocks and trees and sweetly curving cornices along the ridges, the skyline curled over in a lovely almost translucent cornice high above, the forests below one, and the snow and skiing.

I don't know how people get along without climbing mountains. What do they *do* for beauty? It struck me that the ski fields must be rather like music to some people–I don't know the terms to describe it in, but it all was rather like a lovely symphony–the ski tracks like the notes–the sharp beats of the herring-bones and side-stepping, the long swoops of the fine narrow schuss tracks, the rhythm of the curves–the loveliness of motion as those super-skiers soared down the mountain before one's eyes like the best of ski-movies. Skiers cherish the beauty of their tracks like artists or poets–and making them was sublime.

And the perfection of the entire mountain, and the sky and snow, and rocks and trees and their sharp shadows, and the motion and grace of skiing in the great hollow of the Big Draw.

I like climbing on skis. It is rather more like swimming, I think, than walking, because the shoulders do most of the work. There is that swing-swing-swing, and shove-shove-shove, of shoulders and arms and poles, and the legs and skis come up easily. The whole

Ruth Dyar on Mount San Gorgonio, January 10, 1937

body goes into it. It is a rhythm like nothing else one does.

We climbed up the first time, and met another Ski Mountaineer, Clyde Nelson, young, quiet nice doctor (married to a beautiful, nice blonde girl). He and Johnny and I sat in the cup of upper slopes for awhile waiting for the snow to melt a little, and resting. A gang of those tireless Edelweissers passed us, en route to the top. They left their skis, and went on over the ridge but a few hundred feet above us, on top of which they found poppies in the sunshine, and themselves lay in the sun for some time.

The snow was perfect, beautiful, granular spring snow, tiny globes of sparkling rolling ice over a hardpacked surface, on which a person could do anything! I hadn't skied so well in two months or more, and got better during the day, and learned to put a swing in my turns I'd never had. After our first descent, we found Clyde's little camp–he had slept for two nights in the snow alone at the foot of the Big Draw–where we three and Earl had the heavenly impossible luxury of lounging on his tent over pine boughs, the sunshine, and drinking hot tea, and eating cheese, there in the Big Draw. Clyde cooked the tea from snow water melted over his tiny Primus stove.

Then we climbed up again, and I came down first and timed Johnny and Clyde on a special run they wanted to make. Then we skied down to the lunch rocks, and loafed in the sun and ate ryecrisp and cheese, and cookies and oranges, in tremendous quantities. Then we strapped on our climbing skins, and again plodded high up into the Big Draw. I think I had the loveliest run down I ever had on skis; I got so I could really make turns, good turns, going fast, and fun right on down. It was *mah*-velous.

I was pretty tired by then, and left Clyde and Johnny to climb part-way up a fourth time, and skied down to the Edelweiss Hut, where I loafed and talked for awhile, inside on the straw, but I began to get so petrified with tiredness, that I hurriedly skied on down before I solidified entirely. I even enjoyed that horrid run down through the trees. And then, at the edge of the snow above the meadows, took off my skis, and trod over the wet springy turf, and slippery springs, and stepped over the ringing tinkling brooks and tiny falls, down into camp, where our pine bough bed was matted with people back from the ski fields–Mary Jane and Heinz; Ingeborg and Ren; two funny fellows, Herb and Harry, who were going to stay up a week, and had been very comical the night before groaning about their huge packs, and remarking that here they were with all this food, but they had left their Menu at home, so they would probably starve.

I went off into the woods and washed the caked masses of sunpaint and tannic acid off my mug, despite which applications I was severely sunburned. About 5:00, we started down the trail, the green woods shot with sunshine. It is fun packing out from the Meadows, swinging along down the easy pleasant trail, exhausted and exhilarated and contented. Driving out of the mountains we were all rather delirious with happiness–all of us skiers of greatly varied ability, Earl and Johnny and I had each had the best time skiing we could remember in our whole lives (or so it seemed–I can recall having thought that other weekends were the best of my whole life)–the sheer joy of skiing over that perfect snow, combined with the physical, mental and spiritual exhaltation, and the lovely camp the night before, and the exquisite beauty of the mountains that day, and the companionship, and everything else, went together to create probably the nearest to perfection that can be attained.

Life certainly can't always be like that–but twenty-four hours of it is really enough to make one feel good in retrospect for days and days.

We were utterly ravenous and bottomless, and wrapped ourselves around a large supper in Redlands, and drove on home in a deep stupor.

This morning my eyes are tired, my face is a bit on the bloated side, though nothing like that San Antonio sunburn some time ago. (My sunburn is all in the wrong shape for a formal dance Friday–I got a horrid little triangle rather off-center on my chest, not to mention an oddly striped red neck. Oh well, Johnny knows quite well where I got it, and will have to put up with it. I can hardly wait till the dance.) My shoulders are stiff enough to give quiet testimony to the extraordinary amount of use I gave them climbing yesterday– hardly anyone ever climbs clear to the top of the Big Draw three times in one day, especially when they start at the Meadows.

# Strawberry Peak

LOS ANGELES, CALIF.

MAY 31, 1939, WEDNESDAY

*Dear Marg,*

Monday night Johnny and I did something quite drastic and went to a movie, a fine program consisting of Warner Baxter in "The Cisco Kid," and "The Hound of the Baskervilles." The latter was pretty good, having some very fine scenes of a magnificent toothy hound bounding and howling about the foggy moors. Basil Rathbone made a good Sherlock, though rather too well-fed. The Dr. Watson was rather too old and doddering, since he was in reality, young, thin and able-bodied.

Yesterday was our day to climb the North Face of Strawberry Peak. We told no one where we were going. Johnny and I dragged our bodies out of bed around 7:00, dressed in our climbing clothes, ate breakfast, loaded our crud into his car, and shortly after 8:00 were on our way under a murky sky.

Strawberry Peak is in the Sierra Madres, the mountain range north of Pasadena, and we drove up the Angeles Crest Highway, which you will recall is the road to Mt. Wilson, only we didn't go as far as Mt. Wilson. The drive took less than forty-five minutes from our house. We got up above the low clouds, and were in the summer sunshine of a hot morning. The Sierra Madres (Mother Mountains) really are lovely–the many ranges and peaks and deep gullies, sharply eroded, covered with dark green dense brush that is blue with distance and mists, and the canyons filled with streams, rocks, and beautiful timber.

We parked the car by the roadside, and loaded our lunch, canteen, our climbing shoes, and our climbing hardware (nine pitons, four carabiners, and a piton hammer) into Johnny's well-worn little brown rucksack. The rucksack weighed an amazing amount, but of course he insisted on carrying everything. I carried the rope, in a neat coil, over my shoulder. We set off up the trail to Strawberry. It was a fine trail, about four or five miles long, rising steeply but with an even grade, first through the canyon, then up and up the long ridges and shoulders. One could be thankful for a trail upon scrutinizing the dense thorny brush, higher than a man's head, which impenetrably covers the hillsides. It was a hot morning, and we plodded on up and up. It was wonderful to be out in the mountain solitudes, the clear fresh quiet unbroken except for birds and insects, and the breeze in the pines.

We rested occasionally, and eventually got up on the ridge where the real trail ended. Strawberry Peak is a mountain about 6,500 feet high I guess, which sticks up in a lump shaped like the fruit it is named after. We approached it from the south side, which drops sharply into the canyon-bottom, rocky and brushy. Ordinarily it is climbed by the long gradual ridge to the southwest, which we too followed to the notch just below the final rise to the summit. We scrambled up a steep hillside, and then followed the firebreak along the ridge. You know how all the ridges on these dark green mountains are threaded with firebreaks, that look somewhat like roads, where the brush has all been cleared off. The firebreak was just beautiful to walk along: it was like the Primrose Path or something, being sandy, covered with lovely deep pink phlox, and tall graceful blue flowers as high as our shoulders, and other flowers, all waving in the sunshine

Ruth descending below critical pitch of the Black Buttress Route on
Strawberry Peak's north side, June, 1940

and the fresh breeze that blew over the crest, and to either side of the cleared space were trees and brush, and far off in every direction stretched the blue blue mountains and canyons, very topographical like paper-mache, green with brush and blue with mist and distance.

Shortly after 11:00 we came to the north where we could see the cliffs dropping off the north side of the peak. Now, frankly, I had been told they were vertical, but I was surprised to see for myself that the north side consisted, quite literally, of a solid vertical flat wall of rock, and nothing else! Its height varied, but at the highest spot it must have been several hundred feet of magnificent granite. Why our climbers have not invaded it before is beyond me. The climbing is very comparable to Tahquitz, and it is more accessible. Gosh it was fun being one of the first climbers on the thing.

We sat down under some pines and changed hiking shoes to climbing shoes, ate an orange apiece and a couple of pieces of rye-crisp and a swallow or two of water–to tide us over till lunch, heh heh–and left everything behind a rock except our ample supply of iron and the rope. We then descended a good long ways over hunks of granite and coarse talus, to the base of the cliff. Unlike most scouting parties, we decided to start at the very bottom of the cliff and take it the hard way. It was very educational for me in route finding on new rock.

While tripping over the boulders down to the foot of the cliffs, I found a tiny fawn lying asleep among the rocks. We didn't know if it was sick or just playing possum. It lay so quietly, even when John touched it, and then suddenly let out the most awful scream, and sprang up and went tumbling over the rocks on wobbly little legs. We were quite worried over what to do with it, but finally did nothing.

Well, at the foot of the cliff, having picked out a break in the rock by which to ascend, we roped up and John led off. It was probably the most serious rock climbing I have ever done, as it was tough going, and new route finding and all. I know I learned more, about leading and route finding, than I ever have before, and feel more a seasoned responsible climber now. It was good hard granite, but not all cleaned off like the much-climbed routes at Tahquitz, and we had no little difficulty with falling stones, dirt, and crud. Handholds that looked perfectly good would suddenly come loose, and certainly inspired caution!

I wasn't in very good condition I found–I hadn't done anything for a month, and hadn't actually climbed since last year–but felt better and better as the day went on. We climbed for about five hours, interspersed of course with long waits on virtually non-existent belay points. Johnny had to do a lot of driving in of pitons for protection in leading, I belayed him as well as I possibly could, usually anchored to a bush or piton. The rock didn't take pitons well–the cracks weren't deep enough. When I came up after him, I would hammer some of them out of the rock and bring them up, because after all they cost money, and then too we needed them. Dirt and filth kept cascading down upon me until I was so dirty it didn't matter anymore.

It was so marvelous to be climbing again! To be inching and squirming up the rock, in contortions nothing else can call forth! To be perched on a precarious ledge, handling the rope, able to look practically between your legs down to the foot of the cliff, and off across miles and miles of mountains, with blueness drifting in the air between them! To touch the granite, the hard gray granite, stained with black and orange lichens, with little bushes, and blooming hen-and-chickens, and sprays of pink sweet flowers, growing in its crevices way up there on the cliff! To feel the clean remote breezes in the north shade, breezes which feel different on a cliff face! Climbing has *everything*–beauty, exhilaration, physical and mental inspiration, excitement and danger tempered with skill and self-reliance and physical conquest, comradeship, teamwork, the sky and the air and the mountains and rocks!

There was a very grave time when our route was practically blocked by a large wedge of rock in the crack above, where John had to go, which had split loose when he was driving in a piton, and the 100-pound boulder was kept from crashing down on him literally by the piton only! It was a trap for anyone that might come later. Finally John braced himself, and pulled out the piton, and the rock eased down on his head and shoulders, and he heaved it over the cliff–it went crashing and splitting down the cliff, and his hat floated after it, and he was okay, but it is one of these things that makes even a hardened climber a trifle anxious!

At last, late in the afternoon, below a very difficult pitch, both of us pretty tired, and feeling that for one day of pioneering a new route we had done a good job, we decided to rope down. Roping down from pitons is a pretty serious game–safe, but it pays to be serious about it! The first piton was good and solid. The second rope-down gave me a feeling I had never had in climbing before. I wasn't afraid, for I think I have a singular lack of nerves in climbing, or I couldn't do it and enjoy it so. But I was balanced with my back against a perfectly smooth slant of rock, with my feet on a very gravelly little ledge protected by nothing but a small piece of sling rope tied from the carabiner around my belt to the piton. The piton was securely driven to the rock, but after all, it was only a fine blade of steel, stuck into the cliff like a nail in a wall, and through it was tied a thin piece of quarter-inch sling rope, and through the loop of the sling was doubled our climbing rope and John roped off.

I stood quietly on my little ledge, and watched that piton gently, almost imperceptibly sway, while the person I was very fond of slid and climbed easily and softly down the rope. Not long ago we had been discussing the inadvisability of getting into the habit of roping down in short jumps, since it would be very bad when roping down from pitons. Not anything in the world would have induced me to spring vigorously down that rope! When Johnny reached the ledge below, I reached out very gingerly till I had the rope, and passed it between my legs and over my chest and shoulder, and extracted my knife to cut the sling rope I was tied on by, and then ever so gently and tenderly and carefully climbed down to the little ledge right below the piton, and with ever such caution slid down the rope and rock to the broader ledge beneath.

From then on down, two more rope-downs, the rope around solid trees, brought us to a sloping ledge we could walk down. And we climbed over the boulders, up the hillside, back toward our knapsack. The five pitons we brought back had taken such a beating being hammered into cracks that wouldn't take them, and hammered out again, that their steel blades were all twisted and distorted in a wonderfully funny way. Hammered flat, however, they will be as good as ever.

Never have I seen two such dirty people! Dirty Dyar and Messy Mendenhall. We were black and gritty, and our hair thick with gravel, and our faces smeared, and even our teeth gritty! We were so dirty we quite enjoyed it. And there we were, two horrible specimens, at 5:30 in the evening: we had had very little sleep the night before; we had been exercising vigorously for eight and a half hours, and had been operating under a rather extreme nervous tension, and it suddenly occurred to us that besides that bite to eat at 11:00, we hadn't had a bit of food or a drop of water since an early breakfast. Yet we felt excessively healthy and good!

We climbed up the crud to our knapsack; we carried it over the rocks on the ridge, and dropped down under some pines, in the cool wind, and drank from the canteen and laid out our "lunch." The great expanses of blue mountains were all misty in the low rays of the sun, and the hollows between the ridges were filled with glowing white haze. We ate an absolutely enormous amount of food, enough sandwiches, fudge, rye-crisp and oranges to founder a man; and though we hadn't felt precisely hungry before, yet all this food had no effect whatsoever on us: we felt just as though we hadn't eaten anything at all!

After eating and resting, we started down the firebreak into the west, with the bright rays of the setting sun gilding all the waving lovely flowers. The sun set redly behind the lovely blue ridge of Iron Mountain and the silhouette of a great fir, whose long branches, some naked and dead, some soft and covered with living needles, reached in front of the sunset. Above Strawberry, the moon rose, almost full, and very bright, in the blue sky. Quickly the California night fell, and the brilliant stars came out, and we swung down the trail through the moonlight.

The wonderful fragrances of sage and other spicy underbrush filled the night air. The clear song of crickets, and the flutter of a bat, and the deep, steady croak of frogs, and the grate of our boots on the trail, were the only sounds to break the quiet. Everywhere were beautiful vistas and silhouettes, of rocky canyons filled with white moonlight, and stark black trees and ridges against the sky, and shadowy undergrowth with the white trail winding through it. We were sure-footed creatures, the way we tore down the trail in the moonlight or shadows, over rocks and gravel, swinging around switch backs, skirting crumbling precipices with the foot-wide trail clinging on the very edge, prancing over rocks in the creek bed, without a single stumble or misstep!

When we reached the road, it filled us almost with resentment to hear an occasional car tear along the highway. Stopped in a drive-in place in Highland Park to consume hamburgers and milkshakes, and got home to much needed baths; I even had to wash my hair, I couldn't stand it's nastiness; and to bed quite exhausted but contented.

This morning I emptied handfuls of gravel out of my socks, and my overall and shirt pockets and put them in the laundry bag; hung my piton hammer on a nail in the wall; emptied and dusted my shoes and put them in the closet; washed the orange juice and gravel out of my jack-knife; combed my still-moist hair; and so eradicated all the visible signs of a good day!

*With love,*

# Banner Peak Bivouac

LOS ANGELES,
JULY 5, 1939 — WEDNESDAY

*Dear Mother,*

Twenty-four hours ago I was picking my way across the 45-degree slope of a glacier, at around 11,500 feet elevation, at the western base of the Minarets, roped, crampons strapped to my ski boots, John cutting steps with the ice axe, the sun beating down on the glacier, the High Sierra all about us. Now the dismal dirty noisy neon-signed depression of Fourth Street lies beneath my window. Well, the mountains are still there! Your daughter is back alive, having lost nothing much but about one and a half inches off her waist-line in three days!

We had quite an eventful trip, as you can imagine. It was unfortunate that we had to work Saturday morning. It is a drive of around 330 miles. John and I had our schedule worked down to the last detail, and quite an ambitious plan too. We would reach the end of the road by midnight Saturday, be up at 5:00 Sunday morning and pack in seven miles and then tackle the East ridge of Banner Peak. Monday, our one full climbing day, we would scale Michaels' Minaret (the farthest and one of the most difficult ones). Tuesday morning we would do some work on the glacier, pack out and come home. It all went fairly well except we skipped Monday, as you will see.

Phil Falconer was supposed to arrive at noon by train from San

Diego, but he couldn't get reservations on the streamliner, so had to come up by Greyhound, which took exactly twice as long. With Bill Wallace, we dropped downtown and picked Phil up, complete with bushy shaving-brush plume on his Alpine lid, rucksack and squeeze-box.

I don't recall a great deal about the trip up. We drove north through the brushy mountains of the Southeast Tehachapis, along the rolling desert and highly colored barren mountains south of the Sierra. It was cloudy, and not hot as we had every reason to expect. There were lovely vistas of tender lavender mountains, of bold harsh gray mountains under cold bold gray and white clouds, of plum-colored cones across the desert.

It was late at night, and cold, when we turned off the highway and drove along the dirt road that wound off into the mountains. The Sierra looks from the highway like sheer rock. However, the canyons are filled with lovely forests and streams and meadows. All this was lost on me as I was in an intense stupor, and only heard many extravagant and gasping remarks from the fellows upon the absolutely awful nature of the winding dirt road, which fell off precipitously to the left.

Around midnight, we got to the end of the road and went to bed. Sunday morning came cold and clear. John and I got up at 5:00, and shook with cold while we ate shredded wheat and cold milk and bran muffins for breakfast. Frost lay in the meadows in the open. By somewhat after 6:00, we had shouldered our pack boards, put on our feathered lids, and were swinging along the trail. It was easy going, first a long gradual drop into the canyon, then up gently or along the level, for around 7 miles of trail, through woods, along charming green lakes, along streams and lovely leaping white cascades, with high cliffs on either side, and presently the jagged black skyline ahead showing us the Minarets and Banner and Ritter, which we had studied pictures of for so long, towering volcanic rock, with snow and glaciers hanging at their base. The Ritter Range differs from the granite of most of the Sierra by being very ancient igneous rock. To the left was the 11,000 foot black sharp line of the Volcanic Ridge, to the right grayish cliffs, ahead of us the Minarets, very sharp precipitous rocky needles and jagged ridges, and to the right of them, the tremendous rock cones of the twin peaks, Mt. Ritter (13,162 feet) and Mt. Banner (12,963 feet), connected by a snowy saddle.

We got into the camp about 9:30. Above Lake Ediza, on a bend in Minarets Creek, in a little grassy meadow at the foot of pinkish cliffs and under tall lovely hemlocks, the R.C.S. had set up camp. We picked out bed sites for the night (optimistic people), prepared our knapsack for the day, and about quarter to 11:00 set off to climb the East Buttress of Banner Peak.

Our fault, I guess, if any, lay in over-eagerness and over-ambition, and in under-estimating the difficulty of the Underhill-Eichorn route made only once before, in 1931. Most of the other Minarets climbs are easy, but I think this route surpasses the East Face of Whitney. Anyway: it took us about three hours to reach the base of the actual climb, going up fairly easy slopes of rock-strewn meadows, crossing brooks, climbing up talus. Probably it is not peculiar that we felt a little tired. Climbing is not always unadulterated fun, though you soon forget that part. Each foot of altitude was being gained at the expense of heavy legs and strained breathing, and we stopped frequently to rest, lying down and falling instantly asleep for a few minutes in the sun. It was hot, flat against the heather in the sunshine, though the wind was quite cool when we stood up.

At 2:00 o'clock we reached the deep red chimney at the head of a snow slope, and started climbing, unroped at first. As soon as we were on the rocks, we felt wonderful, fresh and exhilarated, and remained feeling good the rest of the climb. The rock was wonderful. About 3:00, sitting on a kind of ridge near the top of the chimney, we ate some snow and lemon drops, roped up, and started climbing up beautiful sound blocks of steep difficult rock on the outer ridge. All those tough weekends of training we've put ourselves to at last paid out. We were feeling in the absolute pink of condition, when we needed it. I don't think I have climbed so well, or with such confidence, enjoyment and sheer physical lightness and joy, this year. The Sierra is so mahvelous! Dropping below us lay an ever increasing vista: the island-dotted meanderings of Garnet and Thousand Island Lakes, the glaciers, the sky filled with beautiful fluffy clouds, and across Owens Valley the green-blue of Mono Lake, and the craters about it, and the White Mountain range beyond, and north and south the peaks of the Sierra thrown up like waves of the sea, ever changing in the light.

The rocks grew more difficult. We had thought we could gain the summit, or pass the hard part of the climb, before dark, and then make a long but safe descent another way by moonlight. Around 6:00, when it was getting so cold we had to put on mittens when belaying, and shivered while waiting, we got into such tough work that we knew we would definitely have to bivouac on the rocks if we went on. We started down. We now thought we could get to the head of the chimney by dark, and then climb down by flashlight and moonlight. However, when the rocks went dull gray and the light failed about 8:00, we were on a ledge of rock with the cliffs dropping off blackly and emptily to the Banner Glacier on the north of the ridge. To go on down by darkness would certainly have been unwise. I have sort of vaguely wanted to bivouac on the rocks for a long long

*Ruth on Hanging Glacier, Minarets, July 4, 1939*

time, yet when the time comes, no one would ever bivouac who could do otherwise. I think one must love the rocks very much to sleep on them!

A couple of rope-downs above us, we had noted and spoken merrily of the best place to sleep. So in the last waning light we climbed up again, and set up housekeeping. Birds were tweeting and retiring about and below us. For a bivouac, we really had a good place. There was a large ledge about fifteen feet long and four feet wide, and a fine cranny behind a big slab of rock, a space about four feet long and all of sixteen inches wide on the bottom, widening out higher up, where we could escape from the wind. We set up our happy house in this space. John arranged a large slab of rock for a door. We prepared the floor with the rope, and a fine harvest of grass which was growing thereabouts in surprising quantities, this being less cold than rock to sit on. I put our spare belongings in the closets (some cracks about two inches wide in the rock). We then sat down to a generous supper consisting of the last relics of our lunch—two pieces of rye-crisp, a slice of sausage, a couple of bites of cheese, a few dried apricots, plenty of chocolate bar, and lemon drops. By the time everything was in readiness, it was after 9:30 and we were both very sleepy.

No doubt it is lucky we were so tired: on four hours of sleep we had been doing the most strenuous and exacting exercise for the past fifteen or sixteen hours. Huddled together in a peculiar position for warmth, we instantly fell asleep. Fortunately indeed, it was not a very cold night (around freezing, I imagine, with no wind). I had on three pairs of wool socks and my ski boots, mittens, my flannel shirt, sweater, ski jacket and parka. At no time were we really cold. The night wasn't as bad as it ought to have been. Only once did I really feel lousy—about 11:00 o'clock when my stomach felt as if it were lined with wool. It was worse sleeping on a bus.

We would sleep like the dead about an hour in a terribly cramped position. Then we would wake up abruptly, unable to stay in that position another second and trembling with muscular cramp, and stand up, and roam about the ledge in the moonlight, and stretch and stretch, and howl with silly laughter because it was all rather funny. At 2:00 o'clock we ate some of our famine supply of horrid Sontag Drugstore bargain chocolate, quite ravenous, lemon-drops, our one precious lovely delicious orange, and John climbed down a ways and fetched some frozen rocky snow, which was the one thing that saved me from death by thirst.

It was a very queer place to be, at night, and really quite beautiful. I made the most of looking about me, since I was there! Above, below, and to either side, rose or dropped the precipitous, almost vertical black hunks of rock. Once across the black sky I saw a falling star. Above, the huge square overhanging tower was blocked out against the stars. Down below us the Banner Glacier shimmered whitely in the moonlight. Far and away in the moonlight stretched the grays, the blacks and whites of lakes and snows and peaks. At 2:00 a red star rose rapidly over White Mountain Peak. Before 4:00, the east (how glad we were to be facing east) was filling with an orange light, and the rocks were turning from black to dull mysterious gray. We went back to sleep, and at 4:45, I opened my eyes to see the blessing of pale sunshine lying against the rock at my elbow.

After such a night, we shouldn't, in all justice, have felt very good. But both of us felt ridiculously healthy, almost as if we had had a normal night's sleep in bed. We felt cheery, and merry. The peaks stretched off in beautiful blue lines. The sun was so warm, even at its pale 5:00 a.m. stage. We stretched, ate snow and lemon drops for breakfast, limbered up, changed boots for tennis shoes, packed the rucksack, combed our hair, and I patched up my face as best I could with lipstick. Before 6:00 we started roping down. The descent was longer than we had thought. It was quite as well we hadn't tried to go on by dark. We roped off pitons and off projections of rock, climbed and explored, eventually reaching the big red easy chimney, climbing down it, crossing the pitted softening snow slopes, at last drinking *water* lying cold and fresh in rock hollows, then descending the heather slopes sweet and blossoming in sunshine and by brook side, and about 9:30 strolling grinning into camp.

No one was much concerned over us. Art I think is convinced we had planned it. One of the Ritter parties hadn't gotten back till 9:00 the night before. The Clyde's party hadn't gotten in till after 1:00 a.m. Not a soul climbed this day. Camp was kind of funny that morning, with everyone sitting around amid the grass and sunshine and mosquitoes, quietly and earnestly eating. John and I actually hadn't had a square meal since Saturday. Occasionally people would ask us with a trace of mirthful sarcasm how we enjoyed the night. Of course the fact did not escape Comment that this was Johnny's second Fourth of July bivouac in succession–he having been in the party of nine who last year spent such a bitterly cold night at 14,000 feet on North Palisade.

John made me a lovely new bed in the woods, under the tall slim hemlocks, and I went to sleep, though rather brokenly because the sun was warm and the mosquitoes very annoying.

There was a cutting wind, and I was glad not to be bivouacking that night. John had built a wonderful windbreak of logs about my sleeping bag. The wind sighed in the trees, and waterfalls roared softly across the rocks. Between a frame of lovely slender hemlocks, the

Great Dipper hung, bowl down, in the sky, and beneath it, faint and conical and dark against the sky, jutted Mt. Banner, its foot wreathed in snowfields and glaciers, and halfway up the East Ridge I could see where we were the night before.

John and I, having missed a whole day of climbing, and being the only truly industrious climbers there, got up at 4:20 a.m. Tuesday morning to go glacier climbing. We walked for two hours to the little precipitous glacier, where we roped up, strapped the vicious-looking spiked crampons to our boots, and climbed. Ice work is so unfamiliar that I felt very awkward and uneasy. We were very careful, being inexperienced, and worked up over the forty-five degree ice slope (kind of dirty old snow, to look at). I wish we had had longer. By the time we had to go back, we had just gotten to the beautiful blue minute crevasses and the tumbled weird formations of the only ice-fall in the Sierra. Below us, Upper Iceberg Lake filled a hollow between the Minarets and the Volcanic Ridge, so high up it was almost like a crater, and Lower Iceberg Lake was filled with wonderful blocks of blue ice and snow. But we had to go home. We descended a steep tongue of snow to the rocks, had lunch and changed shoes, and went on down the rocks, along the shore of Iceberg Lake, over a notch in the ridge, and back into camp.

It was 12:30, and everyone had already packed out. As if just waiting till we left, great ragged cold gray masses of mist began to wrap Banner's and Ritter's harsh red-black peaks as we turned our backs on them and swung down trail. We passed any number of beautiful falls, cascades, streams and lapping lakes without stopping for a drink. And then long after the last nice creek, got so desperately thirsty that we had to stop and strain brown stagnant water through our teeth. We stopped to photograph the marvelous enamel green-and-

*John Mendenhall and Ruth Dyar, Minarets. July 4, 1939*

white Forest Service sign tacked to a tree which reads ominously: "HAZARDOUS ASCENTS-INEXPERIENCED CLIMBERS WITH-OUT GUIDES SHOULD NOT ATTEMPT THESE PEAKS." Since no one ever heard of a guide in the Sierra this was rather silly. Still, three people have lost their lives in the Minarets–Walter Starr, who was an avid solo climber, was killed on Clyde's and is cemented into a crevice up there, and a young couple fell off the west side of Banner.

Phil and Bill, waiting at the cars, were being regaled by an old-timer who had helped wall up these three corpses into the mountains, and who was eagerly waiting to saddle up his horses and go and wall up John and me.

Again we had a cool cloudy drive. The peaks jutted out magnificently along the highway. Johnny knows every peak and its history and legend and elevation, in the Sierra, it seems to me. I got to bed after 2:00–twenty-two hours after rising. Now I must get to my work. I am kind of sunburned–tanned thoroughly on the chin and paling perceptibly toward the forehead due to the hat, but otherwise very healthy in spite of all.

*Much love,*

# Tahquitz, Traitor Horn

LOS ANGELES, CALIF.

AUGUST 28, 1939 — MONDAY

*Dear Schmickface,*

I fear I am sleepy in an excess, but maybe that won't inhibit my letter-writing abilities above the ordinary. My hands are so stiff from climbing that I scarce can type.

Guess what I did after work Saturday noon–I went and tried on some wedding dresses. It was quite fun. Then I went home and put on my overalls. Are you coming to my wedding, pretty one? It would be kind of cute if you could.

My, we had a good time yesterday at Tahquitz! It is so nice the way John and I keep on having a better and better time together. We climbed the Traitor Horn, which is the worst climb on the rock except the Mechanics' or Booksellers' Route (this last has been made only twice: pioneered by Glen Dawson and Jonesy, climbed last summer by Carl and Johnny, and actually is so ghastly, and so utterly unprotected, that there is no justification to it, and it probably will never be climbed again!).

We arrived in Idyllwild about 10:00 p.m. Art asked me what we were going to climb, and I said the Horn, and he went into a long ominous discussion with me about exactly how to belay John in case of a fall on the critical point, drawing diagrams of pitons, ropes and me, in the dust, by flashlight. Since I already was filled with foreboding, that didn't help my frame of mind.

It was a fine, fresh cool dawn to which we arose. To tell the truth, I don't think either of us was overly anxious to climb the Horn. John led it, the first Tahquitz climb this season, the time I wasn't climbing on account of my ribs, and had a heck of a time on the hardest pitch. Carl Jensen fell off of that pitch the same day. Glen Dawson later in the season wouldn't lead it. No one but the best climbers have made the climb at all, and all of them have the healthiest respect and awe for it, and it is worse than the Piton Pooper. I looked forward to it with the greatest foreboding, wondering if I could *climb* it or would have to be hauled up on the rope. No girl had even tried it. Still, neither John or I are the kind to not do such a thing just because we don't relish the thought. However, we started out the day in a rather somber frame of mind.

We made the usual plod up the dirty little trail, which gets deeper with dirt and gravel every climb, because of the way people butch it up coming down. We left our lunches and hiking shoes under a rock at the foot of Tahquitz, and went around to the right of the rock, where I hadn't been this season, where the Finger-Tip Traverse, the Mechanics' Route, and the Horn all begin.

The early morning was cool, and to the south lay the great valley from which rose little peaks and ranges in blue relief. The first part of the climb was straightforward, fairly difficult work up a long steep crack. It seemed very soon that we reached the approach to the first horn, where I anchored to a piton above me, and sat on the rope for a piton belay, my feet wedged uncomfortably in the ledge-less crack, while John made the delicate traverse, climbed up on the horn, and disappeared around the corner. Both the first and second horns jut out of steep slabby rock, white, and shaped much like the horn of a

*Ruth on Traitor Horn, Tahquitz, August, 1939*

rhinoceros.

I then climbed over the first horn and came around the corner, and the crux of the climb was before us. I had a small platform a few inches square to "stand" on. I was anchored firmly to a piton above me. The formation of the rock is very peculiar, as we were in a sort of room of rock with three walls rising square, sheer, and holdless above us, and tremendous precipitous slabs dropping off to nothing below us. The place was littered with seven or eight pitons for protection for the leader and for direct aid to the climbers.

John led off. He traversed delicately up a very steep slanting face toward the horn, threading his rope through carabiners which clicked into pitons in a satisfying way. He was confronted with a steep sheer face of rock, almost overhanging, flat as a wall, skewered with four pitons. He climbed it, got one leg over the horn, and was sitting on the horn, where he rested for a bit, then stood up, and attacked the tricky pitch off which Carl fell. A moment later he gave a great howl of triumph, shouted "I've got the handhold, I've made it!" and went on up, giving the victory cry of Tarzan on top.

Now came my turn. I undid my anchor from the piton above me, clinked the carabiner into my belt loop, and with John's good upper belay, and his encouraging coaching, started the traverse toward the horn. At one point, a person had to lean far out, seize a sling rope in a piton, and swing brightly out over blank rock, then climb up on that piton. The pitch getting up on the horn looked right ghastly. Standing with one foot on a piton and the rest on nothing, I pretended to be resting, but actually was getting more and more tired, because I didn't want to go on. However what must be, must be. In a way, it wasn't so bad. I had to get my right foot up on about a level with my neck, and thrust it far out and into a sling rope hanging from a piton, snap the rope out of a couple of carabiners (rock climbers go through the most awful contortions), push off of something with my left foot, and then, somehow, get my right foot out of the sling, my leg over the lovely sharp convenient shape of the horn, and heave, and there I sat on the horn!

It was a marvelous exposed spot, rather like straddling a sawhorse over several hundred feet of space, blank slabs dropping below, each foot hanging over space. By that time I felt quite lighthearted, and sat there resting and jesting, while John took a few photographs.

It was a comfortable, airy place to sit, or to stand (it was kind of ticklish standing up), and one might have spent the day there in comfort. But the worst pitch was yet to come. John is so comforting and so confidence-inspiring at such times. He belayed me and told me just what to do. First I stood up on the horn, my feet on a knife-like little ridge dropping off to nothing, my hands resting on a hold-less hunk of rock as high above me as I could comfortably reach. The thing that had to be done was to edge along a little ledge to one's left, which is wide enough to stand on comfortably–except that the rock overhangs it in such a way that you can only put the very tips of your toes on the ledge and then the rock pushes you out in such a way that you even wish you hadn't a buckle on your belt.

On the top were a few little buttons of granite which I had to hold on to with my right hand, and then swing around and reach a hand-hold with the left hand. I knew I couldn't hold on to those silly little roughnesses in the rock, but John said I could. I knew there was no use fiddling around, so I dug in with my right hand, swung out on the ledge, and suddenly had a good hold with my left hand, and was able with a sudden soaring of joy to climb up on top and join John.

We both felt so darn good at our accomplishment that we were in the very peak of good spirits all the rest of the day. We had quite a day's workout planned out, to get in condition for Whitney next weekend. So we climbed over the top of the rock, and climbed *down* the White Maiden's Walk-Away by the Jensen variation. Climbing down is much harder than climbing up, and while one doesn't relish it, one ought to practice it. Anyway, we eventually got down, and about 4:00 o'clock sat down on our rock, in the breezy shade, to have our lunch, a Spartan simple affair of sandwiches, water, cucumber, lettuce and oranges. After eating, we milled around, and then tramped down the dusty trail and road to the car.

We drove out of the mountains into the most gorgeous seething rose sunset, above purple mountains and black fruit orchards. It was one of our best days!

My hives are almost gone, and now I have only the usual assortment of bruises, scratching and scars, a blood blister on one finger, a cut on one thumb, and the dregs of some poison-oak, for injuries. Next weekend–Mt. Whitney.

*Much Love,*

# Mount Whitney, Third Needle, First Ascent

*Dearest Mother,*

Well, here is your daughter back alive from Mt. Whitney. We had a marvelous ascent, making a new route up the East Face.

It is 220 miles to Lone Pine, which we reached before 6:00 p.m. It was a hot afternoon, which we didn't notice, taking turns driving across the great desert, with its colored barren mountains on either skyline. At Lone Pine we turned west on the dirt road which winds across the barren plain, out of the tender green charming little valley where Lone Pine sprawls. The road switch backed up and up, out of the sunset, and the jagged line of Mt. Whitney and the pinnacles to its south lay sharply against the western sky.

By the time we had eaten it was dark, so by flashlight we put the finishing touches on our packs, which weren't very heavy, changed into hiking shoes, shouldered our packs, and started up trail.

Due to our Strawberry training, we are strangely more adept at trail travel by dark than daylight. At a slow steady pace we started up the long rise across a dry hillside, then switch backing ever upwards through forests and meadows and along brooks and between cliffs. At first we had only starlight. John went first and murmured "Rock" everytime he came to a projection in the trail so I wouldn't fall over it (which of course I would have done in my own clumsy way.) The trail was softly gray in the starlight. After about forty-five minutes we stopped to rest. Already we had gained much elevation. The road must end at about 8,000 feet, and Mirror Lake is 10,000 or 10,500–we forget.

Suddenly in a brilliant orange glow, the misshapen moon oozed up behind dark pine trunks, and quickly rose in an oblong silver disk along the high dark flank of a cliff, disappearing as we switch backed toward the south, and then reappearing with a forewarning of a silver halo as we switch backed to the north. At our second resting place, a pack train passed us, smelling rather like mule, the packer riding a horse and whistling, leading two laden mules, and a short distance behind four stodgy businessmen riding up on horses. We hailed them cheerily, but contrary to all mountain etiquette, they rode sullenly on without returning the greeting, which annoyed us. I had no doubt who was having more fun–we two ragamuffins toiling up on foot under heavy packs, or those four men, the first two riding in sulky silence and the second two discussing their office.

The granite walls towered higher and higher over us against the stars. The southeastern walls were lost in a vast towering gloom, a shadowy shapelessness brooding over us to our left. To the right, the high cone-shaped peak of Thor gleamed with an almost holy whiteness in the moonlight, shining and vast and clean behind the sharp etching of pines. The air was rather balmy, and filled with clean fragrances. We slogged on up the trail, at an easy pace, tottered over logs and stepping stones that crossed singing streams in the dim light, talked softly–of the stars and the cliffs, and of all the mountaineers in Austria and Germany and Briton and France who were being called from the clean heights to War.

We slept below Mirror Lake, arising at 5:30. Thor and all the

*Third Needle of Mount Whitney (far left), East Face Route,*
*first ascent by John Mendenhall and Ruth Dyar, September 3, 1939*

peaks to the west suddenly bloomed like Talisman roses in a glorious sunrise glow. Thirty-two degrees by my little thermometer. At 7:00 a.m. John and I started out of camp. A short distance up the trail brought us to the small green oval of Mirror Lake lying in its cup of cliffs. We skirted the right shore, and soon it dropped behind, shining in the morning light under the pines, the hollow filled with the blue haze of breakfast smokes.

The climb began–the plod, plod, plod, up and up and up, the legs heavy, the breath coming short; almost immediately we were above timberline, and stepping up and up over the slopes covered with low bushes, prickly red-fruited wild currant, and a little purple blossom which had wild sweet mint-spice, the same fragrance I remembered from last time–stepping over pink rocks, gravelly spaces in the bushes, wet green grass growing thickly where tiny brooks trickled over the hillside. It is charming the way there is spring in the High Sierra in September.

We came to the great glaciated slabs of granite sweeping down from the pass between the rocky ridge of Pinnacle Pass on the right and the soaring granite turrets on the left. We wove back and forth, up and up, our tennis shoes sticking neatly to the steep slabs. We climbed up and up, the valley dropping and widening beneath us, the purple Inyo mountains opening up across Owens Valley, and lakes appearing and as we climbed higher, range after range of aching blue Nevada peaks and mountains spreading forth beneath us.

We topped the granite slabs, and to the west suddenly rose that incredible jagged skyline of Mt. Whitney and its pinnacles, vertical spires of pale granite, deeply slashed with gulleys between them, rising from the slopes of granite wasteland. Everywhere granite, pink or gray or buff–the pinnacles sharp and clean, and leaning crazily,

against the bright deep blue of the high sky–we ourselves in a wasteland of granite blocks, some stained black with rivulets of water. Still
we climbed over the rocks, coming to tiny green lakes in the hollows,
and then quite a large lake, of strong dark green flapping brightly in
the sunshine and wind.

We stopped occasionally to study the route before us. It was
around 8:30 or 9:00 when we finally roped up. We stood on a point
of rocks and looked at the sheer sheer East Face of Whitney proper,
and howled.  We heard answering shrieks, and picked out on that
wall of granite a tiny black figure, moving, against the skyline.  It
looked ghastly. We hardly liked to watch them. We begin to see why
climbers are regarded as insane by the public.

Our climb, an endeavor to pioneer a new route up the East Face
of Whitney, lay up the gully to the south of the third pinnacle.
Whitney's face has been climbed by two routes–about 1931 by the
old East Face route, about 1937 for the first time by the PeeWee
Sunshine Route.  Even now we could see the PeeWee, a gigantic beak,
hanging off the face near the summit.  The face is 1,700 feet of flat
rock wall.

Our climb was not very hard.  Our summer of unremitting climbing paid dividends now.  Much of it we moved continuously, that is,
roped but both moving at the same time.  There was one very difficult traverse, harder than anything on the PeeWee route, as ticklish I
think as anything I have done.  We sat against a rock in the faint pale
14,000-foot sunshine eating lunch about 11:00.  There was a biting
cutting wind blowing, with that tang and smell that means winter.
Out of the wind, in the sunshine, it was warm.  But that thin air holds
no warmth–the shade was bitterly cold, and the wind was merciless.
We munched our rye-crisp, cheese and sausage, our maple sugar, and

then moved on up into the deep chimney.

There was a really fearsome overhang blocking the vertical chimney above us. So deep in the hollow were we that right below the overhang rose a huge pyramid of snow and ice, cold and shaded, and water dripped hollowly. The walls were precipitous. The only way out was a traverse along the northern wall out onto the ridge. John got up on some virtually invisible footholds, leaving the pack, and hammered in a piton. I sat in the chilly shade and belayed him. The traverse was delicate in the extreme. His feet kept slipping, slipping, and the holds were rounded and practically non-existent. He inched over, drove in another piton, pulled up a couple of feet of rope and held the rope in his teeth so as not to destroy his precarious balance while he clinked the carabiner over the rope and through the eye of the piton. Driving in a piton from such a position is no joke! Then he oozed over the nose of the ridge, and while he stood there I took his picture.

John got over the nose of rock and was on a good belay spot. I permitted him to haul the knapsack up on the rope. I had a very sprightly time following in his footsteps, hammering out the pitons as I went. I virtually slipped off every inch of the pitch, and I was shaking with cold, and my hands were numb, but finally got up into the sunshine beside John.

We had another ticklish situation a ways above there. John got up on a long sloping lead to the north, I belaying him from a practically useless stance, and finally he had to climb back down. It was a holdless shallow crack, and what hold he had came off in his hand and he gave quite a ghastly gurgle as he almost lost his balance. He then drove in a piton for an upper belay, and climbed down and I went up an easier way right above me. We had a 120-foot rope and

I had about 40 of it wrapped about my chest to get it out of the way. I now let out the whole 120 feet, my hands so numb I could hardly handle the knots, and John worked over so he could give me a good upper belay, and I climbed up where he had been and took out the piton. Then with the protection of an upper belay I made a hideous traverse across the top of a flake, oozed over into a rounded shallow crack, and somehow got up into the broken rock above, and then up out of the chilling wind, into the soft blessing of hot sunshine. When I was climbing that pitch I remarked that it was very hard or something, and John said cheerfully that That Was Nothing. Yes, we simultaneously agreed, that was just it–*it was nothing.*

A few more walk-up pitches, and a long well-protected traverse along a cold ledge, and suddenly we were up. We unroped, walked to the top of our pinnacle, and shook hands. We built us a little beacon and were pleased. We had completed our First Ascent. It was about 1:00 o'clock. The sky was blue and fair, the Sierra was tossed up about us in endless miles of blue and purple waves. The wind was clean and cold. We walked up the trail to Whitney's summit, over a vast tableland of chunks of rock, a waste of gray granite.

The summit of Whitney is disgustingly commercialized. Pack trains haul up people who can't walk nine miles. Hikers struggle up. Cowboyish fellows in chaps were selling Coca Cola; tourist-like people were reading *Life* and *Look*; a portable radio was parked on a rock playing jazz. Someone told us War had been declared by Britain and France. In spite of one's self, some of the far beauty of the mountain tops fell away; in the mountains, the youngest, the strongest, the most skilled, the bravest, win–in war they die.

*First ascent party on top of Monument Peak, Ruth in foreground, December 31, 1939*

Chapter Three
# Marrying John
# 1939-1940

*We loaded up the ropes, and roared, beneath a cloudy sky, out to*
*Stoney Point, in the San Fernando Valley, which is filled with*
*truck gardens, and mushrooming real estate developments of*
*acres of little shining cheap houses for $100, $50, or $25 down*
*and so much a month.*

Ruth Dyar (1939)

One night after work in the spring of 1939, Ruth and John drove to Van Nuys so that Ruth could be introduced to her future in-laws, Walter and Blanche Mendenhall, who had moved to Southern California from Missouri in 1919. Walter, an angler and ardent hunter, was Editor and President of the politically conservative newspaper, *The Van Nuys News,* predecessor of *The Valley News and Green Sheet* and later the *Daily News of Los Angeles.*

In 1939, Van Nuys was a little town of about twenty thousand people in the San Fernando Valley, about eighteen miles north of downtown Los Angeles. Located on Valerio Avenue, the Mendenhall house was east of the present-day 405 Freeway, south of a major flood control channel. The big square Spanish-style house, kept night-dark inside, was surrounded by six acres of citrus, pepper, and palm trees. The first things Ruth saw that evening were Blanche's two pet desert tortoises, named Erp and Arp, weighing seven and fifteen pounds respectively; Ruth described them as "wondrously homely, and live in a little pen where they dig holes like gophers."

Ruth and John were married at the Mendenhall house on September 22, 1939. John's brother, Ferdinand, was Best Man. Ruth's brother, Conrad, gave her away. In a letter to her father after the wedding, Ruth wrote, "I saw a reassuring line of Ski Mountaineers standing aside to let us in the front door. For some reason it was very nice to see Carl and Dean and Art Johnson, and Doug and Dottie and Jonesy and Elsie and all of them." Conrad and Ruth were "both shaking so hard it was a wonder no one noticed, but we got down the aisle with dignity. John accidentally said 'I do' instead of 'I will,' so I also said 'I do,' too. For an awful second the wedding ring would hardly go over my knuckle, but it did." Afterward, they "fled out into the backyard, ran down the dusty

*Ruth Dyar, her mother, Else Dyar, and John Mendenhall, September 16, 1939*
*Ruth Mendenhall cuts her wedding cake, September 22, 1939*

weedy back road under a half moon as if demons were after us, and found the car parked in a lot a block away. It seemed strange that we were Married."

After their wedding, Ruth and John left the Base Camp commune, and rented a house in South Pasadena. The couple decided that one of them would "study and work" (John), while the other would keep house, maintain their climbing equipment, and pack for climbing trips (Ruth).

In 1939 and 1940, Ruth and John's mountain climbs became more serious, more hazardous. Ruth's parents worried endlessly about these dangers so she assured them over and over that she was "cold-blooded on the cliffs," and that she and John were extremely cautious and took good care of one another. Nevertheless, she kept telling her family scary stories. She described in vivid detail how Carl Jensen "made history by falling off the hard pitch of the Traitor Horn, dangling upside down into space on 6 feet of rope. A bunch of rocks fell off, and those watching from below scuttled for safety, during which Brinton broke a rib." She told her sisters about the English film, *The Challenge*, which depicted Edward Whymper's first ascent of the Matterhorn in 1865: "The rock-climbing curdled even my blood. The cutest part was where four of the seven men fell off the mountain and the rope broke. The bodies thudded and bounced and catapulted off the Matterhorn in just the cutest way."

Strawberry Peak provided a rappel over a "truly terrific overhang, the rope hanging straight down in mid-air, and there was also nothing but mid-air long below the end of the rope. It was mighty sensational, swinging around like a spider!" Again at Strawberry Peak, she told her mother, "I probably shouldn't alarm you by telling you of my Fall, but I might as well." Though Ruth's mother kept hearing the news reports of climbing fatalities, Ruth reassured her by saying that such people were not "real mountaineers" and did not know what they were doing.

That winter, a junior college student named Bill Dootson slipped off a saddle on Mount Baldy and fell 3,000 feet down a sheer and gleaming ice wall into Lytle Canyon. (Mount Baldy has undoubtedly accounted for more winter-time accidents and fatalities than all the rest of Southern California's mountains combined.)John Mendenhall and Homer Fuller, who were at the ski hut, and who had ropes, ice axes, and crampons, climbed down the ice wall that night, found blood on the snow near the bottom, and soon located the injured Dootson. He was too heavy to be dragged back up, so they took him down the long canyon, through ice fall after ice fall. The next day, they turned the victim over to a CCC rescue group, then climbed back over Mount Baldy, descended to the hut, then down to their cars. They had not slept for forty-eight hours, and were so tired they did not think they could make it. The rescue was widely reported in the newspapers.

Ruth always said the Baldy hut was the most peaceful place in Southern California, but this is how she described the night the two rescuers were gone: "you have to know what these beastly California mountains are like–their steep ridges drop sheerly and very, very steeply down into canyons, perfectly bare. Right now their north slopes are *ice*, solid glare ice. People are always falling off the Devil's Backbone; of the last six who fell off, five were killed and one broke his neck." Ruth described the night the rescuers were gone: "Outside, it was one of the most weirdly beautiful nights I have ever seen. The half-moon was extremely bright, the wind bitterly cold, and high up above to the southwest, on the almost vertical-looking bare white slope of that great slalom bowl, the ice glittered in the most wicked way–I never saw snow *shine* that way–it reflected the moonlight with all the silver brilliance of water, or as if there were a white light inside the hill. It was very, very beautiful–and very, very cruel."

Besides going to Tahquitz every chance they got, and to Rubio Canyon above the city, Ruth and John made various climbs in the desert, including the first ascent of Monument Peak in the Whipple Mountains. *The Los Angeles Times* ran an article about the climb on its front page: a photo of the summit team appeared over this caption, "Left to right are John D. Mendenhall, chairman of the climbing group; his wife; Arthur B. Johnson, Paul Estes." Another desert trip took Ruth and John to Signal Peak in Arizona's Kofa Mountains, one of several rugged rhyolitic ranges near the Colorado River.

In the summer of 1940, Ruth and John traveled to Mount Confederation, in the southern part of Canada's Jasper National Park. This attempt at a first ascent failed due to weather. This was the first of their many expeditions into the Canadian Rockies. Only one other climbing team from Southern California had ever ventured so far afield. –V.M.C.

# San Antonio Pinnacles

ALPHA AVE.

SO. PASADENA, CALIF.

OCTOBER 30, 1939

*Dear Mrs. Ull,*

We had a nice trip up at the San Antonio ski hut this weekend, at the work party. John and I hit the trail around 4:30 Saturday afternoon. Neither of us had been up since Easter–little did we think at that time that when we next returned, we would be married! It was a warm balmy afternoon. It got dark long before we got up the trail, but in our experienced way we skipped through the butches and over the rocks and crud without even noticing them. The hut lights streamed warmly down over the pine-tree grown knoll, and when we entered we were greeted with a great cheer from the prostrate masses.

Among the assembled twenty was Murray Kirkwood, of whom I have heard for a long time, late of Princeton, now a teacher at Pomona. He looked more like a tall Byronic dark-haired chit of 22 or so than the 28-year-old Rhodes Scholar which he is. He had a little sawed-off girl friend from London or something named Lavendar whom he insisted on calling Spike, to her dismay.

After supper and dishes, about 8:00, John and I donned jackets and a coil of rope and set off in the moonlight for a little rock climbing in the pinnacles–a slightly weird project. There was a cold gusty wind howling over the slalom bowl. The moonlight was very bright.

The mountain ranges across the vast canyon were black and solemn, and as we climbed, the San Gorgonio group rose palely above their shoulders. The climb to the pinnacles is nasty, as the slalom bowl is an extremely steep slope of nothing but loose sliding talus and scree, which is very dull to climb. An hour's toil up the stuff brought us to the foot of the pinnacles, and we roped up and climbed. It was a lot of fun, though in the main the pitches were too easy for sport or too hard to try in the moonlight. It was much easier climbing in the moonlight than I had expected, and it was wonderful up there on the shadowy crags under the clean sky pricked with a few bright stars, with the bitter cold wind whistling through the teeth of the pinnacles.

About 10:00 we came out on the skyline–from which easy slopes lead to the summit of Baldy–and scuffled down through another notch, sliding downhill with rolling grating masses of scree, the wind whipping dust into our eyes and noses. Below the pinnacles, the slopes weren't quite so precipitous, and the descent was easily accomplished by sliding along with the crud. The slalom bowl was vast and empty, and looked like plowed ground tilted crazily up on end, rising in a great swoop to the jagged pinnacles against the stars. We got back to the silent hut about 11:00. People were on the mountain practically all night, as Koster came up from Harwood, arriving about 2:00 a.m., and Joan and Tweege and Rob Roy got up at 4:00 and climbed to the summit for sunrise.

John and I slept outside under the pines, in a kiting wind that tore at our hair all night long, and rose around 7:30 to warm blue skies and still howling wind which made the wind mill of Brinton's Folly whirr busily. There was nothing for a female to do at the work party, so I gracefully resigned myself to it, after doing up a mess of dishes left by others, and lay in the sunshine on the lockers reading Alpine

Journals. A smear of useless people wandered up from the Harwood Lodge Hallowe'en party. John and some other fellows hauled monstrous logs out of the woods. Others completed the girls' new gaboon, composed some quaint fire-escapes and performed other little tasks. All day the mountains to the South across the canyon were marvelously deep blue, beyond the pines, from the mist that filled the canyon. The wind was cold. About 2 p.m. John and I shouldered our packs and tramped down the summery trail.

We got home at a respectably early hour, had baths, and luxuriated in our cozy Sunday supper over the paper. We like our home.

*Well, write to your pretties. Much love,*

# Rubio Canyon

ALPHA AVE.,

SO. PASADENA, CALIF.,

NOVEMBER 13, 1939 — MONDAY — 11:00 OR 12:00 A.M.

*Dearest Ma,*

I can't type. If you could see your child now! I am a wreck–hardly "a shadow of my former self." I can't say I'm "not all I once was"– because I'm much *more.* In brief, yesterday while climbing I got into a mass of angry wasps, exactly like in the funny papers except it wasn't funny. It didn't do me any good. My left arm & hand are phenomenally sausage like, so I can't type!

Around 11:00 yesterday we went to a picnic of some of the fellows in John's engineering class, in a park near Cal Tech. John played games with the fellows, and I visited with the wives–ten or twelve Mrs.'s and their assortment of ornery squalling homely children. About 2:00 o'clock we departed from the picnic and went climbing, stopping at a service station to change from civilized clothes to overalls.

We went up Rubio Canyon, one of the deeply gashed canyons in the mountains north of Pasadena. It has some fine waterworn granite walls dropping from the dry brushy mountainsides. The canyon is dry now except for a few smelly puddles, and the City of Altadena pipeline which is strung down it. The old tracks that used to carry a Pacific Electric train and cable car up to Mt. Lowe start up this canyon. After the resort on top burned, and autos became more popular anyway, the line was abandoned.

It was a hot, muggy afternoon. We hiked up the right-of-way, leaving it at the foot of the Incline to continue up the canyon, roping up to climb occasional pitches. We had fun, and the climbing was getting good about 4:30 when we thought we'd climb one more pitch and start back before dark. John climbed it, and then I followed, and here I was suddenly attacked by a swarm of wasps, who had probably been aroused by John's passing, and further stirred up by the rope. There was nothing I could do but climb as fast as I could up to John where I had outdistanced most of them and could battle at the rest. My arms, neck, chest, back and scalp were on fire. My hair and shirt were full of furious yellow-jackets (or so it felt), and there were even a couple in my pants. For some reason I had no stings on my face, which was lucky.

By the time we started back, it was already dark. We dared not return via the wasp route. Even I could see how monstrously funny was our retreat down Rubio's Canyon. I felt just like hell. I could just *feel* the poison coursing merrily through my system, feeling slightly sick and faint, and every sting on fire, and chills and fever flitting over my hide. However, I followed along silently after John, since there was certainly nothing else to do. It was warm and dark, and the canyon was lovely when one looked at it. We had a long series of rope-downs to get to the floor of the canyon, off trees, and a piton which when he was driving it, John could see only when he struck sparks. Between rope-downs I would lay my head on my knees and suffer. Then we would hike down the rocky canyon–roping down falls. It was all very unconventional roping off any pipe or valve that the Altadena water system had to offer, and even sliding down an occasional pipe and once, like monkeys, down a section of railroad rail which was conveniently leaning against a cliff.

Eventually we reached the tracks, and tramped down the ties. As soon as we got to the car I felt worse, of course. There is just something about John that is so *comforting* to have around. When we got home I took a bath and plastered on some soda, and felt too lousy to eat so went to bed. Ah, my stummick was squeamish, my left arm was bloated, all my bitten areas ached and burned and stung and throbbed, and where I wasn't stung I had busted out in a sympathetic case of hives, and it was all very jolly. Even my eyes were heavy and droopy and nearly closed! I never felt *that way* before. I made John *sing* to me when he came to bed last night, but not "Last Night the Nightingale Woke Me."

I did not get up at 6:00 this morning; I stayed in bed till 10:00, and am going back soon. I feel better today, because my wounds and limbs are merely numb and bloated, and itch some, instead of burning and pricking so. For some reason I don't feel the ones in my wig. My left elbow and wrist joints won't bend at all well, and my neck glands are stiff. I wish you could see my chubby hand–it looks like mumps. However, all for the sake of something, I agonizedly put my hair up on curlers!

with Love,

# Monument Peak, First Ascent

### Alpha Ave.

### So. Pasadena, Calif.

### January 2, 1940 — Tuesday

*Dearest Fa',*

With a painful burst of concentration and intellect, I managed to write "1940" instead of "1939" for the first time. This is a record. Anyway, this will serve to wish you a happy birthday from your pretty daughter (if any).

We had a singularly fine New Year's weekend. I suppose it is the ambition of every climber to climb something that has never been climbed before. Since practically every summit except a few in places like the Himalayas, have been attained, we are reduced to making "new routes"–that is, finding a new and difficult way of getting up something that we could climb easily by some other route. However, this weekend we climbed Monument Peak, the last unclimbed summit of any worth or difficulty in the Southwest since New Mexico's renowned Ship Rock fell to the San Francisco climbers a few weeks ago.

Monument Peak isn't very big, but it is one of the most spectacular-looking things I have ever seen or thought of climbing. It is situated near the Parker Dam on the California-Nevada border, and it is a very vertical finger of basalt sticking up out of the desert, thin and spire-like, with a rounded top and a profile from every angle which is actually as vertical as a pipe, with a few minor overhangs

*Monument Peak (note climbers on summit), December 31, 1939*

thrown in. The west side blends into a ridge about 225 feet from the summit, and the south, east and north sides drop into the desert for probably a good 300 feet more. It is hardly any wonder not many people have tried to climb the thing. In addition to its general contours, it is made of rotten red basalt which isn't good to climb on. John and a friend made an attempt on it in April of 1937, when he was working in the desert nearby, and two of our very good climbers, Glen Dawson and Bob Brinton, tried it and turned back a couple of years ago.

We left L.A. about 11:30 Saturday morning in the car of Paul Estes, one of the newer R.C.S. climbers who had also thought of going out there so we took him along (as it were), and his brother Al. The Estes car is one of those beastly little tin Willys, which is on the verge of collapse though quite new, and doesn't go up hills very well. Art Johnson, who was also going to climb with us, went out in his car, a comic but efficient Model A, bringing Maxine Holton along for company. We went to Riverside, then south toward the Imperial Valley through Banning, Indio, then east again across the desert, a 300-mile trip in all.

The desert was beautiful–the flat floor of it covered with the long stringy red branches of the blooming ocotillo, greasewood and creosote bushes, round red-spined cacti, fluffy-looking, but viciously fish-hook spined cholla, and expanses of purple and yellow desert flowers. From the desert floor rose the red and purple desert mountains, bare and rocky; John knows the names of all the ranges–Eagle, Granite, Old Woman, Whipple, Coxcombs. As we whisked eastward, the sky behind us was stained in magnificent brilliant colors behind the ragged skylines. To the south the Colorado River appeared, and the air took on the smell of water instead of sage. Immense aqueducts, with many miles of tunnels through the mountains, carry water westward from the Parker Dam region. John worked for several years in this region with the Metropolitan Water District and later for Consolidated Steel.

After dark, at the little shack town of Cross Roads, we turned north on a gravel road, which got rapidly worse and worse, and which wound along through desert, sandy washes, and cliffs. Just as it got dark we had been able to see that high gloomy thin finger of Monument Peak on the northern skyline. We found a little dirt track leading off into the desert which led to an old mine. It was dark, and the Willys's back end made terrible grating noises where it scraped bottom going through the dips. After grinding along up the Copper Basin Mine road for a short distance, we stopped because what road there was, was washed out in a few places, and there we camped.

The desert was vast and mysterious all about us. The night air was warm, the stars luminous and bright. We built a tiny fire of greasewood in the midst of all the silent sagey emptiness, with the black looming forms of buttes and cliffs on the skyline, and sat in the dirt eating stew from the thermos bottle. Then we stirred up the sand in the wash bottom and went to bed.

We had a fine long sleep on the wide clean desert, with the moon rising bright above us, and weak but whiney mosquitoes zooming about our ears. Mosquitoes are so disconcerting because you can't stand their whine, yet the minute they stop you have a horrid premonition that they are eating you up, even if your head is completely buried on their special account.

We got up about 6:00. John and Art laid out a great assortment of climbing hardware (twenty-eight pitons, eighteen carabiners, four piton hammers, 400 feet of rope—a 120 foot and an 80 foot climbing rope, and a 200 foot thin roping-down rope). We finally started off across the desert for the Monument, which thrust up before us spire like and impossible.

John and I went a little ahead of the others, first along the little mine road, past the shafts and dumps of the old mine, then across the rolling desert, with its little pale green uplands dotted with weird cacti and bright wild flowers, and through the raw deep watercourses, dry and rocky, toward the high red ridge of basalt south of us. It was a lovely morning, neither hot nor cold, the air fresh and bright, the desert dropping beneath us. Presently we started to toil up a very steep canyon, choked with red-brown rocks and talus, and after quite a bit of hard work emerged on the ridge, in the notch where the Monument joined the ridge. This took about an hour out of camp.

When we had all gathered on the ridge, and Johnny had gone on a few scouting treks off to the south to get a different perspective of our climb, we sat about changing hiking for climbing shoes, and contemplating our possible route. As someone once said of a Himalayan peak, "It wasn't a *good* route, but it was the *best*." The first part of the climb wasn't especially hard–it started from a cave and worked diagonally up and to the right over a jutting boss and onto a ledge beneath a white yucca stalk which by some freak of nature was growing calmly from the cliff. John and Art contemplated, but condemned as too hazardous, a chimney back a little to the left, which ended in an overhang just below the summit. It was this chimney, however, which eventually led us to the top.

Well, about 10:00 o'clock came that great moment when we roped up: John leading–he always cuts a fine romantic figure in climbing costume, rather like the pictures one sees of people dashing about the Alps; second, as alternate leader and the strongest man to

*Summit of Monument Peak.* The Los Angeles Times *published this photograph January 10, 1940, with the caption: "CLIMBERS–Here are the four Sierra Club members who finally conquered Monument Peak. Left to right are John D. Mendenhall, chairman of the climbing group; his wife; Arthur B. Johnson, Paul Estes.*

back up John, little short Art Johnson, homely, cat-like in his motions, wearing brown shirt and hat, competent climber and mountaineer; third came Paul Estes, a silent, thin, blonde fellow, with a pock-marked complexion, cheeks almost death's-head thin, a certain dry sense of humor yet with a disconcerting habit of saying almost literally nothing, even when a direct question is put to him in a crucial moment of climbing—Paul carrying the rucksack; last, Ruth in a red-plaid flannel shirt and with the coil of reserve rope over my shoulder and a piton hammer in a hip pocket.

Being fourth on the rope for half the climb, I couldn't see everything that went on among the leaders, John and Art, who of course were the heroes of the climb; I sat on ledges in the warm sunshine and admired the view, and jerked out pitons as I came along behind. It was a hard climb—the technical difficulties wouldn't have been so great in sound granite, but in the treacherous brown basalt (quite different, by the way, from Spokane's brand of black lava), it was tough.

The exposure, which is what climbers mean by looking off into nothing, exceeded anything I ever saw on a climb. On most climbs, of course, the angle of the cliff is sufficiently mild so when you look down, you see the rock receding to the bottom, or at least for some distance beneath you. At no time on this climb did you see anything at all between the ledge you were on at the moment and the desert several hundred feet straight down. If you threw a rock over, you almost forgot about it before you heard it hit, since it didn't bounce off anything on the way down. Falling rocks whirred like swallows. The leaders moved with utmost caution, feeling and testing every hold, picking out rotten loose rock and throwing it off, tapping and tapping the decaying rock with their hammers to tell by the sound how good or how bad it was.

At the ledge the leaders had now gained, John and Art changed leads, the customary procedure on a rope where there are two men of approximately equal ability, to give each a turn at the glory of leading. At the far right-hand end of the long narrow ledge, they drove in a good piton, through which Paul belayed Art. At the far left-hand end of the ledge–after deciding the rock above was too loose to attempt–Art and Johnny maneuvered a two-man stand, which is a little trick climbers use on rare occasions when the holds are simply out of reach. It was a sort of little overhang, up around a corner to the left. John braced himself with his head in a nook of the rock and nothing for 500 feet below. Art climbed on John's shoulders, reached the holds above, got up on the precarious little shelf. I heard him utter an exclamation, saw a great handful of loose rock hurtle off into space, gathered that one fine hold had simply given away. His other handhold was sound–otherwise he would have swung out into a great arc from the cliff face, held into the piton by Paul's belay. Then Art got a piton in up there for protection, two in fact, worked to his left across a small ledge, found himself in the chimney we had condemned from below–with the surprises that rocks hold for one, an astonishing deep fine chimney, of sound rock, where one could go up easily with back and knee pressure; out of the chimney he had to make a little traverse, protected by another piton, to escape from the overhang, worked up a smooth but fairly easy little chute, and suddenly was bellowing triumphantly that "the peak is ours!"

And at 2:00 p.m. we all stood on that high spire's tip, where no man–ever–had stood before! It was quite a sensation. How blessed is the climber to be able to do something like that–while a million people watch Pasadena's Rose Parade, ninety thousand see the Rose Bowl game, masses go to the races, thousands pack downtown streets and get drunk, and the Finns kill eighteen thousand Russians.

It was the most satisfactory mountaintop I ever saw, since it went up to one definite little point, and there wasn't much else up there. There was probably an area as big as the inglenook, covered with soapy sliding little rocks, where one could walk precariously around. Art built a large cairn, which fell down at a severe look and had to be built again. We put a brief account of the climb, and our signatures, on a piece of paper, closed them into the conventional tobacco tin, and deposited it in the cairn. We were much photographed by ourselves, each other, and the ground crew. We sat down to our lunch of squirrel food–rye-crisp, sausage, cheese, raisins and chocolate, and a couple of welcome canteens of water. We sat in the sunshine and breeze, and looked out over the immense expanse of purple desert mountains, in relief like paper-mache maps; across the ribbony curlings of the Colorado River, the Copper Basin Reservoir reflecting its enclosing red-purple buttes and blue sky like a postcard, beyond it the blue curlings of Lake Havasu, dammed up by the Parker Dam. It was our Matterhorn, perhaps as near as we'll ever come to Whymper's first ascent. But we remembered the way Robinson, in "Mountains and Men," said of the triumphant Whymper party, "But look North, little men, where the cliffs and the grizzly green ice of the Matterhorn Glacier await you"–and we descended as carefully as we had gone up.

Art scouted till he found a rare piton crack in the crumbling ledges along the summit, and drove in a sound piton. Through its eye he doubled a sling rope and tied it firmly about the center of the roping-down rope. We rarely belay the person roping down, but in this case John belayed the first three down because of the hazardous and vertical nature of the descent, and the loose rocks which the climber couldn't help kicking off and which the ropes themselves flicked off from time to time. It was frightfully steep–for a long distance the rope hung straight down with the force of gravity, instead of lying against the cliff. At sundown we gained the ridge, our companions, our canteens, a little more lunch, and solid ground.

At the last quick twilight, we slid down the steep talus chute. Going back from a climb is always fun–especially with Success behind. One feels tired, but it is a good solid muscular tiredness, with only uplifting happiness and contentment in the mind and heart and soul. Footsoreness, tired muscles, bleeding knuckles, somehow only emphasize how able-bodied, how lean and well and strong, how light-footed, you feel returning from a climb.

Behind us that still vertical, still impossible and impregnable looking spire of Monument was silhouetted against the clear light of the evening sky, tipped by our tiny cairn, a great star and a small one in the sky to its right.

Across the warm sweet desert, with the soft cool evening air about us but our wrists prickling a little with sweat, through the rocky gullies and the spiny desert shrubbery, under the brightening stars, we tramped back to our camp, and four of us stuffed our bodies into Art's Model-A and roared off over the desert to the Sierra Club camp, for motives not quite clear but probably mainly conceit. All along the Colorado River the night smelled wonderfully like wet mud. Finally it got to be 1940 in Arizona, and we got into the car and went back to California, where it was 1939 for another hour. That is the first year I saw in twice!

*Happy birthday again and much love,*

# Mount Confederation, Canada

Alpha Ave.

South Pasadena, Calif.

September 4, 1940 — Wednesday

*My Dear Constantine,*

I have but recently finished one of those little snacks which no one but a Dyar (or a man of resource and courage) could consume successfully and with relish a couple of hours before dinner: a large slab of frosted chocolate layer cake, wet with cream; two big angular juicy slices of dill pickle; and one and a half cups of potent coffee.

Canada seems very very far away. It is a peaceful 4:30 of a sunny, breezy, coolish South Pasadena afternoon. The neighborhood reeks with quiet, since during my absence the people on the other side of our duplex were evicted by our mutual landlord. The local lawns are all frizzled and brown, a la California which trustingly but unwittingly relies upon the heavens to provide sufficient water for their miserable yards of Devil's grass (which in truth is sort of gray at best).

Wednesday morning, two weeks ago, soon after breakfast we started out on the familiar road from Spokane to Eastport, the rose bushes by the roadside laden with berries and the forests a fine sight to our California trained eyes. At the border there were the usual jovial exchanges with the Customs, and off we went again northward. We were not troubled with the view, as forest fire smoke blotted out everything except the woods along the roads, all the way north that

*Ruth en route to high camp on saddle, Mount Confederation, August 24, 1940*

day and the next, and we arrived in Banff about 9:00 p.m.  Banff is wholly a resort town and hence is flavored with the same atmosphere that hangs over places like Catalina Island.  Finally we found a spot in the woods to lay down our sleeping bags, and slept.

We thought we would take a crack at climbing Mt. Confederation, one of the few remaining unclimbed peaks in the Canadian Rockies, and since our information as to its very existence was vague and hazy, we drove up after breakfast to see what information we could garner form the Alpine Club of Canada.

On a forested hillside above the town, we found a lodge perched in front of a semi-circle of little cabins.  The hostess, a smooth skinned and big bosomed lady in pearl gray, cordially showed us over the lodge.  Upstairs were offices, and two long identical rooms with fireplaces, known as the writing room and library. Books, trophies, ice axes, and photographs lined the walls in a charming fashion. She gushed along in a British accent, and presently we realized that she thought we were going to rent a cabin there, upon which point we were obliged to disillusion her. We then mentioned Confederation and another unclimbed peak, and she cried in dismay, "You aren't going to try *that*, are you! It's never been Done, you know," and called in alarm for Major Tweedy (the secretary-treasurer of the Club).

Major Tweedy was as English as anyone could desire, and I found myself unable to regard him as anything real, but only as something in a book or movie. He was perhaps 40, a big stocky fellow, rather crippled with what was doubtless merely arthritis, but what one preferred to think of as gout. He was dressed in impeccable, crisply pressed brown tweeds, a brown and yellow plaid woolen waistcoat, and a magnificent English accent complete with "beastlies" and "damneds." He started out crusty and brusque, but gradually grew friendly and helpful, and was soon dashing all over the place scurrying through books and maps to find what we wanted to know. He even gave us a large topo map.

Eventually we escaped from the Major, drove on north through the haze of smoke into Jasper National Park, and reached Sunwapta Falls, where at 5:00 p.m. we made up our mighty packs, slunk guiltily through the perfectly groomed mass of wealthy rubbernecks fresh from a rubber-neck bus, and started out through the unmapped wilderness of the Athabaska River Valley.

It was *real* wilderness. It made the trail-threaded and pack-trained High Sierra look like a city street. It was a big blank white space in the middle of our topo map. I suppose we were the only two people in hundreds of square miles of rivers and rocks, mountain peaks and great snowfields. The Canadian Rockies are wonderful –enormous, glacier-hung peaks, each with its own individual rugged shape, are everywhere, with vast timbered river valleys running between them, huge lakes lying at their feet. They are remote, inaccessible, seldom climbed, unbelievably beautiful.

We had been told we had a "16-mile trail-less pack-in" before us. Probably no one had ever backpacked up to Gong Lake before, but two or three pack trains of horses had gone in so there was a kind of trail (except where we lost it) all the way–better than we had hoped for. Many trees had fallen since the horses. The first part was along the trail that leads to Fortress Lake, a large and famous lake just over the Alberta Border in B.C.

Almost all the forests we saw have been burned over once, twice, even three times that we could trace in the vintages of burned logs. Great old black trunks would be nearly rotted away. Younger smaller ones would be piled up in the traditional jack-straw fashion. Young Lodgepole pines were again growing, straight and thick and brave. The trail was marked with the passage of elk, of caribou, of moose–they leave a deer like hoof mark as large as a cow! We found a huge elk horn about 5 feet long in the swamp. We didn't see any game, as they doubtless heard our loud passage miles away. The "earth" is peculiar–it seems to be almost entirely white or yellow-white, well-compacted ashes–which sticks to everything quite beyond the powers of mere dust or mud. We found the going easy at first, hiked briskly along the level trail for two hours, about 7:30 found a campsite by a little stream, and slept our first night in the wilds.

Friday morning, August 23rd–ten days, 2,000 miles, a lifetime ago–we were up, to our usual little routine of making-breaking-camp duties. I usually cook supper while John makes beds, etc. On the contrary, he cooks breakfast mush while I pretty myself while sitting up in my sleeping bag (it is always a final shock to draw my lower limbs from its downy confines). One's appearance gradually degenerates on a pack-in trip. One wears the same shirt (mine a new handsome red and black plaid from Mrs. Tansy's skilled sewing-machine) night and day, sometimes inside out for that civilized touch at night; the hair gets full of down (down, but not out); all one's clothes gradually look as if they had been slept in–because they have. However, one patiently carries on with lipstick, and the comfort that everyone there gets looking worse at the same rate. John grew a darling beard, which looked more like Robin Hood every day.

Friday was a strenuous day. The narrow little trail wound over the flats of the Athabaska River Valley, through woods and downed timber. The trail became gradually worse and more obscure. We lost it once crossing a large stream, and definitely in a great swamp, where mucky moss and shallow brooks flowed under a crisscross of small tree trunks. We became deft indeed at skipping along on thin swaying rotting unstable logs, balancing our packs on our backs, and feeling like Northwest Passage at the very least. We would follow game trails. We would go into the traditional blood-hound character of the detective, bolstered by all our woodcraft long dormant in woodless California, and peer and sniff and cast to right and left, seeking an axe blaze, or the lowly but unmistakable evidence of horse manure in the trail. Those packs on our backs (our elephants) had become heavier and heavier. We were weary. Despite the cloudy day it was hot. And the trail began to climb steeply uphill–back and forth, up and through trees, exasperatingly always up, and never did Gong Lake appear over the next rise.

The valley of the Athabaska is probably the most magnificent place I have ever seen. That great river flows from the huge icefields which feed its headwaters, northward, swollen by the waters of the Chaba, the Sunwapta, the Whirlpool, the Maligne Rivers, and others (off my map!) to the North Sea. At the very head of the valley lies

*Athabaska River Valley and Gong Lake*

the magnificent white cone of Mt. Columbia, 12,294 feet, the highest mountain in the Canadian Rockies, surrounded by the great Columbia icefields which also drain to the south to form the Columbia River. We could see other and still other great peaks as we climbed higher–at the head of the valley were sprawling rugged Mt. King Edward, and somewhat westward the black jut of Warwick, the faint far shimmer of Ghost Mt., the distinctive shape of Chisel Peak. The shimmering white Athabaska wound and meandered and interlaced itself among its gravel flats. Between Chisel Peak, and the marvelous black glacier-hung striped limestone ramparts of Fortress Peak, we could see the east end of the curling Fortress Lake. We could look up the valley of the Chaba River as it flowed down to the Athabaska. We could see unlimited miles of rivers and lakes, forests and rocks and snow and ice.

At 7:00 o'clock in the evening we finally looked down upon Gong Lake, probably a mile or so long, the same queer milky green of all glacier waters, its shores an indescribable and almost impenetrable wilderness of large dead trees, ghostly gray, stacked and crisscrossed upon each other higher than one's head, and still-standing, close dead gray trees, weird with fuzzy gray dead branches and moss; dense undergrowth; young trees; all encroaching into the very waters of the lake itself on all sides; and the waters for many feet out into the lake were solid with floating driftwood like a great ring of a raft.

Somewhere on those rank and inhospitable shores was a camp-site. We dropped packs in the jungle of dead trees, and John cast eastward while I cast westward. I found it–first a can, then an axe mark on a tree, then the welcome horse sign, (as they politely say in books), and then the cleared circle on a little point of land–like an oasis in a desert, a bare space 30 feet across, a fireplace, a can dump, two places once cleared off for tents. I struggled back to the packs, shrieking my discovery at John. We made our little camp, wearily; and after a smoky supper, crawled into our welcome sleeping bags.

Saturday was a beautiful warm summer day (our last and only one). We used it (and as it turned out, misused it) for recuperation. Directly to the north of Gong Lake bulked the mountain we hoped to climb–the big rocky sprawl and jut of Confederation, 10,000 feet. We planned to establish a high camp on a rocky shoulder some 1,500 feet above Gong Lake, which we would spend the afternoon doing after loafing Saturday morning. We had not taken a canteen, and now–seeing no snow on the mountain's south side–realized our error if we wanted to camp up there. So we trotted out our ingenuity, and spent some time sealing water into cans with adhesive tape: our Klim can, and some rusty old milk cans we found in the dump! We made up light packs, which were mainly our sleeping bags, the tarp, and squirrel food, as we didn't plan to cook, extra clothing, and the climbing hardware. The rest of the food we tied up in a sack and hung from a tree to keep bears (if any) away from it.

About 3:00 p.m. we started off along the west shore of the lake, through the dense wilderness of dead trees. By this time we were acutely skilled in tripping along over logs of any size, shape and consistency. We crossed the broad stream that flowed out of the lake, via logs. We found fairly open climbing up the fringe of woods on the other shore, then over big blocks of talus, steeper looser talus and scree; and early in the evening we topped the shoulder, which was at the far end of an enormous cirque above which rose the northwest ridge of the mountain. (You stop looking at mountains as a piece of 2-dimensional scenery, and regard them more as a definitely 3-dimensional structure, as an architect must look at public buildings.)

The campsite amazed us. Water was the very thing we hadn't needed to bring. Just over the shoulder, beyond a shore of talus blocks, was a funny small round depression perhaps 50 or 75 feet across, at the bottom of which was a tiny meadow of remarkably deep springy moss. It was crossed by a small cold slowly-flowing stream, which appeared and disappeared in the talus at either end. Not only that, but we had firewood; timberline seemed to have receded a little ways down the slope in late years, leaving some fine old stumps and branches to burn. It was a warm evening, and we ate our pumpernickel and Vienna sausages and canned French fried spuds with great relish. We were in bed before dark, and John played his mouth organ till the great silent night had settled over our high, remote little camp.

During the night it rained a little, but when we arose at 5:30 the clouds seemed to be breaking, so we packed up our lunch and climbing stuff, and after breakfast we started up the cirque. It was a two-hour trudge over talus, up a loose shoulder, and into a gully filled at the base with snow, at which point we roped up. The gully howled and re-echoed with occasional stone falls, out of whose way we climbed with as much speed as we could muster—weather and falling rocks are the "objective dangers" of mountaineering over which the climber has no control except to stay out of their way.

Half an hour or so after we roped up, it started to rain—not very hard, but persistently, so we and the rocks were soon wet and slimy. We kept on climbing, as it was not particularly hard going. Wet rocks are unpleasant as well as rather difficult to climb on, but that was not the worst of it—nor the cold fingers that go with cold rocks. A thick wooly fog settled down, so if we hadn't studied the route out quite carefully beforehand, we wouldn't have had an idea where we were going. Sometimes we could hardly see each other 50 feet away on the rope. We hated to turn back—so we kept on climbing, the rain falling softly and coldly, the fog shifting and sometimes lightening a little, but never giving up.

About 12:30 we reached a notch in the northwest ridge, we estimated a possible 700 or 800 feet below the summit. The fog was thicker than ever. On the north side of the ridge we found a relatively dry ledge. Our last stopping place had been on two rather wobbly chock stones jammed one above the other in a dismal ice-encrusted chimney, where the rain didn't actually strike us, but cold water in large drops dripped down on us from cracks above. On our ledge, we dangled our feet over the edge, which presumably dropped a few thousand feet to the north side glacier, but since we couldn't see a thing under our feet but drifting gray fog, the exposure didn't matter. Nearby, a huge old snowbank curled over the edge and hung into nothingness just as our legs did.

We thought that if either the rain would stop or the fog would lift we could go on. But you can't climb a virgin peak in a steady rain when you can't see the route 30 feet ahead of you. You probably couldn't even find the peak. When we stood up after eating, and a bitter wind began to cut through our sopping wet pants as it howled off the glaciers, and when it started to *snow*, we decided to retreat.

The first few rope-downs were as nasty as any I've ever done. By this time not only our clothes and ourselves, but of course the rope, were wet. The rope was dirty and bloated. We were shivering. We were wearing mittens, but when we squeezed our fists, out ran muddy cold water. John roped off into the fog, and then tried to pull the rope down. It was so sodden that it wouldn't come, so I rearranged the sling rope, with stiff cold fingers, till it would come. Then I put the rope about me, and backed off into the dark slimy dripping chimney, fog thick below, and a sudden flurry of businesslike snowflakes swirling and beating wetly about me.

Of course, it was all quite a lot of fun.

We roped down. We climbed down. Every single step had to be taken with the utmost caution. It rained. The fog was finally above us–it let us see where we were going, but never where we had been. As we descended, it drew itself down about the mountain like a blanket. Off in the mysterious fog, rocks roared and thundered down the chutes. We hated so to turn back when the climbing was technically easy.

Eventually we regained our roping-up spot, and went on down

the slippery wet talus. The down-sweeping sides of the cirque were an intense green, almost park bench green, with the rain on the lichen-stained mass of debris. The rose quartzite talus underfoot was brilliantly beautiful when wet. We had by now become so tired and so well adjusted to balancing on wet rocks, that we pranced down the cirque, leaping recklessly and sure-footedly from sharp peak to peak of talus block. I had been footsore, but cold and wet seemed to cure it.

It must have been 6:00 or 7:00 when we got back to our high camp. We scattered to our duties, cold as we were, I gathering wood, John tying up the tarp like a tent, with the high end at the big over-hanging boulder beneath whose dry edges we had stowed our beds and food. With the aid of kerosene in a can (which had been left by a preceding climbing party who doubtless brought it for their Primus stove–believing like we did that there was no water or wood) I got a roaring fire going. In fact, the wet logs took hold so ferociously, that within two minutes we had to begin hauling the entire fire a couple of yards farther away. We were stiff with cold and wet. We had no spare clothes. We took off sopping shoes and socks and overalls, and sat about a bit on the maudlin side–I in my long undies and John in his shorts, soaking in the fire's heat.

We had nothing to cook, so I made a foul little stew of water (no salt), French fried spuds, cheese and sausage cut into bits. It was very delicious. We finished up the pumpernickel, and some candy, and got hotter and hotter; and as the rain spat occasionally on the tarp, we felt immensely filled with sheer well-being. We thought we'd climb it again next day if the rain stopped.

Morning brought black skies, more rain. We decided we couldn't climb that day. Since it was that day or never, we might as well go down. I didn't even comb my hair that morning–what was the use when a wet parka hood would be pulled over it all day anyway.

It took another two days to pack out. The descent was long and arduous. The trail–what there was of it–was almost obscured by the rain. We lost it completely after crossing the swamps, and the most exhaustive and meticulous search failed to reveal any evidence of it on the other side. Finally we set off along a game trail, which the elk and moose had worn through the dense stand of young Lodgepole pines. Their hooves couldn't break down the crisscross of downed trees. Doubtless an elk leaps loftily over it all–we did nothing of the kind. We picked our feet up high and stepped over until our legs ached, and our packs grew heavy and our muscles leaden, and we went on. And on.

6:00 o'clock brought us to a flat clearing on the bank of the river, where pack trains had obviously camped before. We wearily dropped our elephants, and cast up and down looking for something to tie our tarp to. The trees were all too little, but finally we rigged up the tarp on poles, in front of a mound which I am sorry to say was indubitably a Grave. The grave (I hope a horse) served as a backing for our campfire. The packers had conveniently left some split wood leaning up against a tree, so I used some of it. With squaw wood, which is the dead wood on trees and which always seems to be dry, I soon had a fire blazing.

It was a bleak campsite. The Athabaska roared between its flat, down-timber littered shores. It was swollen with the rain, and with the natural increase every glacier stream evidences late in the day. Its waters laden with fine "glacier flour" were, in the early evening dusk, as white and shining as skimmed milk. A cold wind blew off the river. Clouds filled the sky though the rain had stopped. But our fire crackled smokeless and warmly.

Tuesday was our last day "out." The weather seemed to be break-ing, the sun showing intermittently despite showers; fog still wreathed the peaks. We had done the worst of the retreat. Though we frequently lost even the parts of the trail which had been best five days earlier, we came through the last fragrant stretch of forest toward the roaring of the Sunwapta Falls between its narrow lime-stone banks, about 4:00 p.m. Just as we had fondly hoped, a rubber-neck bus, filled with slickly groomed tourists, arrived just as we did. In a way we felt sorry for the women shivering in their fur collars and silk stockings, they were so cold. We were battered, tattered, and very happy. We had worn the toes of our shoes through, like children do, and our clothes were wet, ashy, dusty, mossy, and plain dirty. John's beard was well along. We had seen the mountains not as a pretty scene to be looked at through a glass window while a uniformed bus driver said "That is Fortress Peak." We had lived the mountains–the cold and the snow and wet; we had slept on the rocks, smelled them, eaten smoke and ashes with our food, climbed over the downed tim-ber, shivered, drank the rivers and the lakes; they would be part of us, not postcard scenes. The tourists frankly stared, rather more at us than at Sunwapta Falls. A slim chap in a gray well-pressed suit asked, rather wistfully I thought, "How many miles have you hiked?"

We fell ravenously upon Food. Before dark, as the storm lifted, we saw new snow on all the peaks, quite low, showing plainly the limestone's horizontal strata. There was that unmistakable tang in the air that heralds the early days of winter–the smell of winter which is without scent.

We started south, spent a few hours in Spokane taking baths and packing, slept out on the desert south of Pasco where the first mosquitoes of the trip descended upon us with fierce whining hunger, drove Sunday to Redding and Monday to South Pasadena, which we attained at the sensible hour of 8:30–in time to unpack the suitcases and go to bed early. It was a wonderful vacation. It seems now like a dream.

Well, this has dragged on to horrible proportions. How will I ever be able to pay the postage? Did I tell you I was crazy about that darling Mounties cartoon you sent! Did anyone ever tell you about how Pale Thorpe once tied his horse to a tree and then forgot where he tied it; he used to look and look for his horse; and finally, years later, he found it–a heap of bones still tied to the tree.

On this cheery note, we will close. Do write soon.

*Your devoted comrade,*

# Kofa Mountains

ALPHA AVENUE

SOUTH PASADENA, CALIF.

NOVEMBER 18, 1940

*Dear Mother,*

I hope this reaches you tomorrow, as it is supposed to be a birthday letter. However, one can generally depend on the P.O. *not* to take care of these things.

We had a nice weekend in the desert. By the time John arrived home Friday, everything was ready, including me in my clean overalls and the shirt you made me for my birthday. We had more than 250 miles to drive before bedtime, which is quite a piece any way you look at it.

We drove eastward, through Riverside, and on to Beaumont and Banning. The full moon was extraordinarily brilliant, so we could see desert and mountains as well as by day (almost). The north side of San Jacinto was still streaked with snow near the top. I was asleep with my head pillowed on John's lap when we crossed the Colorado River and entered Arizona. At the small shacky spread-out town of Quartzsite, where the Justices of the Peace had many billboards and lights out to lure the matrimonially inclined, we turned south on a washboardy dirt highway that goes to Yuma.

According to Randall Henderson's instructions, we were to drive 17.7 miles south on this road till we came to a small sign pointing east to "Palm Canyon." We found the turnoff with no trouble, as the

Henderson car was parked beside it. The sign was, indeed, a very tiny rickety hand-made affair, stuck on a stick inside an automobile tire. We turned off the road, and laid out our sleeping bags on the fine sandy floor of a broad straight wash. It was 12:45. The moon was shining brilliantly in front of a tapestry of gleaming mottled white clouds. The stars were also in front of the clouds, which I do not understand. The desert is nice and roomy, stretching off flat and empty in every direction, to jutting black and purplish mountain on every skyline. The moon was so bright that I could even see the color of wildflowers in bloom along the wash.

We woke about 6:15 in the morning. The white mottled clouds of the night covered the sky with brilliant pink flecks in the sunrise. Randall Henderson and his son Randy were already cooking breakfast, but we ate cold cereal and milk. Randall is a pleasant, slightly stocky chap, in glasses, about 55. His son was the callow youth stage of his career–a slim youth of 18 or 20, rather pale, a very nice chap. He walked from El Centro to Mexico City last summer. He was there on election day. He hitchhiked home, and caught malaria, among other things.

A little before 8:00, we all had eaten, driven the 8 miles over the foul rocky little road that leads off toward the Kofa Mountains; and donning packsacks and coiled rope, we started east across the desert toward Palm Canyon, a sharp split in the main mountain massif. The Kofa Mountains are named for a mine, the King *of* Arizona. John and I had been under the impression that it was an Indian name. We were at about 1,800 feet elevation, and the summit was at 4,650 feet. It was a big jutting reddish-yellow mountain mass with unusually impressive and precipitous cliffs for a desert mountain. It looked much like the High Sierra in contour, and to its north it tapered out in a long line of sharp pinnacles and aiguilles.

En route to the mountain, we studied desert botany. Of course there were the more common shrubs–dark green fine-leafed creosote, sage, goat-nut, little gray burro bush, small loco weed with its long tapering seed-pods. A few wildflowers, yellow and orange and purple, were coming out. There was a fine assortment of cacti–huge tall cylindrical saguaro; round red barrel cactus; fluffy-looking, pale green, and absolutely devilishly burred cholla; ocotillo which is very funny–a bunch of high wirey thin arms reaching out toward the sky; its flowers are little red banners on each stem end: and the desert "trees"–ironwood with its little oval leaves, cat's claw something like ironwood but with littler leaves; and paloverde, with its light bright green branches and long spines. Everything is prickly, and everything neatly spaced on the rocky sandy ground.

The Palm Canyon, the main canyon on the west side of the mountain, cut in between extremely high steep yellow-ocre walls of volcanic rock. At first we were climbing very gradually up the dry rock canyon floor. After a time, we came to the very high steep canyon that had most of the palms in it, and made a detour up a loose rocky chute to look at them. In this and a few other little side-canyons are fifty-two wild palms, the only ones in Arizona they say. There is no surface water at all, which is unusual in these palm canyons, but the trees look cute sprouting out of the slit in the rock walls.

After this little side-trip, we continued up the canyon. We went rather slowly, as we thought we had lots of time, and Randall (being very vigorous but not quite so young as the rest of us) wanted to rest quite a lot. It was all right with me, as I didn't feel very good. I had a cold, a slight one, that had come on me the night before at an inopportune time. I didn't think it worthwhile to mention it to anyone, as after all, this whole trip had been made for my benefit. I certainly didn't intend that it should alter what I was going to do about climbing. But I did feel kind of dopey.

Randall had a route in mind which we should follow, but he couldn't remember which canyon we ought to take. I must say I didn't blame him, as I myself don't have that uncanny memory of landmarks that seems to guide John by sheer instinct through the most unfamiliar territory. The only point is that we lost quite a bit of time and energy by going up blind alleys.

John decided the best way to continue would be to traverse to the right again, below the rocky teeth and abutments above us, into a canyon which he had noted from below as a likely route to the summit. This we did, finding ourselves to our great pleasure following a nice little path made by wild mountain goats! Their little black oval droppings, and their sharp hoof marks in the dust, were unmistakable. Their path led into a steeply rising narrow chute choked with prickly plants, which probably furnished fodder for the goats. We figured that probably we were on the right route as where goats could go we could go. Really if the evidence hadn't been unmistakable, I would have doubted the ability of the best of goats to get up some of those places–I'd like to see them do it! It was a novelty to be following after them.

We scrambled through the viciously prickly underbrush, and up a chute filled with loose dirt and rocks just waiting to come loose and crown somebody, and finally arrived in a little hollow where a roped climb was necessary to further progress. John tied on, and with me belaying him, made a traverse up and to our left, and disappeared over the edge of the rock wall. The rest of us followed with an upper belay and packs on our backs, and from there we found a very broad sloping ledge under a crowning brownish-yellow abutment, which we followed.

Just before we came to the second place where we roped, I had an unpleasant little surprise. John and Randy had gone ahead of me, prospecting, and when I came along I heard a soft chirring whispering noise in the brush a few feet away, and looking down I saw a fat green snake rattling busily. I had never encountered a rattlesnake, and wondered if I'd know one when I saw it. I did! I hastened out of its way, remarking to the others that there was a large rattlesnake there. We were all rather shocked, as snakes are supposed to have been in hibernation for a month or more, and none of us had been looking out for them. It didn't make as much noise as I thought they did. We figured there was no point in killing it, as no one will ever return to that spot, so Randall took a motion picture of it, and I was sort of nervous about how the fellows got so casually close to the creature. Then we roped up and climbed out of its domicile.

The gravelly ridge was covered with beautiful chalcedony formations strewn hither and yon. Randall says they are the best ones he has ever seen, as ordinarily one finds them washed down by streams, and kind of worn out. Here they are fresh crystals, white and waxy and curly, from their natural mold. I brought a few small samples, and will send Marg some. Randall and Randy more industriously collected enormous hunks of the stuff. Some of them were streaked with carnelian, some with a rich blue. (Randall calls them "chalcedony roses.") Finally we reached the summit, the pale one, upon which was a pile of rocks, boards, benchmarks and old dry-cells. It was 3:00 o'clock. John and I ate the rest of our lunch–sandwiches, oranges, pickles, and drank all but a few drops of our water. Of course we were very thirsty. We felt rather sorry for Randall, who was very tired, and came up slowly, pretending to geologize on the way.

John had the best and fastest way down all picked out–we knew we'd have to do some healthy hurrying if we hoped to reach the floor of the canyon by dark–when that Randy recalled having left his father's $35 camera near the rattlesnake! There was nothing for it but to go back and get it. Randall decided to go down the north side–which would entail a very long walk across the desert, but he thought it would be easier for him, as well as speeding our descent by making the party smaller.

So at 3:30 we three set off for the rattlesnake's place, climbing down as fast as we could, roping down a couple of steep drop-offs, and scrambling down again over boulders and small drop-offs. John stopped to do up the rope, and Randy and I dashed down ahead, racing against darkness which would completely envelop us shortly after 5:00.

It got darker and darker, and we tore down the canyon, skipping briskly down places which we suspected we would never consider going over by daylight when we could see the holds that weren't there. We were very thirsty, naturally. Randy cleverly found a small puddle of water in a little "tank." He said this was a strain upon his gentlemanliness, because he didn't want to poison me by making me drink first, yet it wouldn't be polite for him to drink first. However, it was sweet good water, a few drops left from the last rain, and saved us much suffering. We left some for John (not very much, I guiltily realized afterwards). We then tore on down the canyon–and just as it got completely dark, we came to a sheer steep drop-off of indeterminate depth.

John hurled a few rocks into the depths, and they took an ominously long time to reach the bottom. We dared not risk roping off, lest the rope not reach. It got pitch black. Having had no idea we'd be out after dark, we hadn't brought a flashlight, though we should have known better. We thought we might be able to climb up a ways, and traverse across the mountain into an easier canyon, which, since there was nothing else to do, except stay there, we proceeded to do. This night chose to be overcast and black without a ray of starlight. The moon wasn't up. We felt our way up across the mountainside. I ran into a cholla, and of course the nearest burr eagerly leaped off the plant (they are very carelessly put together) and with a sharp snap fastened itself in my pant leg–and my flesh. One must exercise care and self-control in this condition. John felt around for two sticks or stones, and seizing the burr with these implements, jerked it out of my leg. A fine quantity of little hooked spines were left in me, to be sure, and while I was trying to get them jerked out by feel (they stay in remarkably well!), John got the cholla burr in *his* leg. So there we were, both pulling out spines in the pitch dark. This little event over, we continued our exploration, and finally found our way into another canyon, which John thought would take us downward, though I gloomily expected it to lead to another drop-off.

We now had another inspiration. Anything that grows in the desert will burn beautifully, dead or alive, yet the fire won't spread, so in a glory of wanton incendiarism, we got out matches, and lit every plant we could find. It was really fun, after the way you can't ever build a fire anywhere in this beastly State! It was also about the low point of the day! By the fine little prickly blazes, John could see to explore down the canyon a ways, and we would hurl burning matter down to him to continue the line of fires. Then Randy and I traversed among some burning bushes, and descended after him. By the time our line of fires had gone out, and as we were trying to start some more, feeling around in the dark for good kindling and getting

*Rappelling down Palm Canyon on Signal Peak, Kofa Mountains, 1997 (Photo: Wynne Benti)*

our hands full of prickers, the canyon began to light up just a little. The rocks were showing white, and we realized the moon must be coming up somewhere behind the clouds.

Now we were able to work our way down and down, in the faintest glimmer of light on the rocks. We could see the rocks faintly, but not the spaces between them, and we had to feel our way rather like blind people, never knowing just how far down the ground was. It was very tiring. We couldn't see the vegetation, and kept getting pricked and grabbed and scratched by it. Long since, we had lost all botanical exactitude–everything in the canyon, big or little, was cat's claw to us–and that's the way it acted.

Gradually we found the canyon walls towering higher and higher to either side of us and behind us, and the floor of the canyon flattened out a little, and we realized that we had rejoined the route of that morning, and would get out all right.

It was a great relief finally to find ourselves on the flat desert. There was, however, a long long trudge remaining, over rough rocky spiney country, cut with watercourses, back to the cars. We weren't too sure where they were parked. My legs were so tired I could hardly move them. My head felt funny from my cold. My hands were (I was sure) filled with thorns. We walked and walked and walked. Once we stopped wantonly to set fire to a cholla from pure spite–the things burn wonderfully at the touch of a match, as they are oily, and look very pretty–like something for the Fourth of July. That made us feel better somehow. The dead chollas are very funny–they are limp and black and droopy, more like a dead creature than a plant.

It was after 9:00 when we finally reached the ruts of the road, and soon after, the cars. We immediately swigged down quantities of water and fruit juice and more water. It felt good to sit down. Then John and Randy built some huge fires as a signal to Randall. I wearily fixed our supper. John made our beds. There was no good sleeping place handy, but the hard rocky ground, with the big rocks scraped off, looked as good as any mattress I ever saw. Randy was waiting up for his Dad, and John and I had just gotten into our sleeping bags when Randall called. We shouted a greeting. Then, though fires were blazing, and no doubt the Hendersons were talking and cooking and eating, we fell unconscious and stayed that way all night till about 8 a.m.

We had planned to make another climb next morning. But we had slept too long, and anyway, we were just too tired. John and I felt sort of guilty about being so worn out, but we hadn't had much sleep Friday night, and we'd been a little out of condition, and then I had the cold. So we gave in to being stiff, and sore around the edges, and definitely day-afterish, and decided to drive home that morning instead.

Today I did a little wash, and washed my hair, and washed the bathroom and kitchen floors, and soon must have some lunch and go to the store, and maybe sew a little or something.

*Write soon and much love, Again, HAPPY BIRTHDAY*

*Ruth Mendenhall in Yosemite Valley, probably on top of Washington Column, July 4, 1941*

Chapter Four
# War Years
# 1941-1945

*These would probably have been our great mountaineering years
if war had not come again to the world.*

RUTH DYAR MENDENHALL

"Every headline brings more dreadful news than the last," Ruth wrote to her mother. "How can a person put it all out of their mind for a minute—yet how can one *believe* such terrible tidings. It seems as if I can almost count the days, the time is so short, that I will still have my John. But what will be the use of anything, ever again, if he—so dear and wonderful and fine—goes away to War! And he will go, as soon as War comes."

The United States government had other plans for John, a decision that disappointed him for the rest of his life. He worked on aircraft, ordnance plants, and other defense industry engineering jobs. Between 1941 and the fall of 1945, Ruth and John lived an intinerant life, moving from South Pasadena to San Jose to Wilmington, Delaware; Bowling Green, Missouri; and Birmingham, Alabama—usually moving house several times in each city. Ruth once remarked that she had repainted enough bathrooms, during those peripatetic years, to last her several lifetimes.

The Base Camp commune permanently disbanded in October, 1941, when its members took jobs in the defense industry or joined the military. Ruth noted that the coeducational experiment "did work, which everyone but the originators claimed in advance that it would not."

Ruth and John were invited to a last supper at the Base Camp house. "Joan and LaVere were tearing around frantically remedying the fact that the oven hadn't turned on for the meat loaf, and producing a very excellent dinner under the usual nerve-wracking Base Camp conditions. After dinner I happened to glance around the table,  and every single one of the eight people was sitting at his place, quietly smiling to himself in that secret self-satisfied way of contented people."

*Ruth in Yosemite Valley, July, 1941;*
*With Vivian (age 5 months) Mendenhall, Birmingham, Alabama, 1944*

Before leaving California for the duration of the war, Ruth and John skied, climbed in the Sierra Nevada, and took trips with the Sierra Cub's Bay Chapter, whose members came from San Francisco, Oakland, and Berkeley. A few days after climbing a new route on Mount Whitney's Southeast Face (Southeast Buttress), Ruth and John started the long drive east across the country. Any letters mailed during that journey were probably handwritten, and are lost.

Ruth wrote from their first apartment in Delaware: "My fur jacket is awfully nice. Of course, the first time I wore it, I dressed up very specially and carefully, and then fell down the front steps onto the sidewalk! I didn't even wreck a stocking, but the jolt sort of knocked all the Special feeling out of me." Lacking high mountains in the East, she and John took long hikes, climbed at Devil's Lake in Wisconsin's Baraboo Range, and climbed in the limestone quarries of Missouri, where they decided not to plunge through deep underbrush, for fear of snakes.

In August of 1942, Ruth traveled back West alone, by train, to visit her parents in Spokane, stopping along the way in Montana's Glacier National Park, where she picked up a fire permit at the park ranger station. She took her backpack on a bus to Two Medicine Lake with eighty "highly stylish tourists" who worried about her sleeping outside alone with the mountain goats. She climbed Rising Wolf, a nine mile hike and scrambling ascent to the 9,513 foot summit. The summit register recorded only one other name, that of a ranger a year earlier. Because of fog and a wintry gale, because, "it was my time of the month," and because "the Black Feet Indians' sheep had made such a mess of everything on the ground," Ruth had the "wicked idea"of getting a room in the Monteath Hotel for $1.50 a night. While at the hotel, she opened her birthday present from John, and wrote to him, "John, my darling dear, I opened the elephant-box this morning and now have the two sweet little marble-dust elephants on the table before me. They are *wonderful*. They will look so fine with our others (how will the old ones like the newcomers?). I like their names!! I wish *my* big Elephant were here (MMM-HMMMM!!). I was so glad to have a little letter from you, dear one, with the elephants. You are so dear. You made such a pretty package. Wherever did you get them in Missouri?"

Another year passed. Vivian Margaret Mendenhall was born in Birmingham, Alabama, on August 13, 1943. The months that followed the birth were difficult for Ruth. Looking back, Vivian believes her mother suffered from "severe post-partum depression after I was born." When Vivian was three months old, Ruth was able to do a little rock-climbing, her first in a year.

When Ruth was 32 years old, she began to experience health problems that would plague her for the rest of her life. The South's coal dust and lush vegetation aggravated her hay fever and asthma, making her feel "just a trifle woozy," while her food allergies worsened. In May of 1944, she confided other health worries in letters to her sister Joan: chronic arthritis in her spine, calcium imbalance, and metabolic problems. At one point, she weighed 110 pounds.

Separated by the width of the country from her parents, Ruth kept up a running commentary on the doings of the vast extended family. With no beautiful mountains to talk about, she filled her letters with observations about the "violently green" southern landscapes, food shortages, sewing and knitting, and her baby (who was "tied into a cardboard box" for trips in the car). Ruth remarked that "the war certainly makes a mess of about everything, in a futile way."

In 1944, Ruth and John took one more wartime trip back West,

*Ruth in Yosemite Valley, July, 1941*

to the Tetons, where they climbed the first ascent of Teewinot's West Face. Vivian, one year old, was left behind in Birmingham with a paid babysitter. –V.M.C.

# Alabama Cliffs

8TH TERRACE SO.

BIRMINGHAM, ALABAMA

APRIL 7, 1943 — WEDNESDAY AFTERNOON

*Dear Daddy,*

We have been working on our backyard vegetable garden, which runs in long thick strips along several terraces. I have planted rows of carrots, beets and lettuce, following the hard labor done by John. We plan also on beans, radishes and tomatoes. Of course whether these things will grow remains to be seen–also, if they do grow, whether the rabbits and the neighbors' chickens will leave any for us!

Sunday afternoon we drove a few miles northeast of town, to examine a region which appeared on the topo map to contain cliffs. This area bore rather charming names on the map, such as Stinking Creek, Polecat Ridge, and Hogpen Branch. Gravel roads took us eventually to a paintless and rickety little settlement known on the 1907 map as Weems Gap, but more lately christened Jefferson Park; I prefer the former name, personally!

We had a hike over hills and ridges of open pine woodland, in a gentle, sunny, pitch-fragrant atmosphere so peaceful and remote as to seem almost unreal. We followed old faint roads left by logging operations, the brown pine needles dotted with the blue of pansies and violets and iris, the magenta of phlox, the dainty white of tiny wood sorrels. We finally dropped down into the valley of the Big Cahaba River, a fat, deep, sluggish stream of a dirty khaki-gray color, moving silently between banks of coarse sand on whose surface sparkled bits of jet coal. Willows, yellow with bloom, leaned over the dull surface of the water. I lounged in the sand and sunshine while John scouted upstream for the "cliffs," which turned out to be merely steep canyonsides.

In Birmingham that afternoon, a practice air-raid was going on, ten-thousand paper sacks of sawdust, imitation bombs, falling on the city! Gigantic Liberators, so low we could see their guns sticking out, roared over the house, as if to remind us that the peace of the afternoon really *wasn't* real.

I must quickly proofread this and put it out for the mailman, in the hope that if it goes out Wednesday, it might reach you by Saturday. The mails aren't really very reliable these days.

*Goodbye, and love,*

# Alabama Quarry

8TH TERRACE STREET, BIRMINGHAM, ALABAMA

MAY 12, 1943 — WEDNESDAY NOON

*Dear Ma & Fa,*

Sunday morning we worked at clipping our miserable front lawn by *hand.* It is now about two-thirds bald, a pleasing sight. We can't find anyone who has a lawnmower, and there aren't even any for sale. We did get quite a fancy Wiss grass clippers. The handles are a nice bright yellow like Grandpa's tools used to be. As a matter of fact, the lawn is mainly luxuriant weeds, which can be yanked out and which a mower probably couldn't cope with anyway. Our front lawn is very quaint, being built in terraces almost like stairs–the steep parts are so steep we can't even sit on them without sliding downhill.

Late in the afternoon Sunday we went on a little drive, to a place we call the "East Quarry." We leave the car in a countrified little Negro district, where a few decaying, unpainted shacks in green yards line the roadway, and two Negro churches stand near each other. The older of the churches has the saddest little graveyard I ever saw. The wild-grassed, hummocky graves straggle back into the woods; and hardly any of the headstones are real headstones at all–they are just big rocks that someone has found in the woods and put on the graves. They seem so terribly pitiful, yet rather sweetly loving and devout. Some young girls, very black and shiny in their Sunday white and pink, were fluttering over the graves.

*Ruth climbing the first picth of the "Shore Climb" above the Mississippi River,*
*Missouri, November, 1942*

We followed some little paths through the now almost voluptuous green brushland and hillside. There were queer flowers growing in the steamy green shadows–bright red and yellow; and a vine with queer little purple-black blossoms. Our quarry, near the top of the hill, is a big semicircle of gray limestone cliff, quite rugged, *not* overgrown with Alabama vegetation, and wonderfully peaceful and out-off from the world.

I had quite a wash yesterday of shirts and tablecloths, and now have a nice fat bundle waiting to be ironed; so, pretty soon I'd best do the deed.

*Goodbye, and love,*

# Tetons

8TH TERRACE

BIRMINGHAM 6, ALABAMA

AUGUST 22, 1944 — TUESDAY

*Dearest Relatives,*

It is 4:15 p.m., no time to start a long letter, but the chances are against my ever having several uninterrupted hours for letter writing. Maybe I'd better start sometime. Fa's letter of early August was waiting for me when we got home–it should have come the Saturday we departed, but didn't.

Now the funny papers don't go changing things just because we have been out of touch for two weeks: Dick Tracy, Orphan Annie, Terry and the Pirates, are in just the same predicaments as when we left them. Vivian didn't change either, the little dear, except in a few minor ways. She has now 2 full-fledged top teeth, with two more uppers en route. She can drink very efficiently from her glass. And she has become expert at laying the top of her head on the floor and peering at people between her legs. We scrutinized all the babies between here and Wyoming, and found not any to compare in cuteness with our Poory.

Ak, we surely did have a fine trip! This was a fifteen-day vacation, nine days in the mountains, six in travel. John hadn't even *seen* a mountain for three years. The beginning was quite hectic. John had to go to Florida, to help fix up a grounded bomber. Three hours after he got back, we were actually on the train, and it actually started to *go*. We see and hear so many trains passing through Jones Valley, and there we were, inside of one.

During the night we went to a lot of places like Kentucky and Tennessee, and got into St. Louis around 2:00 p.m., and noted to our horror that people were already standing in line for the Colorado Eagle, the streamliner coach which we intended to ride out on two hours later! This gave us the idea that we'd better get right in line too–which we did, eating our dinner in relays while the other one stood by the suitcase. Within half an hour or so, the line had become a seething mass. When the gates opened, the railway officials began to scream at people not to Push, and not to Sprint. This last advice was particularly futile, as no fat railway man ever could have caught those racing passengers. Naturally, we ran too, and amid piteous pleas not to Push, we got into the coach, and got a comfortable seat, and felt much relieved. And I thought the public couldn't run!

August 23, 1944 Wednesday, 10:30 a.m.: I have finished my daily chores, and even vacced the rugs and written a letter to Aunt Gladys (who, the kindly woman, has gotten herself in for knitting Vivian some leggings). To continue in re our journey:

Those streamliners with the Diesel engines surely do slink along with great smooth speed. The seats were luxuriously comfortable. But here we end the Luxury idea. One hears about crowded coaches, but it is something else actually to see people standing in the aisles for ten or twelve hours, or sitting on the corners of crowded suitcases; and at night to have the aisles so littered with men and little children lying sleeping on the floor that it is a major thing to get to the Ladies Only. On the whole, the train officials' nerves were all shot to pieces, and they were very testy; so it was quite pleasant to have a big black

*Ruth on Middle Teton, August 10, 1944*

waiter snatch up the coffee pot to fetch one more potent poison in an agreeable way.

Might I diverge to remark that, as we went westward, Negroes changed from low animals to mere Porters and Waiters; and by the time we reached Denver, they were only People again, who sat near one on the streetcars and even helped to open windows for white people. It was definitely a relief! Two little episodes I noticed on the train gave me a clue to where the white wimmin in question were brung up: one woman expressed consternation at having to use the same tut as a negress; another white woman urged a slender little negress to sit down while she (the white woman) stood up! (The little negress preferred to stand–all night–so she could be beside her uniformed husband.)

It was almost beyond possibility even to get any water–there was none in the Ladies, and no cups at the other end of the block-long car. There was, however, plenty of cigarette smoke.

Flat Kansas range land, strewn with a few red and white cattle, gradually gave way to the rather mild outlines of the Colorado Rockies, and the great tan bulk of Pikes' Peak. Though the Colorado Rockies are cram-full of peaks over 14,000 feet, they are not very impressive, their skyline being no steeper in the main than that of Mt. Spokane. Denver is a bustling, bright city, located on a vast flat plain alleged to be exactly a mile in elevation (it probably is at some point), distinguished by several extremely modern stores (such as the super May Company, much better than the L.A. cousin), dazzlingly bright green lawns, and street corner fountains that gush perpetually with mountain water. In the distance one can detect the Rockies ringing the city. We took the train for Rock Springs to the north about 5:00 that afternoon, and were in our berth (a very skimpy Upper) by

7:00–it felt so wonderful to undress after all that time, and stretch.

The train had the quaint trait of backing up all the way to Cheyenne, which took half the night! The atmosphere wasn't really too peaceful, as the car was very hot, and very bright with lights, and several frightened and indignant old people had bought the same berth-space, about which they argued unmovably with the conductor for hours and hours.

Promptly at 3:30 a.m. on Tuesday, August 8th, we got off the train in Rock Springs, Wyoming, the night starlit and wonderfully chilly. Despite the hour, the town was well-lit, swarming with activity, and the railroad depot was crammed with bum-like people who had been swept off the streets of Cheyenne, equipped by the government with milkman-like overalls, and exported to central Wyoming to help harvest hay! There were also numerous ranchers about their business, and people sleeping in the park under aged quilts. Trains seemed to pass through every few minutes. Young boys, already beery and coarse-handed, slept on the depot floor. And, I must state, that in my whole life I have never seen so many people wearing nice old blue-jeans as in Wyoming–and that counts the Ski Mountaineers and all the Dyar girls.

We were already on the downgrade of civilization, having donned slacks before we got off the train. We now contacted the Baggage Room, where fortunately our trunk was waiting for us, from which we extracted our duffel bags, pack boards, boots, ice axe, and camera, and left therein our suitcase and store clothes. We breakfasted at 5:30 on pancakes, and the waitress asked if we were from the *Circus*–later John was taken for a hay hand. Rock Springs was less glamorous by daylight.

Eventually, somewhat after 7:00, we got stowed away on a scarred and rickety bus of the Rains Transportation Co. That bus line! Honestlee. It was a little worse than usual, apparently, because all the good busses were busy transporting the hay hands all over the state. We were equipped with the worst bus, and the simple-minded son of Mrs. Rains for a driver. We surely did piddle along, the aisles of the aged vehicle stacked with luggage, a hay hand sitting on our duffel bag (on the crampons, we fondly hoped). The bus driver was also the R.F.D. mailman, so he stopped at every mailbox (they actually were very widely spaced over the range land), and every "post office" all day. That wide, open, rolling sagebrush prairie looked SO WONDERFUL. It was nicely dry and big, with cloud shadows sailing over the land. It rolled off eastward to the Wind River range (a beautiful and inaccessible mountain range, where we are going someday–it contains Wyoming's highest peak, Mt. Gannett). It was like Central Washington, or like Owens Valley in California rolling off to the White Mountains. We had lunch at Pinedale, the U.S. town farthest from a railway (a point of distinction, they seem to feel).

The afternoon moved on. The prairies became more rugged, forested, and canyon-cut. The Wind Rivers diminished southward and changed into the Gros Ventres range. The bus got weaker and weaker, and Jimmie, the driver, wasted more and more time, which he later made up–to our horror–by coasting out of gear down into winding canyons (a practice none too healthy in the best private auto). Finally our bus was met by Mrs. Rains in her newest bus, and she transferred the passengers to her vehicle to continue our northward journey. Though Mrs. Rains' cowboy clothing and at least part of her Pardner mannerisms, were undoubtedly intended as local color for the eastern dudes, still she was really quite an interesting woman, energetic and breezy. Perhaps all his life, she had been too much for her simple son Jimmie. She also had a young daughter driving her busses. Mrs. Rains instantly turned the bus ride into a rubberneck tour and a personal visit. At Jackson, we were supposed to transfer to another bus line to continue the remaining 20 miles or so to the Tetons. However, we were very late, and maybe there wasn't any other bus anyway, and Mrs. Rains took us and the dude-ranch passengers on northward in the late afternoon. Upon parting from her, we made a definite date for her to seek us out in the campgrounds the morning of August 18. It was quite peculiar—we never knew a bus line before that seemed to have no schedule but to be run almost wholly on a personal basis.

Due to a peculiar trick of topography, one does not see the Tetons at all till one is almost beneath them. Then, suddenly, there they are, these great sheer crags of rock and snow, towering unbelievably into the blue summer sky. We have never *seen* such mountains. In area, the range is quite small, nothing like the extensive Rockies, Cascades, Olympics, Sierra. But for sheer, concentrated, rugged splendor, no other mountains we have seen can compare. They actually have no foothills though of course the lowest slopes are rather gradual and covered with timber. But for the entire sweep of six to eight thousand feet above the prairie one sees the great steep masses of rock rise to their wonderfully pointed summits. And a thousand feet higher than all the others, towers the awe-inspiring gray rock wedge of The Grand Teton, like a great axe blade among the hammerhead of the Middle Teton, the pincers of Nez Perce, the saw teeth of Teewinot.

We disembarked from the bus at Jenny Lake Campground. It is a beautiful clear little lake under the tall tree-steeples. The campsites were peacefully deserted. It was about 5:00 p.m., and John decided to start taking our packs up the trail that evening, it being about 7 miles in trail distance and about 3,000 feet in elevation gain to where we intended to camp in Garnet Canyon. While he was gone, I went over to the "museum" and ranger station to see what was there. The rangers are rather lonely this summer, and glad for company. It was quite refreshing to be in one place where mountain-climbing is considered by the officials as *the* respected activity, whereas the ordinary tourist is slightly mocked. The rangers kindly offered to keep a few last-minute articles for us, since we had nowhere to leave such things.

The next morning we started out rather late for our Garnet Canyon camp. John carried what was left of the pack (plenty, I might add), and I the parasite carried nothing. We had to walk on the flatlands for 2 miles, then up about 4 more miles of trail switch backing through deep woods and mint-fragrant fields. We saw many beautiful flowers–larkspur far bigger and bluer than the garden variety, beautiful gentians, some things that I always thought were only asters but which turned out to be *fleabanes*, Indian paintbrush (the state flower of Wyoming), and many exquisite high altitude varieties that I don't know about.

When we reached the spot where John had cached the pack the night before, I did acquire a rucksack of stuff. Soon our trail stopped switch backing, and led off the shoulder of timber into the side of Garnet Canyon, at the bottom of which roared a beautiful white stream, and at the high head of which rose the gray bulk of the Middle Teton, with the curious, thick, black basalt dike rising up its east side like a vast straight pipe.

We found a campsite on a shelf above the stream, among big boulders and great trees. The timberline trees up there grow very huge, a kind of spruce I think, and Lodgepole pines. While John went back for the rest of the pack, I erected the tent between the trunks of five enormous spruces. Luckily a high wind was blowing down canyon that sunny afternoon, so I had it impressed upon me just how firmly one needed to anchor a tent. Cutting boughs for the beds, whittling tent stakes, and so forth took me hours.

We hung our food up in a tree while we weren't around, as a precaution against bears, porcupines and varmints, though the bears haven't been turned into troublesome pigs there as in Yosemite and Yellowstone. We didn't see any bears at all, as a matter of fact, though we heard one at a garbage can down at Jenny Lake. We saw a deer and a moose; and as the valley is an elk refuge, it is the custom for people to have a great heap of white elk horns in their yards–exactly like a gigantic ball of string.

As soon as we got up there, we felt so *wonderful*. I suppose it was partly mental, and partly the rest, and partly the high altitude and cool air. Also, my Alabama asthma disappeared. Anyway, it was absolutely magical. It was so good to be in that high, clean, beautiful country–one thinks one can never forget how it is, and then in spite of everything, its wonder fades when one is gone for a long time. Every pine needle and rock is so clean. The water is so crystal, and so icy cold since it is direct from the upper snows. The thin air holds no warmth–one can be too hot in the sun, move into the shade, and in a moment be too cold.

We had a really good commissary. It was completely dehydrated, but even then weighed over 30 pounds (9 days food, for two people, at about 1 3/4 pounds per man-day). Breakfasts were usually dried fruit, stewed; cooked cereal with Klim; tea, rye-crisp and bacon (oh yum). Lunches were assortments of rye-crisp, cheeses, sausages, candy, lemon-drops, and nuts. Dinner usually had two courses, soup (there is a good variety of dried soups now available), with plenty of butter added for nourishment, and some dish made of rice (previously parched in the oven to make it quick cooking), or vermicelli, mixed with some of the varied sauces, vegetable flakes, and other articles I had procured for variety in flavor. We found several excellent cooking dishes and billie cans to supplement our own meager collection.

We met quite a few other climbers–a party from New York; one from Washington, D.C.; a lad from St. Luke's Hospital in Chicago; the ranger "Timerline"Rapp who was Bill Rice's friend. It is the most curious thing, the way all mountain climbers *look alike*, battered and squint-eyed and sunburned, and all get along together. The Washington boys said Dick Leonard was "lots of fun," but surely didn't ooze hero worship.

Our first night in Garnet Canyon at about 9,200 feet elevation – the night of Wednesday, August 9th–the wind slapped our tent about, boomed down the canyon, and howled in the tree tops, mingling with the constant low roar of the rapids. It was still windy next morning, but the air was warm and the sky blue. We planned to climb the Middle Teton, and Ranger Rapp had suggested our looking up the Chicago youth, Jack Crenshaw, who was camped higher, and who had no climbing companion for the day. We found Jack at the high camping place known as Petzoldt's Cave (after Paul Petzoldt who in peacetime was the Park's leading guide for mountain climbers). Jack proved to be a congenial youth–one soon becomes an old acquaintance on a mountain–and we three proceeded to toil up talus, moraines, and boulders toward the almost 13,000-foot summit of the Middle Teton. On unprotected slopes, the wind was startlingly fierce–every now and then an unexpected buffet would calmly knock one down!–and bitterly cold. The climb via the North Ridge was quite easy. We roped up for only a few pitches, particularly at the head of a steep couloir where we had to cross the snow below a cornice that arched out on the other side. The wind surely did scream with wintry chill through this slot. Ice film, treacherously invisible–"verglas"–lay beyond on the rocks.

Protected from the wind below the summit rocks, we lunched, loafed, talked, photographed, looked at the views. We could see the wonderful tower of The Grand. We couldn't help studying the slopes down which Clyde Nelson and Bill Rice fell to their death two years before–now steep but inoffensive talus, but then (in June) covered with snow and ice. Northwestward lay the hazy mountainous stretches of Idaho, beyond the basin below filled with snow-patches and dancing sparkling green lakes. Other Tetons were southward–the South Teton with its double summits, one pointed, the other square, and the round top of Cloudveil Dome next, and then the "pierced nose"of ugly, stark Nez Perce, and beyond them the rock sides of Buck Mountain, and then Wister. And across the soft flat brown valley in the east curled the headwaters of the Snake River, on their way to their deep canyons. And beyond them the distant, snowy, Gros Ventre and Wind River ranges. It was so fine to be ON TOP again.

We descended by the "easy"or "regular"south side route–parted at the saddle from Jack, who in his decaying tennis shoes intended to climb the South Teton before he returned to his camp. John and I glissaded speedily over steep snow banks and got back to camp about 8:00 p.m., having been up 4,000 feet and down again, and not tired at all. The wind dropped in the night, and it was About Time, we all thought. Climbers do not care for wind.

Days and dates lost all importance, and in fact could hardly be figured out. The day after our Middle Teton climb, I was fixin' to have a rest day, so John climbed the Grand Teton with Jack Crenshaw

*Ruth and John Mendenhall on the summit of Teewinot, Tetons, 6:00 p.m., August 17,1944*

by the Owen or usual route. In the meantime, I was having a lazy day, pottering around camp, washing my hair and some socks, secreting tin cans under rocks, gathering wood, and later taking a bath. All day long, great masses of soft white cloud sailed out of the west, floated over the Middle Teton and down the canyon, and dispersed in the east far away over the valley

We loitered around camp the next day, and ate a tremendous amount of food. In the afternoon we took some of our camping equipment and food up the canyon-side another thousand feet to Petzoldt's Cave at about 10,200 feet elevation. The "cave" is a fine little two-room house under an enormous boulder–perched out on a little shelf which blends on top into the mountainside, drops on two sides down cliffs, and on the other side wanders off to a stream. There are large trees growing around on the shelf, and fine grass which the little coneys gather for their winter hay.

The upper room of the cave was the bedroom, and even had a

raised closet. We cleaned away all the sticks and orange peels, and lined the place with spruce boughs, which not only provided a soft insulation from dust, but also smelled wonderful. The cave seemed a trifle dank daytimes, but was delightfully airy and pleasant at night. The lower room was mainly for storage, or maybe to sit under if it rained, but we sat outside. This was where John's "football back" went bad, as happened occasionally in his youth. So we had to give up the climb. The next day we had a wonderful time doing absolutely nothing, and got so into the mood of loafing in the sun that it was altogether too much effort even to take a picture or fetch water. We saw a humming bird up there.

The next day we had thought of as a day for climbing the Grand Teton. However, a high wind came up in the night, really biting cold, and the sky was heavily gray. Since we hadn't enough food to stay up there any longer, we decided to return to our lower camp in Garnet Canyon. Other climbers were also discouraged from their climbs that day, as we found out later, by the fierce wind on unprotected ridges. I think it was about the day after that that we packed down to Jenny Lake, to have a new situation.

My birthday was the day we hiked 15 miles or so. En route, we discovered that I had left the First Aid kit out of the rucksack at lunchtime. The chore fell upon poor John to go back and get it, an extra 4 miles. What did that nice little man of mine do but disappear, after supper, and walk *another* mile and a half to go to the store and buy some ice cream and cookies for my birthday surprise! I also got a present, to open by firelight.

Of course nobody owns a public campsite. However, at that moment, we were the *only* campers in a quite considerable campground. Somehow we felt sort of bitter when a huge family of balloony men and women, and swarms of screaming little boys, moved into the camp place right beside ours, even situating themselves to use *our* faucet. They had dozens of other places to choose. We abandoned our carefully prepared bed sites, bundled up our sleeping bags, and went off to a remote, stony, but quiet location to sleep.

Somehow the time had now come that it was our Last Day! We wanted to climb Teewinot, the nearest peak–about a 5,600 foot rise in elevation above where we were, quite a day's work. However, we just didn't wake up, and hence didn't get out of camp till nearly 8:00, much too late. Of course we intended to be back before dark–one always does–and especially we did this time, since our flashlight was worn out, and we had to clean up and pack and be gone by 7:00 a.m. the next morning.

The first part of the trip lay along the trail around Jenny Lake and up into Cascade Canyon for 4 or 5 miles. My legs surely were stiff and sluggish from the day before. We then crossed Cascade Creek by a log, and started up a steep gully leading up the north side of Teewinot, whose beautiful, sharp, twisted summits give it a very airy appearance. For some hours we just went Up–up round, glacier-slicked granite, up the loose stream bed, up timbered slopes, up hunks of Spokane-like basalt with the identical type of lichen on them, up talus, up rocks alongside steep and dirty old snow couloirs, the snowbanks pocked with rock falls.

By the middle of the afternoon we reached the saddle directly below the upper North Face. The saddle looked over into a tremendous dropping couloir, snow filled, beyond which soared the snow-draped north side of Mt. Owen, and even higher, the great, beautiful, terrible North Face of the Grand Teton. The place had what climbers call "exposure."

The saddle spanned the space between two summits of Teewinot, a minor one called the Crooked Thumb which John climbed while I lazily took a nap, and the highest summit, which is easily reached from the other side. This side, though, was what looked like a flat, blank wall. Practiced eyes, however, could find flaws in its armor, and soon we had roped up, donned tennis shoes, made a traverse across a snow-patch, and were climbing up the broken cracks, which never (or almost never) are quite as steep as they look. John, of course, had the real work of leading, my part being to belay him, carry the pack on the hardest pitches, and follow along with an upper belay. The rock was rather loose, icy or snowy in places, steep and exposed in others, but not particularly difficult. One pitch involved some pitons for John to put in and me to hammer out. At the unfortunately late hour of 6:30 p.m. we reached the small, crumbly summit.

We signed the register, and in reading it could find no account of anyone ever having gone up the way we went. It is possible that it was done before 1939, but as far as we know now, we are the only folk who had ever been that way. We also ate a second lunch, and our triumphal can of sardines (the only cans we ever carry backpacking), and started down the easier east couloir that dropped to Jenny Lake. We had two hours of light, and another half hour of dusk, which was long enough to take us down the steeper slopes, the little cliffs and drop-offs and the glacier-smoothed waterways. And then, by 9:30, there was nothing left but the faintest starlight, the gleam of white rocks, the rush of the cascading stream, the darkness of brush. That sort of descent is not much fun when one is doing it, though one always looks back on it with grim glee. We rested sometimes near the roaring brook, the fragrance of willows and the soft warm air all around us. By and by the descent grew steeper. As John said, it is not peaceful to be descending wet rotten cliffs in the dark, hand over hand on flowers. The rushing cascades below us, pouring angrily down their smooth boulders, looked so wicked. The sage and other brush cut our hands. Once John stepped back with a gasp, and I saw a black form slide from under his foot into a bush–he had come within a too-literal inch of stepping on a *porcupine.*

Finally we got across the creek, our uneasy impression being that we were crossing on wet slippery rocks right under one waterfall and right above another. We certainly would like to see where we went, by daytime sometime–from a distance the next morning it looked bad enough! By that time, the land was leveling off a little, and we plowed through sagebrush and windfall timber for hours more. Just as we thought the worst was past, we got into a mess of *beaver ponds.* They were stale and stinky, and we were wet to above our knees, and all we could do was strike an occasional match, peer around, and then go squishing onward. After fifteen or twenty minutes, which seemed like hours, we got onto dry land. Then we were cold as if we had been fishing. Quite soon, oh joyfulness, we came out onto a *road.* I was all mixed up and wanted to go in the opposite direction, but John had it all figured out how to get back to the lake. We changed our sodden boots for dry tennis shoes, and trudged along, shivering in the pale starlight, each holding a pair of dripping boots out at arm's length. It was about 1:30 a.m. that we got back to the campground.

We had to have our box of clean slacks that we had left with the ranger. We didn't know which cabin he lived in. John slunk off to knock on doors, with the gentians we had brought for their botanical display as a peace offering, while I got the fire going so we could wash a little. Pretty soon John returned, bearing the box–the ranger didn't care, it seemed, and was very nice about it all. We were so

afraid we wouldn't wake up by dawn–and we *had* to–that we felt sur-
prisingly bright by 5:00 a.m. We ate a little breakfast before it got
light, and then vigorously got everything packed and cleaned up by
7:00 (the wet things were all put in one bag to mould together) and
ready to go–John had to mow his 9-day-wonder of a beard! Soon
Mrs. Rains came for us in the bus.

People often rent hotel bedrooms without a bathroom, but when
we got to Rock Springs we rented a bathroom without a bedroom,
and took hot baths in relays; and put on our civilized clothes. That
jersey dress of mine is wonderful–nothing like being slept in all
night, or crammed into a suitcase for two weeks, affects it at all. We
then ate a huge dinner, and caught the train. In Denver we saw "The
Adventures of Mark Twain," visited a business associate of John's
who is at Boeing's Denver plant, and got in line for the Colorado
Eagle coach.

Instead of telling people not to run and push, the Denver officials
officially urged them to hold on to their bags and suitcases! Again
came the race. Again we got seats. My heavens, we thought the car
was full before. This time nobody could possibly lie in the aisles, it
was too cram-full of standees. The atmosphere was foul with smoke
and liquor. In front of us were two lush females who "sang"and
urged the surrounding furloughed soldiers to sing all night, despite
the other soldiers who implored them to shut up so mothers could
put their children to sleep. Men rode in the Ladies Only and ladies
rode in the Men's Only–to the surprise of many customers of both
places! And all night long, more people got on, and nobody seemed
to get off.

Finally, there we were, back in the somewhat sodden morning of
Birmingham. John went directly to the plant, and I went home. I

was startled to discover that Vivian was even cuter than I had remembered. Rosemary not only cared well for Viv, which was the main thing, but showed a social conscience by washing the bathroom floor, putting flowers in the vases, changing the bed, and running up only a very modest grocery bill. Since I have given up expecting too much of people, this was a gratifying surprise. After a day of diaper washing, etc. my hands got clean again. I got a fine suntan, in the high sunshine, though I kept my face well smeared with glacier cream. Our appetites have been absolutely fearsome–Monday I made a pudding which "serves 8 or 10," which we ate *all* of except one dab, already having eaten a rolled roast big enough for six, and many other things. Our trunk did not come for a week–the Beaver Pond contents were quite ripe! This is certainly going to be *all* for right now.

   *Yours, truly,*

*John (leading) and Ruth Mendenhall on Mount Victoria, Canada 1953*

Chapter Five
# Expeditions
# 1946-1957

*Now I experienced another sensation I sometimes have on difficult climbs in remote places: that of being a different person while still retaining the feeling of "I." It is an odd sensation I have never had except in a particularly realistic dream, perhaps what is meant by the cliché, "rising above one's self." At any rate, it is satisfying to sort of exceed one's usual personality, if only once or twice a year.*

RUTH DYAR MENDENHALL

At the end of World War II, Ruth and John moved back to Southern California, where Valerie Patricia Mendenhall was born in Pasadena, on May 9, 1946. Suffering from severe asthma, Ruth was hospitalized several times, and spent the entire summer of 1946 in bed. Vivian remembers that when she was little, her mother had "some sort of infection" and was routinely in bed.

John worked for Ralph M. Parsons Company from 1947 until his retirement in 1977; his titles were Engineer, Senior Engineer, and, eventually, Chief Structural Engineer.

Most of Ruth and John's Ski Mountaineer friends also returned to Southern California after the war, many of them less interested in climbing then previously. Ruth wrote later that "John and I were among the *very* few whose interest in climbing was so deeply entrenched in our lives, outlooks, and personalities, that despite all the difficulties and inconveniences, we gradually returned to the climbing world. For me it would have been the natural time to quit–I loved and enjoyed my home and children, but could not give up climbing."

John's parents, Blanche and Walter Mendenhall, cared for Vivian and Valerie, while Ruth and John went on weekend climbing trips. Nevertheless, Ruth sharply criticized her in-laws, in letters to her own parents; when her children were still small, Ruth told them savage stories about the elder Mendenhalls. Around this time, Ruth's response to her husband seems to have changed also; from this point forward, if Ruth mentions John in her letters at all, it is in very matter-of-fact terms.

When Valerie was nine months old, Ruth had an unplanned pregnancy. Her doctor believed that this third pregnancy would be fatal,

*John Mendenhall carrying Vivian (age 5) and Valerie (in pack, age 2),*
*Los Angeles, California, September, 1948*

*Vivian Mendenhall, age 5, belayed by John Mendenhall at Stoney Point, Chatsworth, May, 1949*

so Ruth underwent a hospital abortion. Some of the nurses came into her private room and spit on her bed. Ruth never told her mother or sisters about this event. (In fact, she never spoke of it at all, until she told this story to her daughter Valerie, more than thirty years later.)

As always, Ruth's letters recorded routine domestic details. "It certainly is hard to get any 'extras' at all done with little ones, whose needs don't take all one's time of course, but are so unpredictable and constant that one has only a few minutes here and there for squeezing in other activities. Sometimes just getting started and having to stop right away takes all the extra time there *is*. And I, alas, have to sleep almost as long at night as my children, so I haven't any time in the ordinary evening after I do the dinner dishes. (Of course, when I consider that I not only care for two children, and read to them and myself, and garden, and do most of my housekeeping, and lead quite a pleasant social life, and sew, and cook, and loaf, and ski, and climb, and hike, and keep up some photography, and so on, I guess I do as much as I could reasonably expect.)" Ruth occasionally went rock-climbing or backpacking with other people, while John "played father at home."

As soon as the youngest was deemed able (at the ripe old age of 3), the children went along on hikes. For example, in mid-November of 1949, the family trekked to the Baldy Ski Hut. Ruth wrote that "it is all UPHILL–the trail climbs a good 2,000 feet. It was the kind of trail that people sometimes fall off of, and roll down the mountain, so I hitched Vivian on to me with a rope, and held Valerie's hand." Soon the trail was covered with sloppy, slippery snow. "Poor Val's short legs finally gave out on the last steep pull up to the hut, and her father spirited her over the surface of the snow."

Often the family hiked fire break roads and canyons in the mountains north of Pasadena. When the children were 4 and 7, they climbed for about 3 miles and gained about 1,500 feet in elevation. Again that year, "we hiked up Rubio Canyon till we came to the first cliff, where we stopped, the children played house, and John and I climbed a little. We had to hasten down then as it was suddenly deep twilight and we had to hurry out of the canyon. While John coiled the rope, I started down with Val, expecting her to be slow. John and I were both favorably amazed at our daughters, who suddenly took to floating down-canyon in the gloom like leaves. I had a good grip on Val's arm, but she was quick and sure-footed, cheerful, and seemed to have an instinct for the places she had to wait while I climbed down before I could help her."

Ruth found it difficult to become physically strong and to stay that way. She trained by carrying a heavy pack up and down local hills. Describing a climb of Mount Williamson's West Face, Ruth said, "I had the conviction that this was one trip when I wouldn't make it. One of the remarkable things about mountain climbing is the way one can get so tired one can't even sit up, and then keep on going for six or eight hours after that." Descending after this Williamson climb, "John wanted to know if I was ready to divorce him, but I assured him I had no wish to get rid of him till he found our camp, as I was sure I couldn't find it."

Conrad Dyar, Ruth's brother, had tuberculosis in 1953, and spent a year in a sanatorium in Seattle. Ruth wrote to him about climbing Mount Whitney's East Face: "I notice that my fingertips are so sore from rock-climbing that it hurts to type, so please notice the self-sacrifice involved. There is such a terrific difference between being wife-and-mother and being a mountain-climber that I definitely get a split

*From left: Ray Van Aken, Ruth Mendenhall, John Mendenhall, Gil Roberts, leaving a base camp in the Canadian Rockies, August 3, 1953 (Photo: George Harr, Sierra Club-Angeles Chapter Archives)*

*Mount Confederation, Canada, 1947, Chirstmas card*

*Ruth at cooking fire near Mount Brussels, Canada (date unknown)*

*Valerie (left) and Vivian, October, 1949*

personality. Right now my house looks unusually terrible–everywhere one goes one sees dreadful little piles of things like worn-out cheese and dirty dishes on the sink shelf, dirty pants on the guestroom floor, boots in the dining-room, children's tinker toys and other junk on the rug. And this is not to say that I haven't been working at top speed since I got home last evening, because I have."

In 1951, the Mendenhalls built a house on Sequoia Drive, in the San Rafael Hills on Pasadena's western edge. The house was 1950s modernist hilltop architecture with blond cabinetry and picture windows. The radio comedian Stan Freberg lived just down the street.

When Ruth and John climbed in California, Vivian and Valerie were taken care of by paid babysitters, or by John's parents. During one such weekend, Walter Mendenhall took the girls to a movie theater to see Humphrey Bogart in *Treasure of the Sierra Madre*–he told his granddaughters that this was his favorite movie because it didn't have any women in it.

Child care for expeditions into Canada was delegated to Ruth's parents, Ralph and Else Dyar, in Spokane. The Dyar's house on East 12th Street was a large Arts and Crafts style home on a wooded lot. There the Mendenhalls could sometimes visit the noted Austrian mountaineer and explorer, Heinreich Harrer, whose relatives lived just down the street. (Harrer wrote *Seven Years in Tibet*, about the time he spent with the Dalai Lama). Ruth and John climbed in Canada during John's annual August two-week vacations. Travel to other continents was fairly rare in those days, and Canada offered deep wilderness with unclimbed summits, not to mention bad rock and worse weather.

Ruth and John finally made the first ascent of Mount Confederation in 1947 (their first attempt in 1940 had failed, after which six other parties failed before Ruth and John returned). Confederation is 9,741 feet in elevation, located in the upper Athabaska River Valley, in Jasper National Park. Approaching Confederation over big windfalls was far more dangerous than the mountain itself.

In 1948 they made the first ascent of Mount Lowell's North Peak. In 1949 they climbed in the Bugaboos in British Columbia's Purcells Range; one day in the Bugaboos, Ruth and John fell into separate crevasses at the same time. In 1952 they made first ascents of Mount Synge, Midway Peak, and Aiguille Peak; Aiguille, 9,840 feet, located in the Mistaya and Blaeberry River Valleys, was notable for its horribly dangerous rock. John said later, "The rock was so poor that I was afraid to climb and then fall on the pitons, because they wouldn't stay there. By doing it by aid and applying pressure very gently on the pitons, they would probably stay in. Then Ruth and I alternated leads clear to the summit."

In 1953 they made first ascents of the Great Rock Tower and Mount Palmer, with other men from Southern California. In 1954 they and Worthie Doyle and Roy Gorin attempted 12,973 foot Mount Robson in the Fraser River Valley, but failed because of snowstorms and avalanches. In 1957, Ruth and John went to Canada's Bow River Valley, where they ascended the unclimbed Northwest Ridge of 11,625 foot Mount Temple: "It had rained every single day this summer, they said—and I might add the record was not spoiled during our stay." Mount Temple was "the mountain some boys from the East lost their lives on some years back—absolutely no excuse for it, as the usual route is not steep though at the time it was icy."

On the same 1957 trip, Ruth and John climbed Mount Lefroy: "The climb starts in a horrid loose, muddy, wet, icy gully. The weather grew colder, clouds and fog closed in, wind grew sharper and more

*Ruth and Pigeon Spire, Bugaboos, Canada, 1949*

*Mount Temple, 1957*

*Howser Spire and glacier, Bugaboo Range, Canada (date unknown)*
*The Mendenhall route on Mt. Confederation, July, 1947*

steady as time went on. It began to snow, and snowed harder and harder as the day went on." From the summit, they descended 2,000 feet to the hut on Abbott Pass in a blizzard. "First we went down some comparatively easy rocks, though we had to be dreadfully careful, they were so covered with snow and ice. We rappelled down the cliffs, setting our rappels on rock points which we suspected were only frozen in place but seemed sound. The take-offs were very tricky, being from slanting icy rocks above the rappel points. And worst of all, on the second rappel, our climbing rope doubled was far too short, so we added to it by tying on a light nylon line which was rather flimsy." The next morning, Ruth repaired her appearance with "a nasty broken little comb" and her tiny lipstick.

The written record is incomplete for these Canadian Rockies expeditions, most likely because Ruth and John had to pass through Spokane afterward to pick up their children, and thus Ruth had a chance to tell her stories in person for her parents. Her accounts of the Bugaboos, Robson, and Confederation are lost, or perhaps never existed. Articles about Ruth and John's Canadian expeditions were published, however, and it is worth digressing for a while, to consider how these articles might have been produced.

Weirdly, John Mendenhall appears to have appropriated Ruth's journals and letters, in order to publish articles about important climbs under his own name. She typed the final versions for him.

John's prose style alternated between the manly and the florid, quite unlike Ruth's more spontaneous letter writing. One example is a partial letter from Ruth about Canada's Great Rock Tower (everything following page eight is missing). The approach to the mountain began with a grueling three-day backpack; they roped up to cross a glacier, and passed through Diadem Col, as the clouds became dark and "suspicious;" Ruth spent eight pages recording mileages and altitudes, scenic views, wildlife, campsites, everything they ate, and how they joked with their companions. John's account for publication boils the approach down to this: "our climbing camp was occupied on July 30. To the south rose the mighty battlements of Alberta," after which his prose descends into an almost incomprehensible third-person paean to Thorington's *Climber's Guide* ("it is felt that this comprehensive work [has] been very instrumental in helping many to enjoy Canada's great mountains").

When the time came for John to produce an article about Confederation for *The Canadian Alpine Journal* in 1948, he certainly relied on the penciled notes Ruth kept throughout that long journey. She describes another epic three-day backpack, moose, elk and mosquitoes. The climbers "stagger on under heavy loads" (John's pack weighed ninety-four pounds). By contrast, John's article says only that the mountain "repulsed six attempts at conquest" and now "the peak's defenses were anxiously studied...one must move into position and strike upon the first half-favorable day."

Ruth's diary describes the summit day on Mount Confederation: "Wind icy . . . view opens and opens . . . snow cornices, up snowy chimneys, along perilous traverses, north side very exposed down to glaciers . . . screaming wind this time brings snow lashing upwards, up and up, and up final snow dome to summit where no one ever stood before. 1:07 p.m." John's published version of the same first ascent reads quite differently: "I guaranteed my companion that access could be gained to the airy platforms of snow half way up the cliff. What lay above would obviously require careful climbing. There was a chill wind... we lost little time in attacking the most favorable-appearing weakness in the peak's defenses." At last, John wrote, they "stepped together upon the highest point of snow, ending our campaign that started seven years before."

In addition to the Canadian expeditions, Ruth and John did a good deal of climbing in the Sierra Nevada, in the years 1946 to 1957. They returned to Mount Whitney, and to the Palisades, including an attempt on Thunderbolt Peak, which had earned its name when the first people to climb it experienced a close encounter with a lightning strike. Ruth and John climbed Mount Williamson twice. At an elevation of 14,384 feet, Williamson stands apart from the Sierra crest, and appears very imposing from the Owens Valley; this is the peak that looms in the background of Ansel Adams' 1945 photograph taken from the Manzanar War Relocation Center (the picture's title is *Mount Williamson, the Sierra Nevada, from Manzanar, California*). Meanwhile, Ruth and John taught their daughters roped climbing at Joshua Tree and Tahquitz, and skiing at Southern California ski resorts (Mount Waterman, Krakta Ridge, and Snow Valley). The family spent some weekends at Mammoth Mountain, which at that time was considered to be an incredibly modern resort, because it had three chair lifts.

At Mammoth, in 1955, Ruth received a long distance phone call telling her that her father had died of a heart attack while shoveling his driveway. –V.M.C.

# Thunderbolt Peak

PAULA STREET

LOS ANGELES, CALIF.

JUNE 1, 1949 — WEDNESDAY

*Dear Ma and Fa,*

Val and the cats are taking naps, and Vivian has gone to school. I've washed clothes, done some marketing, and washed my hair, which is about as much as a person could be expected to get done in a constructive way in one morning.

John and I certainly had a fine trip over Memorial Day. John had arranged with his mother to come to stay with the children–so we got off alone together on what appears to be our semi-annual private trip, the last time having been New Year's.

We decided to go into the Palisades Region of the High Sierra, on the east side of the range. One usually doesn't go this early into the high mountains, as there is too much snow, but we prepared for cold with plenty of warm clothes and a tent. We left here Friday after supper, slept in the Mojave Desert, and got to the end of the road in Big Pine Canyon, at about 8,500 feet elevation, about 9:00 in the morning. The trail more or less followed the rushing stream, through springlike woods. The higher we got, the farther back into spring we got. By and by, about 10,000 feet elevation, big snowbanks appeared over parts of the trail; and higher yet, the bare patches of ground and rocks became fewer than the snow-patches. We finally came to a place where the bare ground disappeared, and only snowy slopes stretched off to the high places to the west.

All day the sky had been gathering clouds; the higher peaks were fog-wrapped; and a somewhat chilly wind stirred through the trees. John found a camp at one last "island" of bare ground and trees. All around us were sweeping slopes of snow, rising to rocky ridges to which clung a few twisted pines, the ledges white with lingering snowbanks. We were at about 11,000 feet or a little higher, at which altitude the air is thin and clean as nowhere else. Across a little snow-field rushed a glacially cold stream between its snowbanks–the water was apparently below 32 and kept from freezing only by its motion, because the moment we scooped it into a pan, ice crystals formed clear through it and a skim of ice on top. Our small bare island was sandy, with a few hummocks of dead last-year grass; a border of red bare willows creeping low against the snow; a few granite boulders; and many ancient, strangely golden, barkless trunks and snags of long-dead pines (similar in needle to the Lodgepoles, but terribly distorted and grotesque from the high winds)–one great golden trunk, with long bare branches against the sky, still had a few living boughs, but seemed doomed to live little longer.

We pitched the tent with tail toward the peaks for better shelter. The wind was increasing, so we pitched it strongly, anchoring the front end to one of the big golden snags, and the back end to a pole and rocks, and the side tapes to rocks. We cooked our hot thick soup over a fire whose smoke whirled fiendishly in the wind. And before dark, beginning to get quite cold, we gladly crawled into our little tent, and with nearly all our clothes on into our down sleeping bags. By this time, the wind had increased to a ferocious gale, the nature of which we have read about in the mountains, but never actually experienced.

You know how a dish towel can be made to snap. Well, the wind did something on that order–but worse–to the tent all night long. It snapped and exploded, and cannonaded, in the most incredible manner. The wind beat through the tent against us like a huge person pushing and shoving all night. The noise was amazing! Through it we could hear the wind singing and crying in the rocks and trees. We had difficulty in sleeping, and periodically lay awake telling the most ghostly and creepy stories we could think of. We looked out to alternating skies of fiercely brilliant stars, of racing cloud banks, of falling blowing snow. We had considerable doubt about our climbing next day! By daylight, the wind had actually dropped so much that it sounded calm and quiet in the tent–but even then, the snow outside was falling not vertically but horizontally!

In such cold, even the simplest little tasks take a very long time; however, when one sleeps with one's clothes on, it is fairly simple to get up. We had stewed apricots, hot coffee, and hot mush with Klim for breakfast; and by that time, since the storm was thinning a little, figured we would at least climb up and see the glacier which lay perhaps 1,000 feet higher. Our pack with climbing equipment, extra socks, and lunch, had been arranged the night before. We both took our ice axes, and trudged off across the snowfields and up the hills toward the heights.

We crossed the snow-covered glacier–which later in the year might have cracks and crevasses opening down into its ice, but which now was a solid sheet of snow rising first gently, then steeply, to the granite cliffs that form the last 1,500 or 2,000 feet of the mountains. Since the weather wasn't any worse, we decided to climb the couloir between North Palisade and Thunderbolt, an extremely steep chute of snow between sheer cliffs, dark gray in the stormy light, covered with lichens of black or green, all the ledges white with snow, old or new. The air was filled continually with a light veil of snowflakes. By this time we were roped together, climbing one at a time, belaying each other around the shaft of the ice axe thrust deeply into the hard snow. To our boots were strapped our crampons with their one and a half-inch iron spikes that bit deeply and securely into the snow floor of the gully. As John belayed me from above, and I climbed, I found myself moving in a slow rhythm suited to altitudes of between 12,000 and 13,000 feet—jam in the ice axe to hold on to, step, step, step and move the axe up, step, step—and so on, the gully steepening continually, till we came to its head, rocks sticking out of the snow, where in a cramped position we removed our crampons, and climbed out to the notch between the two peaks, and looked over the stormy, wintry bowl far below us, and off to the west where the peaks were dim in clouds. Here the wind from the west was increasingly bitter. We could see flat stretches that were frozen lakes—a rind of pale green ice around the edges, and white with new snow over the middle; small streams of water flowing over snowfields—the purest pale "aqua" in color; forbidding, snow-streaked cliffs and peaks. It was a splendid and desolate sight.

We thought we might take a try at Thunderbolt, which is several hundred feet lower than North Palisade, and also its south cliffs weren't as forbidding as the north facing cliffs of the other peak. Its brownish-yellow rocks were plastered with peculiar, feathery formations of new snow that had been pasted there by the wind. After we climbed a few pitches, though, it was so cold, and the afternoon was wearing on, that we decided to return to camp. The climb down the couloir of steep, crumbly snow had to be made with extreme care. Most of our ascending footsteps had disappeared as the wind worked away at the snow surface.  It was rather a relief to reach the relatively flat glacier, especially as by this time the peaks above had disappeared in fog and snow, and our own visibility was very limited.  We had, however, carefully noted landmarks leading back to camp, and by 6:30 tramped wearily to our sandy, bleak little island.  Hot soup tasted wonderful.

For the second night we crawled into bed with all our clothes on. The socks we had hung up inside the tent to dry were stiff with ice. Even our shoestrings were still frozen next morning.  We felt a little cold that night, probably from tiredness, as it must have been warmer than it was the windy night before.  It was still sort of windy, but in only an ordinary sort of way.

Monday morning the weather was definitely on the mend–but not in time to do us any good, as we had to start back home.  The trip out to the car by trail was so beautiful that we spent a good deal of time turning around to admire the scenery, the fine, rugged, stern crags–still snow covered–jutting against the blue sky.

We got back to Paula Street about 8:00 o'clock–the comforts of a house, modern plumbing, and a soft bed duly appreciated after our rugged little holiday.  John's father was here, and drove Blanche back home soon after our arrival.  Our children, who were either up or wide-awake or both, were duly greeted and put to bed, and then we sat down to a hastily assembled but large dinner of ham, corn, bread and gravy, cold milk, salad, and ice cream, which we got around with no trouble at all.

*With love,*

# Lady Mountain, Zion

PAULA STREET

LOS ANGELES, CALIF.

NOVEMBER 28, 1950

*Dear Mother,*

Zion was *so* different from any place we'd ever been. Of course we'd seen many pictures, but the place didn't really come to life till we reached that great gaudy canyon, with the 3,000 foot peaks of red and white sandstone towering above the aqua river, the brilliant golden cottonwoods, the green junipers with their fat blue berries, the red dirt everywhere.

We had decided to leave real early Thursday morning, and I regret to say that we actually did get up at 3:30 a.m. Ug. We potted the kids and put them to bed in the back seat of the car, where they soon went back to sleep. It is about 475 miles from Los Angeles to Zion, I think, but the trip is rather an easy drive, as most of it is over deserted, straight, desert roads. We were in four states in a single day. When we were speaking of the outskirts of Las Vegas, Valerie asked us slyly when we would reach the "in-skirts."

We entered Utah, which state I had never been in, a country of rolling, juniper-clad hills and mesas, prosperous little Mormon towns, and the red cliffs and flat-topped ridges and peaks. Around 4:00, we reached the park, glowing in the warm afternoon sunshine. Most of the peaks have been scaled in spite of the terrific drop-offs, but from a rock climber's standpoint it is not ideal, as sandstone is quite a weak rock in spite of the way it forms extremely vertical cliffs.

We had the large campground virtually to ourselves. Every night a wild wind came up with dark, and didn't die down till the morning warmed up. We had a fairly festive Thanksgiving supper–I even brought a tablecloth, and the children gathered yellow leaves for decorations, though they tended to blow away.

In the morning we went up to the little "museum" to talk to the ranger. They had a wonderful relief map of the whole park, done in scale, which was almost as fascinating as the scenery itself. I was to go hiking that day, and according to the map, the only nearby trail that went to the top of a peak was the one that climbed the face of Lady Mountain, a "thrilling mountain climb by a steep trail"–and as a matter of fact, it was much more of a rock-climb than a trail.

I left my family, who went on a milder hike, and with a rucksack with camera, lunch and canteen, I crossed the Virgin River by the suspension bridge, and switch backed up the first red dirt banks. The trail soon turned out to climb steeply up various cliffs and gullies, the steeper parts guarded by cables, chains, and footsteps that had been cut out of the soft rock. It was exactly like following a route marked on a picture in dotted lines, as the route was all marked out on the mountain with dotted red lines and *painted* bright red arrows. In theory I thought it messed up the mountain, though I was really glad because I probably would never have found the way otherwise. It certainly was Some Trail, and that's for sure! There were even a couple of sturdy *ladders* at places where they couldn't make it easy or safe enough otherwise. I was on the 6,940-foot summit in two and a half hours, and settled down to enjoy the scenery and my lunch. The climate up there was different, with Yellow pines, Lodgepole pines, and

Douglas firs among the manzanita, cactus and junipers that were also at lower elevations. I could see miles and miles away, across the flat topped wooded mesas that crowned most of the peaks and cliffs, across fearsome gulches and canyons water-cut out of the white and red sandstone, far off into Utah.

I got back to my family about 3:00 o'clock, and we took another sight-seeing drive along the road that climbs out of the canyon going east, and goes through a mile long tunnel, in which a lot of big wonderful windows look out over the changing scenery. My children just love tunnels, so they were quite taken with this one. We had another long windy night's sleep. Saturday John went off climbing. I fed and dressed the children, combed their hair, which hadn't been done since we left home, and drove the 30 miles to Glendale, Utah, to visit with George and Emilie Bauwens, who are building a tourist camp. George is a big rangy German man, the old-time Ski Mountaineer Chairman when I first joined the club. (The Bauwens told us of a Mormon man who had *fifty-six* children and *six* wives!) We went back to meet John at 2:00, and as he had an engineering job undone to work on, we decided to start home that afternoon. We slept out in the desert somewhere west of Las Vegas, and got home around 1:30 Sunday.

*With love,*

# Aiguille Peak, Canada, First Ascent

SEQUOIA DRIVE

PASADENA, CALIF.,

AUGUST 14, 1952

*Dear Daddy,*

I thought I would write you something of our climbing trip, since we did not have a chance to tell you about it. We had an extra fine time, partly because of the absolutely unheard-of-weather. It *always* rains at least half the time we are in Canada; this time we had nine solid days of perfect weather, warm and beautiful.

Our first stop was in the general area of Lake Louise, where a side-road takes one into the "Valley of the Ten Peaks." We had heard of an often-tried and still-unclimbed summit in that area, a secondary summit of Eiffel Peak known as the Eiffel Tower, which we thought we'd try as it was quite accessible. We had a fairly short backpacking trip of three or four hours, made camp near a high small lake, and were all set to get up early Wednesday morning and make our attempt.

Wednesday we spent a long time climbing scree, inspecting impossible cliffs, and more or less spiraling around the mountain, till we discovered the easy approach to the base of this climb. Finally in the early afternoon we reached the foot of the steep, long, loose chimney which had turned back many climbers, and were just about to rope up and try it when to our shock and astonishment, we suddenly

*Ruth on the summit of Aiguille Peak, Canada, first ascent*

saw a man at the head of the chimney starting to rope down! Two brothers, one from Minneapolis, the other from New Jersey, had just made "our" climb! We waited while they came down the chimney, and by that time it was too late to climb it that day. So we decided to drive on north about 50 miles farther, and take a crack at another first ascent we had in mind.

The peak we were planning to climb next, Aiguille, is in a group of terrific looking peaks visible from the highway at Waterfowl Lakes. Aiguille is set back a little behind the others, and all that peeked out was a dreadful-looking assortment of sheer rock pinnacles, one of which turned out to be the summit. It was obviously very impractical to approach them from that side. The alternative was to drive north about 20 miles farther, and pack back south up the Howse

River where there is a trail, well kept for the Canadian north woods. We decided to have our stuff taken in by horse to the Howse Pass, from which we would have to backpack a number of more miles. We got up at 4:00 a.m., knowing we would have to get a good head start on the horses, and soon were starting off along the trail through the dense spruce woods. We passed several small muddy lakes, and saw quite a few moose. We also saw a band of elk swimming across the wide dish-watery expanses of the Howse River, whose east bank we followed more or less the whole way.

The trail was nice, the woods deep and beautiful, the vistas across the river of peaks and glaciers inspiring. Soon after 12:00 we reached the place we were meant to meet the packer, where the trail joined Conway Creek (a huge river). I was glad the packer hadn't caught up with us yet, because our brisk 16 miles had made my legs tired, and I promptly lay down in the grass and had a long nap. However, he hadn't come by 2:00, by 4:00 we were getting anxious, and by 5:00 we were figuring out how we would bivouac for the night and go back the next morning. At 5:15 he came. He said he had corralled the needed horses the night before and they got out, and it had taken him all morning to round them up again. He rode one horse, "Whitey," and had brought two pack horses, as by that time he had to bring his own bedroll to spend the night. When we reached the pass, the packer said he would take us farther, as I guess he felt guilty at having been so late. The instant we crossed into British Columbia the trail more or less was gone. I was quite amazed at how the horses could leap over downed timber. Finally, after 6:00, we came to a place where we decided we'd better camp. We were in a sort of rough meadow, with many little streams now flowing south, the very headwaters of the Blaeberry River (we found the word is the British version of blueberry). The packer decided to spend the night there too, and went about staking out the horses, Whitey, Baldy, and a wild little buckskin mare. We all had supper, and crawled into our sleeping bags before dark. About 10:00 o'clock we were wakened up by a wild galloping. The horses had broken loose, and were tearing around the meadow like crazy, leaping over downed trees and more or less confirming my low opinion of horses in general. Baldy was wearing a cowbell, that clanked loudly through the night. The packer was out of bed and running for rope and bridle, and disappearing off into the hills after his creatures, who as far as we were concerned were never seen again.

Next morning we were all up in a frosty dawn. The packer said the horses had probably gone home, and that he had better "start hoofin" it. He looked ruefully at his pointed, high heeled shoes and said "Those things were never made for walkin'–I can't even get down to the stream in them." By this time we had become quite chummy, and shared each other's breakfast, we contributing apricots and mush, the packer bacon and coffee. I put all his coffee into a kettle of boiling water, and it came out with quite a wallop. Then our packer, rolling a little with the walk of a horseman, disappeared on his 21-mile walk to the north; we made up our packs, and started off through heavy downed timber along the valley of the Blaeberry. We had left the fine tall spruces, and come into an old burned area.

For six hours we fought downed logs, alder and willow thickets, fields of wildfire covering logs and little swamps. We soon left the Blaeberry, which was already shaping up into a real river, and climbed over hillsides, and up the valley of a tributary stream, the north fork of Ebon Creek, where we intended to camp. Ebon was a fast, racing creek, the glacier silt making it already white, and continuous rapids and falls making it whiter. The going got worse and worse till we reached an elevation of probably 6,000 or 6,500 feet, and the woods thinned out into open timberline meadows that were covered with wonderful flowers, paintbrush in cream, raspberry and scarlet, wild asters, buttercups, the last of the dogtooth violets, and many others we didn't know the names of. Finally near timberline, we found a suitable campsite on the bank of the roaring Ebon Creek, with small slender spruce of several varieties scattered about.

This was Saturday, August 2nd. After lunch, John went off to scout the approach of the morrow's climb, and I finished making camp. We got to bed early, and on Sunday, August 3rd, rose at 4:00 a.m. to attempt the unclimbed rock towers of Aiguille Peak.

The approach to the mountain was first a long climb up old stream beds, over small meadows marked with mountain sheep foot-prints, and over the sliding scree of huge old moraines, then skirting along the edge of a glacier. We first climbed the moderately sloped southwest summit of the peak, several hundred feet lower than the main summit, and from there roped up and climbed down steep but firm rock into a deep notch. From here we had to traverse for a long ways across horribly loose, out-sloping ledges, not difficult but requiring extreme care, and over snow-filled gullies. Looking back, what we had already done with fair ease looked impossible, which cheered us up about what lay ahead. Sure enough, a long chimney that from a distance had looked quite out of the question, proved to be a fairly easy route for an experienced climber! From here our route lay over some more ascending traverses, each of us carefully belaying the other, till we came to the "critical pitch," a rotten, over-hanging, sheer crack, and as far as we could see the only possible way up. For two hours, while I was tied to a piton and standing on an extremely uncomfortable small protuberance of rock, John struggled away above at this section of the climb, removing unsound blocks of rock and working to get pitons into the unreliable limestone crevices. At long last he was up. I had been changing feet every fifteen minutes or so, and baking in the sun, and inspecting the far away threads of water below that only increased my thirst. Now my turn came to climb up, taking out the pitons as I went. From there on up, it was only a couple of easy pitches to the top, and soon after 3:00 p.m. we were on the rock summit that hundreds and thousands must have seen from the road below, and only we had ever been on.

I guess the "First Ascent" is the acme of most climbers' dreams–and sort of a last frontier in a well explored civilized world–and most of the ones still available in a reasonable distance from home are either inaccessible or difficult or dangerous. Of course Alaska, the Himalaya, South America have many unclimbed peaks, but we have not the time to go there.

After eating, photographing, and resting on the summit, we started the descent, climbing down a short way and then making a long rappel down the most difficult section. A falling rock damaged our climbing rope about 20 feet from one end, so we cut off the end, and proceeded across our loose dangerous traverses, which were worse going down. The return usually requires more caution than the ascent, even though the route is known, as one is tired, and going down is harder. However, by twilight we were off the mountain proper, and there remained only the long tedious trudge down the moraine and the watercourses to camp, which with tired legs we finally reached at 11:00 p.m., having taken scarcely a step for eighteen hours that didn't require extreme caution.

Ordinarily we don't climb the day after a big ascent, but since we knew there was only one day, Monday, left, before we had to go out, we left camp late and retraced the earlier approach, to take a look at a couple of lower unclimbed peaks on the ridge, which look so fearful from the highway. On the west side, sloping ledges gave a fairly easy access to the summit. We first climbed Mt. Synge, which was not hard but was horribly dangerous, with the loose rocks and melting snow-water on the sloping ledges. Nonetheless, we reached the summit without incident, and looked down the fearful black cliffs and glaciers to the woods and aqua lakes between us and the highway, and did considerable photography. John climbed the one remaining peak we had in mind alone, it being safer, and I went back to camp, being just too tired to make another ascent.

Tuesday we struck camp and packed out, hour after hour over the downed timber, incredible jams of vast logs that had been swept down into the riverbed in the winter. At last clouds were collecting, lightning forking over distant peaks, and several drops of rain fell on us. We made a cold camp in the midst of still mosquitoey spruce woods, at dark. We got rained on just enough to damp us down like a bundle of ironing, and to add the last touch to our battered, soot-stained, greasy GI ski pants that make such wonderful climbing pants because of the comfortable cut, tough cloth, and generous pockets. Wednesday was just a long hard almost grim 12 miles or so, with blisters still popping up on our tired feet. At long last came the welcome sight of our blue Ford on the opposite shore. Baths, clean clothes, hot coffee made over the Primus, caused a great revival in our feelings. By evening we were consuming a steak dinner at the Lake Louise Junction. And one week later I was back in Pasadena entertaining six little girls at a birthday party—a quite different, but just as strenuous occupation.

*With love,*

# Mount Williamson, North Face, First Ascent

SEQUOIA DRIVE

PASADENA, CALIF.

JULY 9, 1957 — TUES., 2P.M.

*Dear Ma (and Marg if there),*

I have been wondering if Marg came over this week. Either way, I bet you are busy, and probably still in the throes of the raspberries.

We had a wonderful time this weekend, and I really must write you about it before the details become hazy. Ever since we climbed Mt. Williamson by one of the west side routes, on Memorial Day in 1952, we have been thinking about trying the north side. Williamson is the second highest peak in the Sierra (14,384 feet). Although the mountain is spectacularly visible from the highway, it is actually one of the more inaccessible peaks of the Sierra because the access road stops out in the desert at an elevation of only 5,900 feet–many of the roads going toward the Sierra on the east side wind up into canyons to 8,500 or 9,000 feet elevation, which makes quite a difference on a summer backpacking venture! A lot of other climbers have been thinking about the north side too, and we knew that several groups of young fellows were talking about going in there this summer, so we only hoped they wouldn't get around to it till we had a chance. This July Fourth seemed the time, as we had four days.

*John and Ruth, May, 1954*

Viv and Val were to visit in Van Nuys, as were the cats. Wednesday afternoon we deposited children, suitcases, cats, cat-food, and other accessories, then drove clear to the end of the Symmes Creek Road, where we left the car, by midnight. We rolled out in our sleeping bags in the sand behind some willows, and slept till the sun came up, about 6:00, when it immediately got hot.

We had no illusions about the day before us—we knew we had a long long trail awinding into the land of our dreams! So we ate breakfast and made up our packs as fast as we could. First the trail wound over very gently rising desert, among sagebrush and other pure desert vegetation. One couldn't actually see the trail more than a few feet ahead, but it was always there, and off to the left, in a gulch bitten through the desert, one could hear Symmes Creek rushing away. After a mile or two of this, one gradually entered the canyon where the creek came out of the mountains. Here columbines and wild roses bloomed along the stream, and willows and birches appeared among the sagebrush. The trail crossed the stream five times, and finally quite a long way up Symmes Canyon, it started its switch backing steep rise to Symmes Pass, which is about 9,000 feet high. Cactus was in bloom along the way, its apricot buds opening out into lovely lemon-yellow blooms, with scalloped pointed petals arranged in three layers around the centers. Manzanita grew with brilliant green leaves, mountain mahogany with its twirly fuzzy seed pods, and Piñon pines with their cones falling thick on the trail. As we rose higher, the Piñons gradually gave way to other Sierra pines more appropriate to mountains than desert. After a long drag we finally got to the top of Symmes Pass, where we had a fine view of the east and north expanses of great Mt. Williamson, scoured from top to bottom with long gullies of snow, and other lesser peaks and wild canyons and ridges all around us.

This is a very sad trail because it goes up and down so much, to avoid hopeless cliffs and canyons too rough to build and maintain a trail. From Symmes Pass one drops clear down into Shepherd Canyon, where cactus again was blooming along the trail, and sage-brush putting out its soft green little three-fingered hands. Then the trail again rises on and on, in seemingly endless switch backs. We intended to take two days to establish our high camp, and the first night's destination was a spot called Anvil Camp, where a bench at about 10,400 feet is covered with lovely pine trees and meadows. We finally arrived around 6:00 in the evening. A couple of young fellows who were going fishing in the high lakes had passed us on the trail, and got to Anvil Camp an hour or so before us. They invited us to use their supper fire, which we gladly did, and then before dark we bedded down on the pine needles with the soothing roar of Shepherd Creek nearby.

The last time we climbed Mt. Williamson we also stayed at Anvil Camp, and were awakened at 4:45 by an atom bomb explosion. So we weren't too surprised when at the same spot five years later we also were awakened by this great explosion rolling from rock wall to rock wall in reverberations like the greatest clap of thunder. About seven or eight minutes before we heard the sound, we had both by chance seen the sky light up with such a peculiar orange flash that we thought we dreamed it–later we got to calculating, and figured it had taken the interval between, for the sound to reach us. It reminded me of how we used to sit on Horse-Heaven and watch a man in the valley chop wood: down would come his axe, and then next would come the chop.

With the bomb for an alarm clock, we decided to get up, cook breakfast, and be on our way. Our next objective was to cross

Shepherd Pass. The trail soon left the bench of trees, with its meadows speckled with buttercups, and the very definite timberline, and wound through the gray waste of an old glacial moraine. Then it rose quite steeply, zigzagging back and forth through scree and snow, up the headwall of the pass, which is more than 12,000 feet high. At the top of the pass we left the trail, which wanders west down again to timberline and various lakes in the high eastern part of Kings Canyon and Sequoia National Parks. Our way still continued upward, over a sort of hill of gravel and boulders, with the splendid granite, snow-marked faces of Tyndall and Williamson and lesser or farther peaks coming into view. We passed near or above many small lakes lying in rocky basins, still covered with ice and fringed with deep turquoise or inky-blue water around the edges. From an eminence along our way, we picked out a small lake (hardly more than a pond) that lay in a saucer-like depression and was *not* covered with ice. It appeared most inviting in the sunshine, and much more hospitable than the deeper, larger, icy neighbors. We had to go down quite a long ways; cross a sort of canal between two lakes where we spied many large trout darting about in the shadow of a snowbank; and then up again over slabs where patches of old glacier-polish glistened in the sun. We finally found our appointed little lake, which was luke warm because it was so shallow in its basin of rock. It was a wonderful spot, at just under 12,000 feet elevation. All around us were the great faces, turrets and shoulders, gendarmes and couloirs of 13,000 and 14,000 foot peaks. Within our rocky saucer it was warm with the very essence of the sun, completely pure and penetrating at the high thin altitude.

We spent a lazy leisurely afternoon. We fixed beds in a gravel patch, gathered the dry dead branches of currant bushes for fuel (not very good fuel, either), washed in the delicious warm water of our

lake, and basked and basked under the flawless blue sky. We also studied with intent interest the possible ways up the North Face of
Williamson–which now from this vantage point lay back at a far more
promising angle than one would guess from the view head on from
the highway. Still, even at best, there would be 2,500 feet of completely unexplored climbing next day. After much study, we decided where
we would start and where we would try to go; made up our pack for
next day; had an early supper of mashed potato (instant) and canned
chicken; and gladly got into our sleeping bags when the sun went
down and simultaneously a chilly wind began to pick at us.

The night was mild for that elevation, and I had a real good sleep.
We had resolved to get started at dawn–but the night never did get
very dark, as a blazing half-moon sailed in the sky half the night, and
the pale bright rocks, water, and snow reflected the brilliant starlight
from then on. We woke up shortly after 4:00 a.m., and ate breakfast
in our sleeping bags. One's Appetite at that high an elevation is apt
to be delicate, and the breakfast tasted sort of horrid to me. Since we
had slept with all our clothes on except pants and boots, it was a simple matter to be up and away.

There is certainly a psychological difference in trying a climb that
has never been made and doing one that has been done before–quite
regardless of the difficulty. In the second case, one can always think,
"If they did it, we certainly ought to be able to."

The pale dawn light was coming over the flat expanse of Owens
Valley eastward and 7,000 feet below us, beyond the wild canyon of
Williamson Creek which consisted of a series of lakes, rapids, and
cliffs down to timberline and out of sight. We now were picking our
way first upward and then downward over scree and ledges toward
the base of Williamson's North Face. We had decided to start up the

*Valerie (left, age 6) and Vivian (age 9) Mendenhall, January, 1953*

snow at the foot of a gully that promised to give reasonable access to the easier rocks above the first band of smooth cliffs that were stained black from snow-water. We found these rocks to give climbing that required care but presented no difficulties. We ascended slowly but steadily for a long way without even uncoiling the rope.

Among the surprises of the untouched, barren mountain face were the polemoniums, which must be to the Sierra what the Edelweiss is to the Alps. It is a lovely blue flower that grows only in the most barren places at high altitudes. I have seen it only in three places–on the screes of Split Mountain, near the top of 12,000 foot Kearsarge Pass, and here on the North Face of Williamson. It grew in thick sturdy clumps, scattered at intervals from 12,000 feet almost to the summit–each clump consists of rather sticky leaf stalks, and the strong groups of blossoms on each stem, a heavenly blue and like honey in their sweet smell. Near the top, they were not yet in bloom, the clumps were smaller, and were covered with the old seed pods and the new buds not yet ready to unfold.

We were rather put out with the weather. The two days we had been backpacking were blistering hot, and here on our climbing day an overcast was gradually covering the sky, and a chilly wind kept coming around corners. We had realized from inspecting our route that the bottom was easier than the top. Partway up we roped up, and had to do quite a bit of searching around for a good route, but the climbing did not get really difficult–just as well considering how one puffs up there! Our pleasantly ascending shoulder between two gullies gradually steepened till we realized we had to work over to the left. We found we had gone too high and roped down a pitch. Then we traversed over some steep sound blocks into a gully, crossed a couple of snow streaks where John cut steps with the ice axe, worked to the left some more, and finally decided we really were nearly at the top. We inspected several more gullies, and picked out the one that looked easiest–a delicate combination of loose rocks and ice–which we climbed up and found ourselves on the boulder-field that composes the main part of the top of Mount Williamson! From here it was only a tedious walk up talus blocks to the summit.

Just as we finished the difficult part of the climb, it started to snow. John decided to climb the East Peak, 14,211 feet, and I said I would rest while he did it. I rather thought of myself as tucked cozily in the lee of a good over-hanging boulder, eating and relaxing for an hour. However, all the boulders turned out to be too downtrodden to provide any shelter from the wind, and anyway the wind kept coming from every direction. First I cleverly opened the rucksack and put on all the clothes in it, including all of John's. These proved to be all the shelter I needed, and I kept warm and cozy. Then I set myself to doing up the rope, which had been moved from place to place in handfuls–always a great mistake with a rope. It is like thread, or yarn, or string, but one really would not think 100 feet of rope could get into such a nasty snarl so quickly! I couldn't even find the ends for quite awhile, and what with the wind, and the cold, and the thickly falling snow, it took half an hour to do up that coil of wet rope. After that I fell into a trance, like a horse in a blizzard, and ate peanuts and sausage till I heard John's hoot across the boulder field. I had to give him back some of his clothing, but I didn't need it as soon as I got up to go.

We descended by the west side route we had gone down by before–mostly just a long tiresome descent down loose scree, with one rappel down an ice cliff. No polemoniums on this side–they are certainly particular as to just where they will grow, though one place looks about as unpromising as another for something that would be gorgeous in one's own garden.

We are always getting back to our climbing camps hours after dark, but this time (mainly because the camp was so high, I guess, and we started so early), we finally dragged ourselves past the last frozen-over tarn and over the last sparse little meadows about 7:00 p.m. We had wrapped all our possessions up in the tarp, so they were nice and dry. The snow had stopped on our way down, and the sky was clearing, but a particularly penetrating, bitter wind was hooting across our bowl which had been so gloriously warm the afternoon before.

We were piercingly cold before we could even get our things put out, and at the earliest possible moment crawled into our down sleeping bags. Once in, we ate a little squirrel food, and in spite of being cold all night we were unconscious off and on most of the time. Every now and then we stuck our eyes out to look at the glorious scenery under the white sailing moon. I even wore mittens to try to keep warmer in bed.

Next morning, Sunday, the storm was gone. Our pan of bedside water, and our little lake so praised for its warmth, were covered with ice, but the sun peeped over the edge of Williamson Canyon with all its benign kindness of two days before. This certainly made it easier to get up! Now all we had to do was go back the entire distance to the car in one day which it had taken us two to cover on the way in. It was 6,000 feet downhill, but there was quite a bit of uphill and that downhill again, thrown in, and probably around 12 miles of horizontal distance.

First we toiled up the cliffs and talus to Shepherd Pass. Then we glissaded down the softening snow in a glorious swish to the moraine. At Anvil Camp we collapsed among the buttercups and shooting stars and ate lunch. Then on down Shepherd Canyon to the Piñon pines and cactus we went, noting changes in two days that were most remarkable, such as a lively little side stream with snowbanks that had entirely dried up! The weather was hot again–we would have loved an overcast and a drop of rain that day. When we had dragged up through the gravelly switchbacks to Symmes Pass, we stopped to study our route, which looked satisfyingly steep and diffi-cult from that angle. Then we went on down and down through the pines to the bottom of Symmes Canyon. By that time my downhill muscles and my feet were Killing Me, as the saying goes. On the way in, we had carefully crossed Symmes Creek with dry feet, but now I just waded across, using the cold water as an anaesthetic and a cushion. The last couple of miles through the sagebrush I was so busy thinking how my feet hurt that I didn't notice it was hot till I got to the car (quite a record for me!). We washed in the stream, changed clothes, and drove to Lone Pine for a dinner that really hit the spot.

It got so late that about 10:00 p.m. we phoned Van Nuys from Mojave, and then we went straight home. Next morning I went out to get the children and cats. Valerie did remark that my cooking was "a blessing" and she hadn't had any for four days, which was quite wild praise from that source!

I haven't done much this week. I had watering to do, and a wash—but there is more wash, and I certainly wish I had gotten my hair washed. It has been hot, and we have been very pleased with the air conditioner! I have had to go to the store. Last night we had a steak, and I am cooking a pot roast this afternoon.

*Ruth and Valerie Mendenhall awake after a miserable night out, Clyde Peak, July, 1966*

Chapter Six
# Family Trips
# 1958-1966

*No wonder practically nobody keeps on climbing after they have*

*a family; and if they do, they don't take their children.*

Ruth Dyar Mendenhall

John Mendenhall spent the spring and summer of 1959 working in Germany, leaving Ruth responsible for her two elderly and ailing aunts, her teenage daughters, house and yard work, and all business decisions. Ruth hurt her back, and suffered from respiratory and stomach infections.

While John was gone, Ruth had a chance to make an historic (and televised) first ascent of the Matterhorn–not the Swiss Matterhorn–but its fabricated Disneyland replica built four years after the amusement park first opened. This Matterhorn towered over palm trees and swimming pools and was the tallest man-made feature on the Anaheim skyline. The opening extravaganza for the Matterhorn and its bobsled ride was attended by movie stars and politicians. Ruth was among the Sierra Club mountaineers invited to climb the 147-foot high snow-covered artificial mountain (approximately 1/100th the size of the real Matterhorn) and to descend by way of spectacular bounding rappels.

"One Disaster After Another" is the title Ruth later gave to her experiences in the mid 1960s. In 1964, at age 52, Ruth was diagnosed with breast cancer and underwent a mastectomy. A year later she had a hysterectomy and other surgeries. Also that year, her brother, Conrad, was killed in an industrial accident. Her cousin Phoebe's older son, Terry Russell (who, with his brother, Renny Russell, had just published the Sierra Club book *On the Loose*) drowned on the Green River in 1965. Phoebe Russell attempted suicide in Yosemite. Vivian and Valerie went away to UCLA.

Meanwhile, Ruth made some modest progress toward fulfilling her early ambition to be a writer. She produced saddle-stitched booklets for La Siesta Press in Glendale, California: *Backpack Cookery*

*Out-of-print La Siesta Press edition of Backpack Techniques*

(1966) and *Backpacking Techniques* (1967). Together, Ruth and John published *Introduction to Rock and Mountain Climbing* with Stackpole Books in 1968. They also contributed to *A Climber's Guide to the High Sierra*, and Ruth published articles in *Desert Magazine, Summit Magazine, National Parks,* and elsewhere.

Another of Ruth's ambitions was to create a family in which everybody climbed rocks. To this end, she called that period "Teens on the Rope" in later notes. She wrote that "there was no real beginning—we had always dragged our kids about with us on trips that we (not necessarily they) considered within their abilities and scope of enjoyment. We certainly forced them unwisely at times. Perhaps climbing is not really a child's sport. Most of the time it wasn't forced on them till they wanted to pursue it." The family hiked and climbed in the Sierra Madre, Sierra Nevada, and Cascades. They went to Europe in the summer of 1961, and climbed in the Alps. They climbed the real Matterhorn and the Eiger by an easy route, although yet another bivouac was involved.

In spite of health and family problems, Ruth continued to attend local Sierra Club rock-climbs. She climbed Mount Humphreys (1959), Mount Gayley (1960), Mount Saint Helens (1963), Mount Rainier, and Mount Sill (1964) with the usual nighttime descent: "Valerie now became very brave, and though she reminded us from time to time that Things were waiting for her in the dark, she went ahead and picked out the trail." In 1965 Ruth climbed Telegraph Peak, Mount Muir, Temple Crag, and Mount Tyndall, followed in 1966 by Mount Langley and Mount Darwin. Ruth decided that she was tired of climbing the same mountains over and over, and would rather finish climbing all the 14,000-foot peaks on the Pacific Coast, which were all in California except for Washington's Mount Rainier.

Vivian and Valerie found other people to climb with, by joining the Bruin Mountaineers at UCLA. As in her early letters to her parents, Ruth continued to report various fatal accidents in her letters, while always assuring her correspondents that climbing was perfectly safe. On a Sierra Peaks Section trip, Don Coyle fell on Middle Palisade and "landed virtually at Vivian's feet, and there was no doubt at all that he was very dead." On Christmas Eve, 1963, "the phone rang, and it was Mexico City calling–would I accept the charges! After a few words from operator to operator in Spanish, there was Vivian, cheerily telling me she had broken her ankle on Orizaba, the highest of Mexico's volcanic peaks, and she would be home on the plane Christmas night." –V.M.C.

# Disneyland

## MATTERHORN, "FIRST ASCENT"
## SEQUOIA DRIVE., PASADENA
## JUNE 16, 1959

*Dear Mother and Alice,*

I think I'll write you a joint letter about our Disneyland adventures before I forget all the little details that made it fun. I wonder if the lengthy 90-minute TV show came to your area last night? Of course those of us who were there were entranced with the whole thing, but it would have been better if it had been shorter. We naturally thought they cut too much out of the climbing–especially as they made a great point of our timing it just so, because they wanted to run it exactly as it was taken. In the end, although they saved it for the climax, they took out quite a bit of both the climbing and the commentary. Even I, who was right there and knew just exactly what everyone did at what instant, could not tell the people apart, so it didn't make much difference who was who–it really didn't, as we were all doing similar things. I think all of us showed at some time, except possibly the fellow who did the lead on the hardest pitch! Such is life (or TV) I guess.

Friday was the day of the filming. Thursday was hot, but Friday dawned cold and foggy. The Wiltses were coming by for me about 9:00, and I managed to get the house straightened a little and the dishes done. That was Vivian's Senior Prom night, and I had her

*The Disneyland Matterhorn, Anaheim, California*

clothes all ready except her slips–which I thought weren't going to get washed, as the drain hose of the washing machine was leaking; I had a change of heart, though, and did them by hand that morning.

Did I tell you of the crisis we had with our pants? We had them all tailor made by a climbing firm in Colorado, and when they came Tuesday, they were not climbing knickers at all, but skin-tight ski pants. None of us could raise a leg in them. We had to send them back (no doubt to the mutual regret of everyone involved). Luckily, Ethel Vandegrift, who owns the only store in L.A. that imports climbing stuff, is an old Sierra Club friend; and she said we could take their whole stock (rather low) of knickers home to try on. This was a god-send because the men did not dare take any more time off from work. I went down and brought ten or twelve pairs of pants home to Ellen's. There were only two pairs of women's knickers–ski pants, not tough climbing material, unfortunately, and they fit us just beautifully. We also got nice long wool stretch socks to go with the knickers. By great good luck, the assortment of men's pants fit them all and pleased them all! We also had new hats.

So when we finally met in Disneyland about 10:00 that morning, we really did look quite sharp, at least compared with our normal climbing garb. Our outfits had several advantages. Everyone knew we were The Climbers, and since nobody but us had any idea what we were supposed to do and were able to do, we were treated with suitable respect. Of course, we did everything we could, to do what they wanted, too. Disneyland has hired a couple of boys about Viv's age to climb the Matterhorn all summer (they get $85 a week), and they turned out to be a handy thing to have around–they appeared to respect us (which I am frank to say the youngest climbers usually don't), and just hung around and slaved for our every wish! We liked them too.

Most of the day was spent in occasional climbs of the mountain, to get the timing right for the three routes, and in sitting around doing nothing and watching the twirling gaiety of all the concessions below. The TV cameras, on various carts and on an enormous crane, were busy filming the dancers, the skater, and mermaids, and so forth. At one point in the afternoon it actually *rained*–the painted mountain got slippery, and the cameras were hastily covered with plastic. After that the light improved, but they waited and waited till it was past 5:00 before they were ready. By this time they had a chunky fellow posing timidly, well back from the edge, with his

*Ruth and John Mendenhall*
*hamming it up, 1958*

Alpine Horn; and a famous old-time skier, Hannes Schroll, nearby yodeling. Poor Hannes was so anxious to be in the picture that he absolutely refused to retire to one of the tunnels when the cameraman asked him to at a certain point–and in the end he did not show even for an instant! I wonder if they did that to him on purpose because he wouldn't cooperate.

We had made our climb many times, so when the final moment came, it went smoothly and easily, we hoisted the American and Swiss flag (it later turned out they had made a mistake, and the Swiss flag was really Swedish!), threw the rappel ropes, and rappeled.

When the gear was collected and we were really down, it was well after 6:00. Mr. Walker, the Manager of Disneyland, asked us if we would stay to dinner at their expense. (I noticed that all the men who work there are quite *young*.) The Wiltses wanted to, and I said I could but would have to phone home. He told me where to find a phone, under the grandstand, and there it was–sitting on a talus block! Seven of us (one climber had gone home, one had his wife, and this included Harvey Hickman who did the commentary with Art Linkletter) went to their nicest restaurant (where they told us to). Naturally, we all ordered their best steaks. I decided I had turned into a real Hollywood Mother: Vivian had left for her Senior Prom, and Valerie, all alone, had had a mustard sandwich for dinner while I had my $4.25 steak.

Next day, Saturday, I wallowed around in all the undone work inside and out, washed my hair, and got my clothes back in topnotch shape. Ellen and I found it very difficult to have to look like models and climb too. Luckily the mountain didn't seem to rub off much on our dark wool pants–poor Ellen did tear hers on a piece of wire in one of the tunnels. One of the things that amazed us that Friday, was how much had been done on the mountain since the preceding Saturday. For one thing, turf had been unrolled around its base, with flowers planted in it, a pretty good imitation of Alpine meadows! Workmen kept popping out of the tunnels to ask our opinion of their handi-work, which they were very proud of, and also to take pictures of us.

Finally Sunday came, the day of the Opening. The girls and I drove down this time, and by chance encountered two of the other climbers and their families in the parking lot (the Wiltses, and Dr. Bill Wagner who was my climbing partner). We sort of milled in together, and milled over to city hall for everyone's free ticket books, information about the time we were wanted, and so on. Then we all milled out and took rides, ran across Sierra Club friends, from time to time attending to a little business in the climbing area. We looked at the reserved seats in the grandstands, noticing labels for quite an assortment of people such as Walt Disney, the Nixons, Joan Crawford, and several admirals who were to open the submarine area! It was a very hot day–my kids were scorched. We had hot dogs and milk shakes for lunch, and after a while Ellen and I departed from our children, so we could primp a little. Then we watched the parade from near our mountain, which parade was very colorful–we were especially enamored with the vast flock of balloons (ten-thou-sand, the paper said, whereas I would have said millions) that were turned loose to float away.

At last our call came, and we all whisked inside the mountain, and climbed the stairs to the middle platform, where we were supposed to wait for the signal to climb. Then we climbed. Then we rappelled, after signing the Sierra Club register that had been cast in the name of DISNEYLAND MATTERHORN USA. When we had descended, Ellen and I were waiting for the men to appear. And who should *seek us out*–that was what pleased us the most!–but Vice President and Mrs. Nixon. Mrs. Nixon said it was wonderful, and how much she enjoyed it. Mr. Nixon said, "You couldn't get me up there!" I thought that sounded like a *sincere* remark, and he shook our hands hard. To tell the truth, the men climbers admitted they were jealous of us later about this. We have been gloating about this ever since.

There was a wonderful free lemonade stand (with several kinds of cold drinks) at the foot of the Matterhorn, and having finished our work, we made full use of this. Then we went to hunt up our families. I thought it would be nice if I could take my girls to the top by the inside route, and Chuck wanted to take his on the bobsled ride on the lower slopes (we had been frightened to death that we would be cut down by a bobsled when we had to cross the tracks). We asked a guard, and he said that of course the climbers could go but not their families. I thought Chuck gave up too easily and also that there were too many of us in a mass (for the information of those who don't know, Chuck and Ellen have three children, 6, 9 and 10). So I got hold of Viv and Val, and sidled up to another guard, and asked if I could take them in and ask inside if they could go to the top when I went for the ropes. He said I could, and pretty soon Chuck looked around and spied us standing smugly in the sacred area. He flew in to find out how I did this, and flew out to find his children again and try again. In the mountain, I latched on to one of our other climbers,

Mike Sherrick, who had to go up for his ropes, anyway, and asked if he would take us. We just went to the bobsled station and said we were going, and they opened the gates and we went. We hastily disappeared into the vast, cavernous interior of the mountain, the height of a fourteen-story building. The lower part has the skyway now running through it, and the two bobsled runs that are like small roller coasters–this section is lined with imitation ice caves. We first took the very exposed little elevator to what one might describe as the attic of the peak. This level has several doors and windows opening onto the outside! Then we went up a lot of steps and ladders, and finally popped out a trap door on the summit, which is like a small metal roof with painted concrete walls around it. We had not been there long when the door opened again, and out came the Wilts family one by one–they had found a new guard and tried my approach. We felt that probably it would be much more difficult at any future date to ever get them on top again–so this was the time!

After awhile we retraced our steps, and then decided we would see if we could ride the bobsleds even if they were reserved for the Press and the Notables. We stood in line with Fred McMurray, and probably other people we didn't recognize. The bobsleds were just terrible, rather like small roller coasters but not quite so frightening. Then we all went to the refreshment stand, and the Wilts kids in the shrill piping voices of the young kept wanting to know How Come We Didn't Have To Pay.

We then hauled our ropes that were to be left, over to the office, and finally split up into families again. Viv and Val and I took another Indian Canoe ride–the Indian Village is new since we have been there. The Indian (a real one) in the stern, had a conversation with me about mountain-climbing. He wanted to know if it made me nervous to have so many people looking. I hadn't thought of it–I replied that I had been far too busy climbing.

I had a few after-thoughts about tramping around Disneyland for two days in my so-obviously mountain-climbing outfit. For one thing, though hot, it was so comfortable. I always have wanted to go sightseeing in boots, wool socks, and knapsack–and I have never come home with my feet feeling so good! And naturally we looked like characters, and couldn't help noticing the heads swivel as we went by. Occasionally people would come up and Speak to us. I also have a beautiful new climbing rope, which ought to please John! If he ever comes home, we'll have to go off to the real mountains and use it.

Vivian remarked after the first practice day: you should have heard all those venerable mountain-climbers, veterans of the Rockies, Sierra, and Canadian Rockies, as they approached the scene of their first publicity-stunt climb. They sounded just like they do whenever they first see their mountain: "Look at the mountain!" "There's the mountain!"

We drove home, between 7:00 and 8:00, with the sun (which seemed to be setting right in the north) right in my eyes most of the way, and trillions of cars on the freeway, and I kept thinking the drivers were all blinded too. However, we got home alive, and Pasadena looked pretty and peaceful with the mountains clear and blue, and the hills and trees.

*Goodbye now,*

# Humphreys Basin

SEQUOIA DR., PASADENA, CALIF.

SEPTEMBER 14, 1959

*Dear Relatives,*

After being gone all summer, John got home I think it was Tuesday, August 18. They wanted him to take a vacation, and take it right away. We had decided to spend it in the High Sierra, which is a beautiful place but we never have been there for more than three or four-day weekends. We studied our maps, and picked out a new area none of us had ever been to–the Humphreys Basin, over Piute Pass, west of Bishop. On Sunday (August 23), I finally got my groceries bought, and everything else as ready as I could. It was about the worst-prepared-for vacation in our history.

We went into the mountains over Piute Pass, close to 11,500 feet. We passed two lovely deep turquoise lakes and by and by began to pass more human creatures–namely various Boy Scouts distributed in various stages of decay along the trail. Their goods were packed in on mules. Apparently our girls became quite a source of conversation–especially because the man in charge was obviously using their example to try to get his boys moving. "What did I tell you about girls along the trail!" he would exclaim in triumph as we plodded by. (Naturally this was more of an inspiration to the girls than to the boys!) The man also inquired into the girls' ages, feeling that the boys were mistaken when they insisted the girls were at least 15

*Mendenhall Family in Humphreys Basin where Valerie (opposite) hits her limit, August, 1959*

and 17 (we figured they took Valerie for 17, since she is now 2 inches taller than her sister). To tell the truth, we saw dozens of men and boys all told, and only two other girls (except for the ones on the Sierra Club knapsack trip) on the entire trip, which seems sort of too bad in a way as girls seem to enjoy mountain activities as much as anybody (maybe their mothers don't see it quite that way).

The trail was very gradual, and finally late in the afternoon we had made the long haul to the top of the pass, and got our triumphal oranges (though it was suddenly so cold and windy we might as well have eaten them sooner). Out of the canyon and over the pass, we were looking west into one of the great interior basins of the Sierra scooped out long ago by the glaciers–a large area perhaps 5 miles across, partly above timberline, covered with countless pale granite rocks, countless groups of little timberline trees lower down, and many many (though not entirely countless) lakes–from a mountaintop later

we counted eighty-five in view at one time, large and small, high and low, dotting the hollows left by the glacier. This is a very dry year, but even so, many little streams crossed the basin, and one could see many more dried-up stream beds. To the north was a long ridge, crag-crowned, of striped Mt. Humphreys, almost 14,000 feet high. To the south were the peaks of the Glacier Divide, averaging around 13,000 feet and with little glaciers at their cliff bases. To the west, the basin gradually drew into a dropping canyon which became black with timber as it lost altitude.

We had originally intended to camp at Golden Trout Lake, which we could see in a sort of triangle at the base of some cliffs a couple of miles beyond the pass. However, it was getting late in the day, and at dusk we left the trail, cut across the dry little autumn meadows toward the stream, and walked into what turned out to be a lovely little campsite, exactly what we needed, situated with delightful privacy and solitude. It had an absolutely wonderful fireplace that had a grill, a chimney, and big flat rocks to put things on. It had some fine flat soft sleeping places on the lee side of the clumps of Albicaulis pines that grow at that altitude–they are a little like Lodgepole pines, but have thick heavy trunks, limbs reaching away from the prevailing wind, and very bright thick needles. We had a tent and a "fly," which we didn't really need as it didn't rain a drop, but we had quite a bit of wind, and it was cozy to have a bit of shelter at night. John collected us a wondrous woodpile, and we made ourselves fine seats by the fire, with a log backrest, and rock cushions.

The first morning there was much like our other mornings–the blaze and warmth of the sun blasted us out of our bags even while the frost still lay white on the short grass of the meadows. It was a flawless beautiful day, with a brilliant sky. The brook murmured by our camp. The shining light rocks of the basin surrounded us, and around our camp was a great variety of boulders, some low for the wash stand, some high for the view. We had a leisurely breakfast of bacon and pancakes, which rise to a wonderful tender delicacy at a high altitude, and then did a little work at organizing our camp.

We had taken three little cooking pots with us, but soon began to find a great variety of useful utensils (all shining clean, for some reason) at other campsites. Val found a big billy can, and a coffeepot. Later we found the coffeepot cover, and later still we found a can part full of coffee (I had only taken instant), so we had some real true Camp Coffee (this is living off the country). We found several little cooking kettles of great character, one made in Italy, one with a good cover, and several small cans, a fine wash basin, a bucket with a hole in it, and later when we discovered the chipmunks were going to take what food they could get, we rustled up some big tins to put the food in.

Soon we girls could not resist going fishing–my only distinction in the fishing line was to catch the first Golden Trout any of us had ever seen. We were very impressed with it. The Golden Trout have a bright orange belly, and orange and dark stripes on the sides. We were told it was discovered as a "sport," a variation of the Rainbow, in an isolated stream near Mt. Whitney, and has been bred and planted for the higher elevations of the Sierra where it seems very well adapted. It has cross bred with the Rainbows, until there is a good deal of variation–some have orange meat, some white, some flat backboned, some three-cornered, some with even four or five branches.

The truth about our fishing was that Valerie, who could hardly catch even one last summer at the Little Moyie, suddenly turned out to be the family fisherman. Not only could she catch five or six to my one, when we were fishing from the same hole, but she found the holes, the time of day to catch them, the *way* to catch them (I doubt if Viv and I would have caught any without her coaching, which we were humbly obliged to seek), but she fed us fish every single night she fished, caught the biggest of the trip, and three or four times as many as the rest of us, also the only one to get her "limit." This was a good thing too, since we really needed them!

How we did love our walk each afternoon down to the small lake above the big lake, where we found the best fishing–the beautiful little stream, the shining rocks, the peaks around us, the clusters of pines, the bright little autumn colors in the meadows, wildfire with deep red leaves, shooting stars now reduced to clumps of yellow leaves. Sometimes John was off solo-climbing while we were fishing. Sometimes we all went on exploring trips to some of the higher lake basins above timberline (we never caught anything up there, but we liked going). Sometimes we found lovely little flowers still in bloom in damper meadows, tiny blue or white ones, miniature Indian paintbrush in a soft raspberry color.

For several days we had good meals, and then we began to notice our supplies were dwindling alarmingly. On about the fifth day we laid out all our food, and found that we had lots of lunch stuff, but not too awfully much but soup (and fish) for dinner and almost nothing for breakfast. This was obviously poor planning on my part! There were several solutions: we could go out early, which we didn't want to do; we could eat very skimpily indeed, which we were willing to do; or we could get some more food from somewhere, which we considered the best thing to do. So one day we set out on what was frankly a mooching expedition. John had already talked to some fishermen who had been mountain sick, and we thought they might have spare food. Then we found a family camping who were going out the next day, and said they "might" have some food left over that they would be glad to sell to us. That evening, as we were finishing our most meager day's meals, the two boys appeared in our camp with quite a fine contribution to our diet: a can or two, several of those Bernard Kamp Packs (including biscuits to be cooked in a frying pan), margarine, popcorn, and most monumental of all, a huge cartwheel of bread that the lady had baked in her big iron Dutch oven (they had, of course, been taken in by a pack train). This bread was really our mainstay! It was sort of a cross between sourdough French bread and baking powder biscuits, and at first it tasted very peculiar. However, we soon found a wonderful way to fix it–to fry hunks of it crisp in bacon grease. I am sure we will never have anything just like that again!

Our weather was simply wonderful. The air at 11,000 feet is heavenly. It is wonderful to bask in the sun. Often we got too hot, and just by moving into shade or breeze would be cold again. Nights were cold the instant the sun sank, which was early in our west-sheltered camp, so we would soon have a big fire blazing, and go to bed at dark. What good nights of sleep we had. Keeping clean soon became utterly hopeless–there was so much soot on the pans, and from sitting around the fire. Of course we kept washing, but it didn't do much good. Mornings we often washed socks, and soon all around camp the big rocks would be covered by small rocks holding down socks to dry. We were always boiling our towels, but they got worse and worse. Val would ask me from time to time if a week at home would get her clean before school began. We thought we were developing wonderful suntans, but it was hard to be sure what was tan and what was soot.

We had a certain amount of social life. A Sierra Club knapsackng trip with thirty-nine people passed through. During the first week the girls received a certain amount of attention from Boy Scouts who would work for hours trying to attract their attention during our fishing expeditions. Of course, the fact was, the boys had the girls' attention all the time, but didn't know it.

Toward the end of the first week we got ourselves worked up to climb Mt. Humphreys. Val stayed home while the other three of us arose at the ghastly hour of 4:00 a.m., and had breakfast by firelight and moonlight. Up till then the weather had been absolutely perfect, but this time was a cold and windy dawn, with light clouds scudding over the sky. As a matter of fact it was cold and windy all day–so windy that Val didn't go fishing, but stayed in camp and kept our stuff from blowing away. It turned out she had lots of fun alone because the chipmunks came and she watched them all day, fed them from her hand, and found out that they were a lot smarter than we gave them credit for. For instance, she actually saw two of them take away our salmon egg jars–first they would roll the jars, then they would carry them in their front legs like a person!

This was Vivian's first Real mountain climb, so it was sort of an event. To get to Mt. Humphreys, we had a 3-mile walk across gradually rising rock and meadowland. As with most mountains, it wasn't as steep as it looked when we finally reached the front of the peak. First we went up talus, then a broad gully of loose talus where nothing more than care was required, then up the black rocks, and finally reached the reddish-yellow rocks. All this time we were in the morning shade and the cold wind, huddled in mittens and parkas. It was colder than ever when we came to a notch in the ridge and peeked down the north side that dropped to a small glacier, and off to the desert of Owens Valley, the dark green patch that we knew to be the trees of the town of Bishop, and the White Mountains beyond. Up on the ridge, we eventually roped up, and had easy though exposed rocks to the summit. In sickly sunshine we signed the register of the 13,986' mountain, then found a rocky nook sheltered from the wind to eat lunch. The descent was easy, and the day seemed to get warmer as we got lower. The wind was still blowing as we walked back across the miles of meadowland between the mountain and the camp, the lovely little grasses of the high altitudes waving in the wind–some of them had purple stems and heads, some had tufts almost like tiny cat tails, some grew fairy circles, or circles that weren't quite complete so they looked like letters you couldn't quite read. We got back to camp in the late afternoon, had pea soup, and chocolate pudding for dessert, and a lovely sleep that night.

Another day we all went on a kind of exploring and climbing trip in the opposite direction, toward a high pass in the Glacier Divide southwest of camp. We passed a high group of small lakes called the Wahoo Lakes. They were nestled in old moraines, among clumps of huge chocolate-colored boulders, the lakes themselves a brilliant dark aqua color, dancing and leaping, which sparkled so bright you could hardly look at them. When we got up into the pass, we could look over into another great basin, with more lakes, and rather a lot of timber, called the Evolution Basin. We climbed a nearby mountain, rather a crud-pile, but almost 13,000 feet high, and geologically different from nearby peaks as it had a volcanic top of black and red lava.

All went well except that during the day Valerie lost the seat of her pants. As we were all alone, this made no difference. However, that afternoon when we were coming through the great talus blocks of lowest Wahoo Lake, we were greatly surprised to encounter a new group of Boy Scouts–eight or ten big, handsome boys with a nice looking man at the head. We were privately greatly amused when one of the boys took out his camera, and remarked ostentatiously that he liked the scenery there with no trees and wanted a picture of it–but we could plainly see that the scenery that he took a picture of was Viv and Val. When we got up to go, to our dismay the Boy Scout troop all did an about-face and came along after us. Valerie sat down on a rock. John, thinking it was getting late no doubt, said, "Come along, Valerie." Val said, "No." John said with fatherly firmness, *"Come along,* Valerie." The Boy Scouts stood there. Val said, "No." I realized that someone was going to have to break this up, so I remarked to the male population at large that she had lost the seat of her pants. Big broad grins spread over the Boy Scout faces, but they were too well bred to laugh out loud. The leader said gallantly, "We will turn our backs." They did, and we went! Crisis over, I showed her how to tie her parka on to cover up for the time-being.

Every day the fish became more numerous, working up from four the first dinner to eighteen at the peak meal, so we began to live it up. Those trout were simply yummy, so fresh and sweet, and all crispy and nice, fried in cornmeal and butter or bacon grease. I will say that during our entire stay there, not one single time did one member of my family say about a single item of food, "I don't like it."

As you can imagine, some of my mornings were spent patching people's pants. Another day John and I climbed Mt. Humphreys again by another route. It was a gorgeous day this time, the climb went fast, as we got back to camp by 3:30. As our children were fishing, we made tea and sat around the fire reading the sooty disintegrating remains of our *Reader's Digest,* which certainly isn't up to camp life the way it used to be before it got so fat with ads.

Alas, it finally came to be the Last Day. We lived it up by eating almost everything left. How we regretted the thought that soon we could not go fishing through the bright meadows each afternoon. The last morning we got up early, but it took about three hours to break camp. This was Friday September 4. Vacation wasn't quite over, but John wanted to go to the R.C.S. climb on Mt. Whitney–having been Rock Climbing Section Chairman all summer, but having also been gone all summer. The pack out was easy because it was mostly downhill, and of course by this time we were in really good condition, having walked for miles, even on our "rest days," every day.

After living so long in the open timberline basin, we felt almost hemmed in by the canyon walls and the willows and aspens of the lower part of the trail. We encountered various people going to the area–a group of Japanese Boy Scouts, a buxom looking man and woman who hold the speed record for running up Mt. Whitney (an odd hobby?), a packer in charge of a string of mules who told me I needed a good mule (I replied that he had told me the same thing when I went in), and as we got farther down the trail the people became cleaner, neater, plumper and paler. We finally reached the car, and were glad to shed our filthy clothes for a clean set–what was our surprise to find that our blue jeans that had fit a scant two weeks before, now hung on us like bags. We measured our waists with string and a rule, and found we had each lost two inches from our waistlines (when we got home, we found that I had lost eleven pounds, John had lost eight pounds and the girls six pounds each, but we are rapidly gaining it back). We lost no time in driving back to civilization and stocking up both on food and groceries. Then we drove south a ways in Owens Valley, and back into the mountains to the end of Mt. Whitney road.

What a shock, after our magnificent seclusion, to have to pry our way into the crowded campground, virtually with a shoehorn! John took off Saturday morning with the climbers. As the pack-in is up a rough trailless canyon, we had thought it too hard for the girls. Sunday we went on a long hike to Meysan Lakes. The trail climbed and climbed, and time after time, we would top a rise and there would be another one! The trail got older and feebler and more obscure, as if almost everyone had long since given up. At about 3:00 p.m. we actually did find the Upper Meysan Lake, a small, deep, blue-green body of water in the cirque, with rather crumbling peaks around three sides of it, and the tumbled rocks of the moraine pinning it in on the lower side.

When we got back to camp, John was already back–having climbed the East Face of Whitney and made the pack-out all in one day. We drove down to the desert, where we found a quiet side-road for a good sleep. Next morning, after a hearty restaurant breakfast, we drove home, where we luxuriated in shampoos and baths all afternoon. Sure enough, by the time school started Val was rid of all her soot (so were the rest of us), though our beautiful tan is still peeling off in spots, giving us a rather piebald look.

The week has gone by in a hurry since we returned–girls have been to orthodontist; Valerie twice to occulist; Mugelnoos meeting; and of course I have washed, washed, washed. I am finally down to the pants and the wool socks. I have to go to the grocery store (again) this morning.

*And love,*

# Baldy Ski Hut

Sequoia Dr., Pasadena, Calif.,
June 11, 1963 — Tuesday 9:00 a.m.

*Dear Mother,*

Over the weekend, I conducted one of my periodic female mountain trips. Val and her fiend Janet Griswold wanted to go to the Baldy Ski Hut to keep in shape for their summer trips, and I finally said I would take them. John was too busy. As Val had finals to study for, we didn't leave till late Saturday afternoon. The girls were so grateful to me for going that they carried all the food. We left the car about 6:00 o'clock, and set out up the steep trail through the woods. As it had been sunny at home, we were sort of surprised to be rained on on the trail. It was of course a much easier trip than last time when we went in the snow and the dark–this time it took less than two hours instead of over three. There were quite a few people already at the hut, so we had a jolly weekend. Our dinner was the standard dinner Val and I have developed for the hut–steak, corn on the cob, and garlic bread.

Next morning I got up about 7:00, roused the girls, and after breakfast we climbed the peak, which is 10,080 feet elevation, about a 1,500-foot climb above the hut. It was a perfectly beautiful day, neither too hot nor too cold, but exactly right for what we were doing. We were quite surprised to read in the register about a man who appeared to have a hobby of standing on his head (his bare

*Baldy Ski Hut, 1971*

head, it said) for photographers on the summit.

One of my little tasks with Viv gone is to feed the two frogs. Their "meal worms" live in a container in the icebox, which keeps them dormant. They have to be warmed up before the frogs will eat them, as they won't eat anything that isn't wiggling. I was rather queasy about the worms at first, but now just warm them up in my hand till I feel them kick. Then a worm is placed in front of the frog. The frog, if in an eating mood, will stare fixedly at the worm for a time, and then suddenly pounce on it–and that is that. Usually one frog gets frightened, or isn't hungry, and sometimes one who has already had plenty will snatch the worms away from the other. They are nice little pets.

*Ruth*

# Mount Langley

SEQUOIA DR., PASADENA, CALIF.

JUNE 2, 1966 — THURSDAY NOON

*Dear Mother,*

L ast week I was very busy. I did a good job with spray starch on those limp ruffly curtains in Val's room. Thursday was the ceremony for Viv's Phi Beta Kappa initiation, with a reception at the campus home of the University Chancellor, which was held on the well kept (but weedy!) lawn. (Imagine having such a large yard that you had to put up an EXIT sign!) This morning I went to the grocery store, had a haircut, and am washing a blanket.

Friday naturally was spent getting ready for our weekend trip to the Sierra. We planned to climb Mt. Langley, 14,042 feet, the most southerly of the Sierra's 14,000-foot peaks. A few years ago I got tired of climbing the same ones over and over, and said I would like to finish the 14,000 foot peaks on the Pacific Coast (I'm not going to start on Colorado and Alaska!). They are all in California except Mt. Rainier. One more to go.

This is a seldom climbed peak, not because of difficulty but due to inaccessibility. There are easier but much longer ways to go than the way we went, which was up a canyon with no trail most of the way. This made the backpacking arduous, but the canyon was just *lovely*, with so many monstrous trees, and not one *bit* of litter the entire way. We walked along an old deteriorated road for some distance, which we had been told ended in a "cabin." The cabin turned out to be a very large, X-shaped lodge of beautiful native stone, which was of course abandoned but must once have been a very impressive fishing resort. We are going to try to find out its history.

From there we traversed a steep canyon-side with the stream dashing down the V of the canyon in white waterfalls among its willows. First we went through arid vegetation such as sagebrush, manzanita hung with its little pink and white lamps of blossoms, and Piñon pines. These gradually changed, as we climbed to Jeffrey pines (which are very much like Yellow pines) and two kinds of firs which I think must be the white fir and the red fir because they are the only varieties that grow in the Sierra. These trees gradually changed into the kinds one finds at higher elevations–first huge specimens of Lodgepole pines, then the Limber pine, Whitebark pine, and the Foxtail pine. The trees were very large right up to timberline, instead of dwindling away as they usually do at high elevations. It was too early for many flowers, though I saw some paintbrush and one or two other earlier varieties. The going was hard going up, very slidy, somewhat brushy, and steep, some of it over large boulders.

It took us almost eight hours to reach the spot where we decided to camp (having climbed up 3,500 feet from the car), on one of the forested, rocky benches at around 10,000 feet, with the stream near-by in the willows (this canyon had so many willows that in some places you couldn't even find the water). There were snowbanks nearby, rather gray from blowing sand so they could hardly be distinguished from the pale tumbled boulders. Still much higher up the canyon rose the snow streaked sides of Mt. Langley right above us. We had a gorgeous campsite, on beach-like sand; and due to the wild nature of the canyon, the place just filled with good firewood.

Instead of having to find it, one had to throw some of it away from the fire for safety.

Bed felt good that night, and we rose around 5:00 the next morning. The climb had no technical difficulty, but it was long, over crud, loose rocks, and icy snow. From the summit we had a stupendous view, looking out over peaks we had climbed and many more we had not climbed. The day was cold and windy, but we were well bundled up and if anything were a little hot ourselves. We got back to camp twelve hours after we left it, and again found it very nice to crawl into our cozy tent, and sleep soundly on our comfy beds, while the wind flapped the tent around us. My husband made me get up at 6:00 the next morning, I regret to say. The drive home was slow because the traffic was very thick. We had plenty of time in the traffic jams to study the motoring public; one pair that amused me was two boys, around 12 and 16, in an old beat-up Jeep, with a shiny new aluminum chaise lounge in the back of it! I bet they thought they were really Living.

*With love,*

# Clyde Peak Bivouac

## July 12, 1966

*Dear Al,*

Did you go backpacking over the Fourth? We did, and had quite a trip. John had picked out a mountain called Clyde's Peak, around 13,940 feet in elevation, one of the peaks in the so-called Palisades region which we hadn't climbed. Valerie came with us. Driving north through the desert Friday evening we saw a *meteor*–speeding across the lower sky with a long tail, till it finally burnt out.

Saturday morning we left the end of the road to go up around 3,000 feet of backpacking, part on a good trail, part cross-country. Even down at the deserty elevation of 6,000 feet, the wildflowers were lovely–at that elevation the pale green foliage of sagebrush contrasting with huge bushes of white lupines for acres, and long-stemmed, rose-pink Indian paintbrush among them everywhere. Crossing the stream was very difficult, and we got sort of wettish around the feet. The trail climbed steadily till it came over a little pass, where we were met not only by marvelous rows of jagged peaks on the skyline, but also by hordes of nasty mosquitoes which prevailed all the rest of the day.

We took off over cliffs, bogs, willow wallows, streams, meadows, canyons–filled with waving dainty grasses and flowers–knee high shooting stars, clusters of magenta penstamen, vivid purple monks-hood and larkspur, asters, daisies, buttercups, paintbrush. By late

*Valerie Mendenhall at the bergschrund below Clyde Peak in the Palisades, July 4th weekend, 1966*

afternoon we reached the upper part of the canyon we were going to camp in, on a mosquitoey meadow with shooting stars and willows and a lot of dead pine wood to burn. That night I stuck my head out into the chilly air, and was startled to see a huge snow-covered mountain blocking the canyon mouth. I put on my glasses and it was still there–even though I *knew* it was moonlight, I couldn't believe it because it looked so much like new snow.

We rose shortly after 5:00, and before long were plodding up the long reaches of the canyon, frozen snow slopes alternating with talus, until finally the sun came out and melted the snow crust and beat warmly upon us. What should appear but seven other climbers from a Sierra Club group, bound for the same peak. A couple of them were old friends, some we knew slightly or by name. They caused us a certain amount of anxiety. They were just far enough ahead most of the day to keep throwing rocks down in our direction–far more than they needed to knock off, loose as it was! They quarreled from bottom to top, wrangled, the stronger ones abandoned the pleading weaker ones and rushed ahead. We crossed the bergschrund, with its rather cavernous depths, together, at a wide snow bridge.

Then they all rushed unroped up one gully, while we, tied together, went up the other one. After awhile we had to get off the snow, and onto the rocks, big steep blocks painted with vermilion and chartreuse lichen, and thoroughly covered with loose crud of every size. We came up with the other group by midafternoon. Their three strongest men rushed off to finish the climb, without one word or reply to the pitiful calls of the rest of the group–who finally wandered off downward.

The climb was long and slow, and when we finally got to the ridge and saw how far off the top still was, we realized we would have to decide either to turn back, then and there, or to go on to the peak and probably spend the night on the mountain. I said we ought to go on, and Val agreed, and since it was probably John's wish he agreed too. Sure enough, by the time we got back to our crampons and ice axes, it was pitch dark and we felt it would be too dangerous to go out on the frozen steep snow. After we had milled around awhile, we found it was already almost 11:00, and were glad indeed that that much of the night had passed.

We had heard water not far away, and to our great good luck had the first drink we had had all day except for a pint of water between us, and periodic snow. True, we had to climb up about 40 feet in the dark, by flashlight, with ice axes and rope, but it was worth it. John filled the canteen (rather, I did and he carried it), and we descended to the ledge below to find our bed. By this time of course it had grown very cold, as it does at between 12,000 and 13,000 feet at night, though luckily there was hardly any wind. When Val started with a routine type complaint, I said "NO! Since we have to be here, let's enjoy it."

We had two rooms, so to speak, one floored with rocks, snow and mud; the other a flat slab that tapered off to nothingness on three sides, and had sort of a backrest at the wall between the two rooms. We thought this bed-rock was pretty good, and we all got tied on by ropes leading from each person back to a protruding tooth of rock. We also tied on the rucksack. We were wearing stocking caps, parkas, extra sweaters, mittens, boots, even eye-glasses. I just lay right down with my head on the camera in the rucksack and immediately began to dream.

With a lot of shivering and tooth-chattering, Val and John lay down too. As the night drew on, we curled up tighter and tighter together. I was in the middle part of the time, and I liked it (Closer, Valerie!). About once an hour we, or first one and then the others, would sit up, shaking, and say it was time to move. We exercised a bit, studied the Great Dipper's change, admired the glorious view with the moon shine creeping over it, had a sip of water. I thought tea would be nice, and for once in her life Val admitted she did not want a Coke. We would look at the time, and finally lie down again in tight formation. And finally when we sat up it was 5:00 a.m. and the stars had faded away.

To celebrate the arrival of dawn we ate a candy bar, and went to sleep for another hour. At 6:00 it was really morning, and we breakfasted on cheese and a little water. It occurred to me a week later that I had never even *thought* of coffee or tea–the cheese seemed pretty good, as it went down without much spit.

Unfortunately we were in a sort of north-facing gulch, and had quite a wait till the sun got in. This was Val's first bivouac, my second–the first being before I was married; but John is the bivouac king of the area, having had many and many over the years, including one Viv was on a couple of years ago (in fact Vivian has bivouacked more times than I have–she's welcome to the distinction!). Finally around 8:00, we got strapped into our crampons and were on our way down.

We had made various estimates as to how long it would take to warm up. Val said two weeks, I said two hours. Actually it took about two minutes, as the second we got out of the shadow, it was frightfully hot on the snow. It took about four hours to get down to camp. We had thought in the night we'd have to sleep there, but No, by that time we felt fine. We had tomato soup, bacon, toast, tea, and other things to eat; packed up and departed. We got to the car around 5:00, little the worse for wear, considering, and were home before midnight.

On the whole, we thought it had been rather fun, and it wasn't even as bad at the time as one might think.

Well, we've been to a couple of parties since. Val has gone back to the mountains. The car has valve trouble and is in the garage. I'd better quit and go to bed eventually.

*Your loving sister of the South,*

*Ruth (right) with unidentified climber, on edge of crevasse, Mt. Baker, 1969*

Chapter Seven
# Growing Older
# 1967-1989

*I always have just loved being free to sit and enjoy the exposure,*

*with no other duties than watching the rope.*

RUTH DYAR MENDENHALL

*Ruth, 1972*

Ruth and John joined the American Alpine Club in 1966. Ruth was elected to the Board of Directors in 1974. She edited the *American Alpine News* between 1978 and 1981. She received that club's Angelo Heilprin Citation for Service. The Sierra Club gave Ruth and John its Farquhar Award for Achievement and Leadership in Mountaineering.

During these years, Ruth and John climbed in the Dolomite Alps (1966), Balcony Peak (1967), several summits in the Kaweahs (1967, 1968), Polemonium Peak (1968), in Yosemite (1968), and the Minarets (1969). Ruth and John completed their list of Pacific Coast 14,000 foot peaks in 1969, by climbing White Mountain Peak (14,246'). East of Owens Valley, White Mountain Peak is not only the high point of the range from which it takes its name, it is the highest desert mountain on the North American continent. The University of California operates the White Mountain Research Station with several high-altitude research facilities in the White Mountains, including a montane station at Crooked Creek (10,200'), an alpine station at Barcroft (12,500'), and a high alpine summit laboratory.

As they had been doing for nearly forty years, Ruth and John taught Sierra Club Rock Climbing Section practice climbs at Joshua Tree, Mount Pacifico, Tahquitz, and Stoney Point. "We set forth with five fellows to instruct them in 'prussiking'–a means of climbing up a fixed rope with short slings. There was a period in my life when I noted a certain amount of animosity from male students, but I have now become sufficiently . . . prestigious? . . . legendary? . . . that they say it is an Honor to be in my class. They also sometimes thank me for talking to them. John actually did the real work, and I supervised and advised from the ground." Ruth confided to Vivian that "we have reached the conclusion between ourselves that we are given credit for many more first ascents than we ever actually did."

The Mendenhalls first met Royal Robbins at Stoney Point when he was about 16; he had a cast on his arm, yet climbed "like a lizard." John and Royal did various climbs together, including the 1953 first ascent of Tahquitz's Human Fright route. John later remarked that Royal always climbed with remarkable skill and meticulous care. In return, Royal says that "What I most remember about your father was his encouragement of me when we were climbing together or when we were at a climbing area such as Stoney Point. His integrity and plain basic decency always shone through, along, of course, with his love of climbing. He was an outstanding example of what a climber should be. He was always very detailed and precise and careful in his climbing, and never let his ego get in the way of the climbing experience. In short, he was a real climber and a real gentleman, and a rare breed in his day and this."

Being a woman climber (and a *better* climber than other women) was a constant theme in Ruth's letters and essays. As children, she and her sisters had climbed basalt formations in Spokane (where they should have had a rope), but their older brother was "too conservative." Their father, Ralph Dyar, owned property in British Columbia which he visited for fishing, but usually only his son and male friends were invited.

When people asked Ruth whether women in the 1930s climbed with men or mostly with each other, Ruth would say that there weren't enough climbers back then to sort them out by gender. She thought that some men felt "diminished" if a woman climbed a pitch they couldn't. Male Sierra Club climbers tended to believe that women were "frail." In 1938, her very first season, Ruth was asked to lead a Swiss visitor up the Fingertip Traverse route at Tahquitz; she was on the verge of declining, until another man exclaimed, "Ruth! You shouldn't! You only had three hours of sleep last night!" So of course she had to lead the climb. "Years later I discovered by chance that I had acquired a modest fame in Europe as a rock-climber."

Ruth certainly did compete against other female athletes. For instance, she mentioned that one woman was a very good skier, but Ruth was extremely annoyed that this other woman "always does every simple thing as if she thought she had an audience's eyes upon her, even to spooning her soup and walking across the room." Another woman was "kind of a dumb rock-climber. I don't like her very well. I haven't anything specific against her; but she is quite jealous of me, and works very hard on the Men when I am around." Female climbers in the Bay Chapter, according to Ruth, "didn't seem to be able to do anything much."

Ruth always carried a comb, and a red lipstick with a little mirror clamped to its gold case, when she climbed. "I struggled unhappily with my long unwieldy hair, my fingers so stiff with cold I couldn't feel the bobby-pins," she wrote in 1941. On Michael's Minaret, Ruth had to tie two rappel ropes together, "and you may be sure I didn't use the granny knot commonly attributed to females!" Ellen Wilts and Barbara Lilley were the only other "really enthusiastic women climbers in our area." At the age of 58, Ruth said that she and John were "the oldest climbers on the rock–and most certainly I outstrip any women climbers (of whom there are never any too many any-

*Ruth and Vivian Mendenhall, January, 1972*

way) by a good many years."

One might well assume that Ruth was deeply incensed by a letter printed in *Summit Magazine,* in 1956, from a man named Kurt Reynolds, from Denver, Colorado: "History records no truly great women climbers.... No experienced leader would willingly choose a woman as member of his climbing team. In fairness to his companions' safety he would not dare. Woe to the climber depending for his life on the instantaneous reaction of a woman, for women are physically inept, emotionally unstable and notably unreliable in emergency. A woman's very presence can mean discord and defeat.... In their mad rush to ape men, women have invaded every field of our endeavor. Let them return to their proper realm of kitchen, children and church—and be there when we return from our mountains."

The printed response, ironically enough, was signed only by John Mendenhall. It read in part, "One can only assume that Mr. Reynolds met with some unfortunate experience or experiences, and his viewpoint has been distorted thereby. . . . [Sierra Club] groups include girls."

Hiking with a woman friend, Ruth said "we both admitted we were not used to walking first in the trail, as when we were little we walked behind our brothers, and later behind our husbands." One time, John was injured on Mount Whitney, and Ruth reported, "I knew he must be in poor shape, when he 'let' me drive over the Angeles Crest. His idea is that I should have a nice straight stretch of highway like a beginner."

Ellen Wilts recalls that Ruth "wanted her Sierra Club and Alpine Club friends to see that she knew how to dress and look nice. I think she was driven to look anything but well-to-do. She was driven to excel in a man's world. She was driven to make a name for herself independent of John. She wanted to appear an above-average woman with interests of a lovely home and two bright children."

At age 59, Ruth told Vivian that her climbing life was "gradually dwindling away due to arthritis." In addition, she lived with considerable spinal pain. Later, she had both ankle joints surgically fused, to compensate for arthritic damage, procedures which put an end to her hiking life.

After John retired in 1978, he and Ruth moved to Seattle to live near her mother and her sisters. Ruth co-wrote another cookbook for backpackers, *Gorp, Glop and Glue Stew,* (Mountaineers Books, 1981). John continued to ski and climb. In 1983, they traveled with Vivian to the Tetons, to visit Valerie and her family; Valerie was working as a National Park Service law enforcement ranger. John and Vivian planned to climb Teewinot, but the night before, he suffered a stroke. Valerie drove the ambulance to the hospital in Jackson. John died in Seattle two weeks later.

Ruth Dyar Mendenhall died from an infection in 1989. While cleaning out Ruth's Seattle house, Vivian and Valerie found notes with Ruth's papers that made it clear she had meant to use these letters to write this book. Apparently she had begun rereading her old letters around 1970, for this purpose, and she discussed her plans for the book in 1971 with Vivian. Ruth left several introductory and concluding paragraphs for the book which never came to be:

Climbing used to be such fun, old climbers so good to new

ones, such enthusiasm. Climbing gave me adventure, a husband, an outlet, spice in my life, lifelong friends, scope. Now is a time of growth, specialization, foreign expeditions, and public interest in climbing. But then were the great beginnings, and the best climbing friends one could have had. Nowadays the climbers swarm over the earth–but in our heyday, the new routes, the unclimbed summits, lay closer at home, and perhaps were even harder to reach. Those were my high old times.

Would I like to do it all over again if I had a chance? Yes, if I could start when I did or even sooner. Heavenly days! Of course I would do it again. And in a way I have, reading my letters and writing this book.

Was I born 30 years too soon? Well, not really. Would I like to be young again and be one of today's top women climbers? In a way, of course–climbing days have been among the great days of my life. But still, those starting now cannot live the early days of roped climbing in the United States, the great days while the sport came of age in California, and California methods and equipment have spread all over the world. They cannot climb as I have with the rock climbing pioneers of California.
–V.M.C.

# Bear Creek Spire

Sequoia Dr., Pasadena, Calif.

July 9, 1969

*Dear Ma,*

I am home from the jury on my lunch hour. I have been serving now for six days, and have not been on a jury yet! The Superior Court in Pasadena seems extraordinarily dead. When I was on the jury in L.A. a few years ago, I was on a jury every single day, and it was fascinating. I consider it unhealthy to *sit* and breathe cigarette smoke all day long. At least there is no smoking in the courtrooms, just the assembly room. Anyhow, I have made some progress on my afghan (though not much).

We had a lovely July 4th weekend in the High Sierra. The R.C.S. had a trip scheduled in an area I had never been in, and John just once long ago—considerably farther north than where we usually go, so it was a long drive but a short backpack. The end of the road was at 10,500 feet, about 2,000 feet higher than the usual roadhead—so we did in the car what we usually do on foot. It couldn't have taken more than a couple of hours to walk in on a quite level trail that had once been an old mining road. The club had set up camp at the lower end of a beautiful lake, and we found ourselves a spot beside a tiny dashing stream, among rocks and Lodgepole pine trees somewhat stunted by the elevation. The peak which we (and a number of others) had in mind is called Bear Creek Spire, a fine-looking mountain but

*Bear Creek Spire from the Rock Creek drainage (Photo: Wynne Benti)*

not in the least spire-shaped from any angle I have ever seen it, 13,710 feet high.

We got up Saturday at the horrid hour of 4:40, when it was just getting light; had the usual nasty little climbing breakfast over the campfire; and were off across the frozen ground, icy swampy meadows, and snowfields before 6:00. The sun was already lighting the peaks, but we had a long gradual approach over the snow. As happens in the higher elevations where it takes so long for the snow to melt, it had formed dreadful sun-cups, a foot or more deep–one had to either step over the intervening ridges into the pits, or step on the slippery edges of the ridges themselves. This seemed to go on for hours, though the higher we got, the shallower the sun-cups, and eventually the snow softened up a little. Several groups were headed for "our peak," but they were either separated by some distance or bound for different routes.

It was nice to finally get on the rock, which was a very easy ridge at first, gradually getting steeper and steeper until we put on the rope, and then were puffing and panting at the elevation as we had more strenuous climbing. The beautiful blue polomoniums, that smell like honey and grow only above 12,000 feet in the rocks, grew all along the upper part. We got to the summit about 3:00 p.m. Four members of the Wilts family were just departing–Ellen hasn't climbed for a long time; they had their son, who is 20, and their youngest daughter, 16, with them.

When we came over the crest, the warm weather was blown away by a bitter wind on the west side, so we were not disposed to linger. However we had to climb the "summit block"–there are quite a number of mountains in the Sierra that have perhaps easy routes that are often climbed, but the very tip-top may be a smooth, not very easy, chunk of rock that many of the people do not climb at all since the registers are placed below the summit block. However, so far, we have always gone clear to the very tip-top.

After the first pitch, which we rappelled, the descent was merely a walk–though rather a long one! The lake was a long ways away. Others had trampled a path in the sun-cups. We came back into camp about 8:00 o'clock, and had the unusual and gratifying experience of having somebody give us each a cup of hot soup! *Nothing* ever tastes so good! This had a lot of noodles in it, which posed a problem when the liquid was gone. I noticed John eating his with his jackknife, but since my knife is almost impossible to open, I used a little piece of flat wood I found.

It was a quite cold evening, with a cutting wind, and we were very anxious to go to bed! We had brought our old tent which I made in Missouri in 1942, and which is really rotting to pieces, but we thought maybe it would last one more time. It seemed like home, with the familiar ridgeline inside where we have hung our wet socks through many a trip in the Canadian Rockies. After we had crawled into our sleeping bags, John lit the little gasoline stove, and we heated water and made cocoa. We accomplished this without either burning the tent down or spilling anything (probably because I made John pour). This tasted very good as did the many crackers we ate too. Then we threw everything we didn't want outside including the rocks we scratched the matches on. I remarked that I was going to sleep now; and turning on my side, I went to sleep–not always done as soon as said!

The evening we got back from our trip, Glen Dawson brought us twenty copies of our book to autograph–which seemed a chore for a minute; but then, as I said, *last* Fourth of July I stayed home and wrote the worst chapter in the book (Chapter III) so it was sort of nice to be signing the finished product this year.

I'd better quit, and put on my shoes and lipstick, so I can return to enforcing law and justice.

*Ruth*

# White Mountain

SEQUOIA DR., PASADENA, CALIF.

SEPTEMBER 6, 1969, SATURDAY NOON

DEAR VIVIAN,

Da is in Van Nuys inspecting his property, and I might as well write you a letter to tell about our Labor Day weekend before I forget all about it: our last 14,000 foot peak on the Pacific Coast.

We were supposed to go to the Palisades with the R.C.S., but Da had to go to a Structural Engineering Society committee meeting Friday night regarding a program on earthquakes he was involved in. I wasn't very surprised when he phoned about 10:00 p.m. saying it was just too late now. We went to bed too tired to care, and the next day we reorganized for a different kind of trip. I have been trying to induce Da (for at least two years) to go up White Mountain so we could finish off the 14,000-ers of the Pacific Coast; he never got very interested as it isn't really a "climb," and I was beginning to despair of ever getting there. However, I timidly suggested it as an alternative this time, and to my pleased surprise (after a long silence) he said Yes. So we went!

We really had a good time, and it was quite different from what we expected. First, as you may know, one drives into the desert mountains just east of Big Pine, and through the Bristlecone pine area that has become quite a fad in recent years. These trees are not unlike other wonderful timberline trees we see during our climbs

*White Mountain Peak (Photo: Wynne Benti)*

and backpacks, but are the only ones I know of that people can drive to. They apparently startled the botanical world in the 1950's when it was discovered the older ones run about 4,000 years old! In this particular place, at least, The Bristlecones grow on white dolomitic soil that doesn't support much else–*they* just like it! The atmosphere was *lovely*, so dry and cool. The views off to the Sierra were just wonderful–the Palisades were right opposite. We found Jim Gorin, whom we haven't seen for years–he had to give up climbing on the advice of his doctor, and is now bombing around in a red dune buggy he made on a VW body. Jim buzzed around and told us all the gossip, such as the fact the penguin-shaped gentleman who was monopolizing the Chief Ranger, was the president of the Audubon Society; it was rumored he wasn't looking at birds, just getting ready to write a book.

There is only one campground, below the Bristlecone area and miles away from the "end of the road," but we found we could sleep beyond the boundaries of the government area. A person is *supposed* to drive to the gate that shuts off the Naval experimental stations on the mountain, and then walk the 6 or 7 miles to the summit. However, we found we had taken the wrong car–the road had been fairly bad most of the day, and about 3 or 4 miles short of the gate became impossible for the station wagon. So, we decided we would have a LONG WALK. We parked well above timberline, with the pines below and strange whitish barren hills above. The ground there was so pretty. It was paved with colorful flat stones much like a stream bottom, all laced together with tiny dwarf plants–phlox, asters, daisies, sagebrush, rose-colored wild buckwheat–none more than an inch high at most.

Next morning we rose at Dawn, (chilly) and soon were off on our long, long walk. The road was a white dusty line looping over the hills, rising gradually, and only occasionally presenting switch backs. Sometimes we walked in the dusty ruts, sometimes in the–shall I say–Arctic-Alpine-Desert Tundra beside the road when it wasn't very rocky. Sometimes there were grassy meadows along the way, so pretty with the red or whitish grass shining in the early morning sun. We passed a round tumbling-in "stone corral." The views of the Sierra, with huge piles of white clouds above the bluish peaks, were wonderful. We walked and walked.

We passed the gate, and walked on. We were almost to the first Naval station (4 miles short of the peak) when we heard growling behind us, and saw a bright clean red-white-and-blue Chevron gas truck grumbling up the hills with much gear shifting. It stopped beside us, and the driver asked if we wanted a ride, so we climbed in, and rode to the bleak brown buildings of the Barcroft Naval Station, where the truck was disgorging the winter's supply of gas. Another truck was coming far behind, having more trouble on the hills, and behind it we noticed an orange VW station wagon. At the Naval Station, according to the gas truck driver, they are trying to put a person into hibernation and "even experiment on themselves." All we saw was a young man who came to a door, and we heard the rather out-of-place sound of a rooster's crow.

We walked. After awhile, what should draw alongside but the orange VW truck–the driver asking if we wanted a ride. We got in. What the gas trucks had achieved with five gears, it achieved with sheer momentum. The driver, a Sierra Club Desert Peaker, seemed to drive with a remarkable lack of worry about his car! He jounced wildly over the ruts and rocks, churned up hills, cheered himself on. He and his 11-year-old boy had been climbing other desert peaks further north, and when they reached this area he had suddenly noticed his gas tank was almost empty. He had been figuring up his two gallons of white gas when he caught up with the gas trucks. At the Naval depot he had asked if they had gas (rather than diesel fuel), and one of the drivers took his huge hose and squirted ten gallons of gas (free) into his tank. This was quite a find, 75 miles from the nearest gas station. It put him in quite a good mood.

When we were a mile or so from the actual peak, a 4-wheel-drive jeep coming from the peak's direction drew over and said we couldn't go much farther. True–there was an alarming downgrade, and after that the road is (this year) completely impassable. There is still snow on it, and we found the installation on top is abandoned at present. By this time, we were definitely all one party. The boy set off ahead (and was mountain sick on top for his pains); the men strolled along chatting; the lady (me) came along behind, not quite able to keep up. We had about a thousand feet to climb, perhaps a mile in distance, and were soon on the rather littered summit, where we had lunch; and saw a bird (which I thought was a Clark's Crow and the Desert Peaker thought was a sparrow), a mouse, and a sickly orange ladybug the color of salmon berries, with elongated brownish spots.

We had long-since been offered, and accepted, a ride back to our car. It was even wilder than the ride in (it was 9 miles long). The boy was turning pale and taking long breaths, and his father told him not to get carsick on the *up* grades where he couldn't stop. We jounced; everything inside the car was in frantic motion. Clothing, boxes, maps, flew all over. Something hit my head and fell on my lap–an alarm clock! After a bit, we began to wonder how we would get *out* of the locked gate–the fellow had come in after the gas trucks, and hadn't realized it was always locked. As we approached the Naval station, a Jeep pulled out and started downhill. The VW owner yelled, in his Massachusetts accent, "Serendipity! Good things happening as you go along." (I really knew the meaning of the word, but had never heard it used out loud.) However, much to our dismay, the Jeep did not stop for the gate, but made a sudden detour around it, through a rocky gully and along a hillside! We drew up. The men walked around to look. The boy said, "Daddy, don't try it." The man said, "We can't stay here all night." Alone in his little bus, he tried it, and did it–it looked very funny to see the little orange vehicle speed along the almost trackless hillside.

Back at the car at 1:00 p.m., after not so much a climb as a ridiculous adventure, a parody on a climb! We figured we had walked about 8 miles, and as my knees and feet weren't even tired (yet!) I guess I could have done the 20 all right; but was glad I didn't have to. The drive home was *hot*, and we got home about 9:00 o'clock, the car filthy with dust inside and out.

*With love,*

# Tahquitz

SEQUOIA DR., PASADENA, CALIF.
APRIL 25, 1970

DEAR VIV,

We went to the Tahquitz climb this weekend. I feared it might be a little early in the year, but Saturday was a truly lovely day. The woods still look a bit wintry, as the oaks have not leafed out at all, and there were little patches of snow in shady spots from the fall earlier in the week. There were big banks of old snow along the base of the cliffs, so we had to rope up to get to the first pitch on the Trough. The idea was to take a short, easy climb the first day–but there were two exceptionally slow ropes of beginners ahead of us, so we headed off across the From Bad Traverse–a nice climb that never gets you very far off the ground. It comes into the Maiden just below the piton pitch. We then climbed the Maiden below another slow rope. It was a gorgeous day, with the countryside spread out below in soft blues; the sun shining beneficently; little saxifrage plants already out in the cracks, but nothing else growing yet–actually, there was a good deal of snow in the cracks, but it didn't seem to be on the holds and made good eating with its peculiar sterile flavor of new snow. I don't know what I'll do when I get too decrepit to sit on belay ledges (or at least to get to them)–hire someone to haul me up a couple of pitches?

That evening, we went down to visit Bud Couch for a short time (we have tried before and couldn't find his house; even now, the

Physicist doesn't know his house number). The Kamps' were there–Bob was one of the trip leaders, and had two large paper signs saying LEADER pinned to his hat, which made him look rather like the Mad Hatter; also Michael, whom we had seen at the rock; and Mike Dent. The men related boyhood games that made rock climbing sound like a panty-waist sport.

Sunday morning seemed somewhat colder than the day before, and a wind had come up. We took off for the Finger-Tip, and Bill Dixon caught up with us. It was exceedingly cold on the rock. Being tired from the day before, and so cold besides, I had trouble with the layback. A couple of times in past years, I climbed the slab to the left instead; last time I found I couldn't do the slab so I did the layback; this time, I tried the slab again and just whizzed up. Up above, we sat for a long time on the belay spot below the Finger-Tip, while the first rope groped its way across. The wind was very high there.

I had sort of a vision of Truth when I started up the traverse–it suddenly looked to me like pure clean *rock,* in perfect focus, steep and smooth, without very good holds! I didn't think of looking at the Exposure while I was in such a clairvoyant mood, but quickly climbed on my way. We were anxious to finish the climb and find a spot out of the wind. We were nesting among some sheltering boulders at the top when Michael and Mike Dent came over from Jensen's Jaunt–they were soon down on the Mechanics Route. We had lunch, then walked down the back, and gradually wended our way home.

We stopped in Riverside to see Val, who was boning up for her final Masters Exam. She was, characteristically, sure she'd flunk.

*With love,*

# University Peak

SEQUOIA DR., PASADENA, CALIF.

JULY 7, 1970 — TUESDAY 10:30 A.M.

DEAR MA,

I haven't typed for so long that I can't even run my typewriter. John had a horrible cold which he had caught from his mother (who doesn't believe in germs). He had been looking forward to our July Fourth weekend for so long that he was determined to go anyway.

We got off during the evening Thursday, slept in the desert, and went on to the mountains next morning. We were bound for University Peak, 13,588 feet elevation, west of the town of Independence. The road goes to almost 9,200 feet, at a place called Onion Valley, and the backpack is around three or four miles, mostly on a good trail, past cascades and small lakes. We camped at a high lake called Bench Lake, where we found the perfect campsite on a very private knoll above a lovely little green lake, surrounded by high altitude pines of artistic twists and gnarls. Although the sky was overcast much of the time, it never actually rained till after we had left. Both being very tired, we went to bed and to sleep at 6:00 in the evening.

We had 3,000 feet to climb to reach the top of our mountain. We got up at 5:00 on Saturday, and soon were off on the rather easy, non-technical ascent.

This is the time of year when one finds the wonderful clusters of blue polemoniums in bloom between about 12,000 and 13,000 feet

*University Peak (Photo: Norman Clyde, eastern California Museum Collection)*

elevation. They blossom in their honey-scented loveliness on the most sterile and impossible-looking talus and scree slopes! There are other small high elevation flowers, but most are in a low cushiony form. The polemoniums grow a foot or more tall, and the luxuriant flowers are in clusters of light blue ranging to deep almost purple-blue.

At one point, as we were resting on a rock, we saw a coyote on a big snowfield below, dodging back and forth rapidly as if chasing either birds or small varmints. We were on top soon after noon, and had a good descent by sliding down many long snowfields. We achieved the ultimate in luxury by arriving back in camp by 4:30 in the afternoon. After tea, I felt quite rejuvenated, and had completely recovered from being tired *before* the trip.

Sunday morning we ate a large breakfast of bacon and eggs, and broke camp. We had seen very few people during the trip, rather odd for such an accessible spot on a three-day-weekend.

# Old Damnation

Sequoia Dr., Pasadena, Calif.

September 7, 1970—Labor Day

Dear Mother,

We got home late last evening, and are busy getting back into the swing of living. Our house looked nice, since I left it that way. I'll have to go to the store pretty soon, but thought I'd get a letter off to you to mail on the way.

We had a really nice vacation, quite varied. We had some good mountain weather, and some very poor. I figured I walked at least 35 miles, some backpacking, some hiking, some climbing–and saw some lovely country. We first backpacked into the Goodell Creek area, where the trail was so poor, and led to such prodigious bush-whacking before we could approach a peak, that we gave it up and went back.

Next, we picked out another area on a map that had a trail leading into an area where the lowest lake was called Thornton Lake. The trail appeared to have been designed by a man with a direct mind, as the upper part went straight up (sort of rock-climbing on dirt, with twigs for handholds) and then straight down to the lake. We might not have fully appreciated it if we hadn't been in such vilely thick brush before! We then made our way along the shores and up the intervening gullies of two more lakes, arriving at the upper one with a gasp of delight at what we saw: a virtually untouched Alpine lake, lying in a stupendous granite and snow cirque. Small floes floated in the water.

MERRY CHRISTMAS 1985
RUTH D. MENDENHALL

*Ruth in Morocco, 1985*

We camped in a lovely meadow that appeared mostly untouched by human beings–we found the old remains of one fire in the rocks. We put up our tent in the grass and sedges, and John built a fine fireplace in the old spot. There were quantities of wood from the timberline hemlocks, and many flowers. The most prolific and useful vegetation was the huckleberries, which were in their prime everywhere!

One day up there we spent resting; the night following, and the next day, it rained–so we put a day of snoozing and lying in our tent on top of the rest day. We reached a relaxed state of hibernation wherein we were able to sleep about sixteen hours out of twenty-four.

The day after that was gorgeously clear–and for once in my life, I was quite alert at 5:00 a.m. We made an easy climb of the one respectable peak accessible from the lakes, 6,900 feet, and called Damnation by Becky in his old guidebook. Since Damnation had been moved on the map to another lower peak, we called ours Old Damnation.

We had the most superlative view! Baker and Shuksan were to the west and northwest; the Pickets to the north and northeast; and in the southerly direction we saw a great line of glacier-draped rock peaks, and also the meringue-like mass of Glacier Peak. There were also long lines of smoke from the great forest fire that was raging in the Wenatchee National Forest. We returned to camp by walking along the top of the cirque, which was easy and very fascinating–over the granite, the snow, the little gullies covered with brilliant green moss just like velvet. It was fun to step on (when one had to), as one left a perfect green print of one's Brahmani boot soles. The many little north-facing gullies, wet from melting snow patches, were bright with a great variety of flowers.

Sunday morning the air was filled with acrid forest fire smoke. We packed out, and drove to the Cascade Pass region. We spent two days and two nights there. On each day, John got up early to take a whack at an 8,000 foot peak which I felt was too long for my creaking knees. I climbed the trail (twice, on successive days) to 5,300 foot Cascade Pass. It was the easiest trail in the world–thirty-five switchbacks, the numbers cut into logs at the turns, so you could amuse yourself with keeping track of where you were. Upon leaving the area, we had a wonderful dinner at a small cafe in the town of Marblemount. In fact, my Camp Appetite lasted all through the next few days while I was visiting–something I haven't had a chance at since the olden days in Spokane.

It poured rain all over the Northwest next day, and we drove to Seattle to visit the relatives. It was nice to see them all. We then settled down to our drive home. It was cool all the way, even in the California desert. We enjoyed the passing scene of forests and rivers, gradually changing to farmland and desert. It is a long time since I have made that pleasant drive.

*Valerie (age 1) and Ruth, Los Angeles, California, spring 1947*

## Epilogue
# Growing Up Afraid

In Jack Kerouac's *Dharma Bums,* Japhy Ryder says,

*"It's impossible to fall off a mountain you fool."*

Boy, was *he* ever wrong!

I called her Mama and never thought too much about her being a mountaineer. She called *herself* a housewife. At home she always wore a housedress and an apron. She washed and curled our hair, drove us to doctors and dentists and music lessons, made us hot Jell-O when we were sick, decorated our rooms, and tried (and completely failed) to make us clean our rooms. She sewed dresses for us and for our dolls. She arranged to have special soles put on our Buster Browns, so we wouldn't be pigeon-toed. she taped our lips shut at night, so we wouldn't be mouth-breathers. She fed our cats and changed their dirt-box. Before company dinners, she bought the food at Safeway, cooked it, polished the silverware and silver plate, cut and arranged flowers, and ironed the linen tablecloths that went underneath the lace ones. If anything broke–a toy, or the toilet–she fixed it. She tried to comfort us those times we hid from our father's anger. She helped with homework. She starched the petticoats we wore for Cotillion dances. She wore a suit, hat, high heels, and gloves, to attend meetings for the PTA, the Structural Engineers' Association Ladies' Auxiliary, and the Sierra Club. She typed our school reports when we ran out of time. She read aloud to us every evening until we each went away to college. My parents' trips to Canada and their occasional disappearances into the Sierra Nevada were a mystery to which I paid little attention. Sure, I knew that my mother climbed: but what I knew about climbing (even though I climbed, too) was mainly that it was terrifying and perfectly insane.

Vivian and I were playing house with our family of little plastice dolls (whose names were Mother, Father, Sister, and Brother) in a shallow stream, while our parents climbed in Rubio Canyon. I think we were 8 and 5 years old. If Ruth wrote a letter about the accident, she did not set it aside with the other letters for this book. John was leading over a block of granite the size of a kitchen stove, when the block came loose. Ruth yelled, "Children, *run!*" As we had been taught, we ran in to the base of the cliff, while the percussive sounds of rock-fall filled the canyon, along with the bitter smells of broken rock and crushed bay leaves. Ruth, the belayer, was yanked upwards against her anchor piton. John cracked a rib. We figured they were dead and we were next.

Decades later (1985), Ruth responded to a request for information about past rock-climbing accidents: "Regarding your recent letter asking about rock-climbing accidents and safety, I climbed from 1938 till about 1972, but not in recent years. In my thirty-five seasons of climbing with the RCS I never experienced an accident or even saw one happen with my own eyes." Excluding their personal trips, perhaps Ruth had never seen or experienced an accident on an officially sanctioned RCS trip, but she knew that they happened. Perhaps "accident" was just a normal event to Ruth, or, as John once said, "We had a few close shaves, but that's to be expected."

Vivian and I were taken to see the movie *White Hell of Pitz Palu* (the German or Italian version). I must have been 5 or 6, because I was too young to read the subtitles. Our parents were all excited about what a fine treat this would be. Ruth reported that "Hitler's girlfriend, Leni Riefenstal, was the heroine. It was a real wonderful picture. It was 100% climbing, and quite grim at that, so I naturally enjoyed it." Vivian remembers that the film "left an immense impression on me." What I remember–or think I remember–is one climber holding the frayed end of a broken rope, while his or her spouse's broken body bounces away into the black and white abyss.

One time I asked Mama what would happen to us, if they never came back from a trip. She said, "Aunty Al and Uncle Phil will be your legal guardians." I did *not* want to be part of that family, in which the boys tortured me, the aunt humiliated me in public, and their house wasn't as nice as ours.

After my mother died, I found, among her mountaineering papers, a wrinkled scrap of paper torn from a larger piece, bearing a penciled note in my father's handwriting: "Sat. June 6. Will attempt N. Face Williamson. Probably by couloir just west of 14,211. From Symmes Pass to North, this suggests a Y, vaguely." Below is his little drawing of the route. On the back, in my mother's writing, it says "Cats. Commissary. Cereal." I believe this piece of paper was left in or near their tent, in case somebody had to come looking for them.

Vivian remembers that on the Friday night in 1957 when our parents were leaving for Mount Williamson, "Ruth wrote a page describing exactly where they were going . . . she put it in a *sealed envelope,* and told me to open it only if they didn't return. Other parties were also about to try for that first ascent, and Ruth didn't want word to get out." Vivian was 14 at the time.

Not long ago, a friend of mine asked if I ever felt that my parents had abandoned me, when they went away to the mountains all those times (starting when I was just a baby). I didn't know how to answer. It was just normal–that was the way things were. In fact, I had no idea until I was writing the introduction to Chapter 5 of this book, that my parents had gone on *so many* expeditions to the Canadian Rockies. Now that I have been a mother myself, I think my parents' leaving me so often and for so long with other people . . . cold.

Here is a letter I wrote to Vivian when I was 16: "We packed in 9 miles up Milk Creek yesterday, Wednesday, with the intention of climbing Glacier Peak. It *rained.* Drip, drip, drip. Ugh. The trail was, for the most part, thru dense forest–very beautiful. Last 2 miles were thru dense, dense thick, numerous, omnipresent, *weeds*–up to one's neck and higher. Hard going. Had a H___ of a time with the fire (when we got there) but finally Ma got it going.

"This morning it had stopped raining, but it was *foggy*, so we came out late afternoon. Got a glimpse of the peak, tho–*very* beautiful. It has lots more rock (bare) than the other volcanoes. Also a huge glacier all full of crevasses and icefall. The trail back was *LONG* and I got many blisters–several of which popped.

"But maybe all the agony was worth it, as I am firmly ensconced by the fireside, and cannot walk–therefore cannot *WORK!!* Hooray–these parents work you like slave drivers–'Get the water' 'I need more firewood' 'Put up the tent' 'Wash the dishes' 'Brush your teeth.' I could go on forever. We'll drive out tomorrow, with the intention of going to a motel and seeing a movie. Goodie."

My parents took me up my first roped climb, the Trough at Tahquitz, when I was about 5 years old. This is an easy roped climb of half a dozen pitches which the *Climber's Guide* says is "an ideal introduction to climbing for the dubious beginner." Believe me, I was more than "dubious." I was stark staring horrified at the exposure, and I cried from start to finish, which made both my parents extremely angry with me. To this day, I suffer from an abnormal fear of heights. Nevertheless, I kept on climbing throughout high school and college, sometimes going on long solo climbs where I ought to have been roped. I spent summers in Yosemite Valley. I married Michael Cohen (who in his teens climbed with the Sierra Club at Stoney Point, then later climbed El Capitan, and mountains in Alaska and Afghanistan). For a while I kept on climbing with him, still crying from start to finish. Why? Because climbing was what my friends did, and I was good at it. I didn't know what else to do. One summer day when I was in my early twenties, sitting on a beach beside the Merced River in Yosemite, I told Chuck Pratt how scared I was. He told me I had two choices: I could lead and fall and learn to trust the rope, or else I could quit climbing. The very next day, I took my sketch pad and ink pens, and hiked to the top of Yosemite Falls. I drew some pictures of purple flowers, and had a can of Deviled Ham for lunch. Now, *that* was a perfect day! Michael and I still climb lots of mountains, but only the nice kind that you can walk up and you can't fall off.

So. As soon as I got married, at the age of 22, I never used "Mendenhall" for my middle name (until I started work on this book, so as not to confuse anybody!). It was a relief, particularly at first, to be rid of that too-identifiable name. Even now, I meet people who knew and admired my parents; they say how lucky I was, to grow up in the Mendenhall family and get to do all that climbing. Yes . . . but I believe it is important for me to say there was a downside to it, too. Climbing took precedence over most of the things *I* wanted to do, such as art or music lessons. And there is always that troublesome question for any parent: am I teaching my child something necessary and beautiful, or am I making my child live *my* life?

I will say that I learned many good things from my parents. I always know where North is, and will never get lost (at least, not for very long). I know how to tie a bowline, pick a route, and start a fire in the rain. Now I paint watercolor landscapes. I am a good enough skier. I feel stronger and safer in the mountains than anywhere else, even inside my own home.

I will say that the single most important thing Mama ever taught me was this: "If you ever think you need a rope, ask for one. Just sit down and don't move until somebody gives you a rope."
    —*Valerie Mendenhall Cohen*

# Appendices

## APPENDIX A:
## RECIPIENTS OF RUTH DYAR MENDENHALL'S LETTERS

*Elsie Josephine Kiesling (Dyar).* 1887-1981. Mother ("Ma," "Ma'," "Maw"). Spokane, WA.

*Ralph Emerson Dyar.* 1884-1955. Father ("Fa," "Fa'," "Pa," "Paw," "Daddy"). Author and newspaperman, Spokane, WA.

*Conrad Emerson Dyar.* 1910-1965. Brother ("Con," "Constantine"). Chemist. Married Janet Palmer Olson. Port Angeles, WA.

*Joan Wilhelmina Dyar (Clark).* (1915-?) Sister ("Judpud"). Musician, Married Nathan C. Clark. Los Angeles, CA.

*Alice Mary Dyar (Bier).* 1917-1996. Sister ("Al," "Eloit"). Married Philip N. Bier. Seattle, WA

*Margaret Thekla Dyar (Ashworth).* 1920-2001. Sister. PhD Bacteriology, college chemistry teacher. Married Paul Ashworth 1952, widowed 1955. Bremerton, WA.

*Vivian Margaret Mendenhall.* 1943- . Daughter ("Viv" ). PhD Zoology, Wildlife Biologist, U.S. Fish and Wildlife Service. Married Jim Johnston. Anchorage, AK.

*"Schmickface"* cannot be identified.

## APPENDIX B: WHO'S WHO

*Applewhite, Adrienne.* Children's author, one of the first women to climb the East Face of Mount Whitney, married Dick Jones.

*Austin, Spencer.* Photographer, wrote  article about the Bugaboos for the *Sierra Club Bulletin* (1938)

*Bauwens, George Otto Paul.* German skier, made early winter ascents of Mount Baldy, taught engineering at USC, built three ski huts and chaired Ski Mountaineers Section. Married Emily, ran a motel in Glendale, Utah, in the 1950s.

*Blakeman, Seth.* Member of UCLA's Ski and Ice Hockey Teams, Navy Pilot in WWII.

*Brinton, Robert (Bob).*  Professor of Chemistry at UC Davis, civilian expert for the military in WWII, married Mary Mies of Davis, CA.

*Bryan, Ingeborg (Inky).*  Radio singer, good skier.

*Cohen, Michael Peter.*  Yosemite climber, mountaineer, skier. Environmental Historian (titles include The *History of the Sierra Club* and *Pathless Way: John Muir and American Wilderness*).  Climbed Snow Creek on Mount San Jacinto with John Mendenhall, December, 1967, to prove he would be a worthy son-in-law.  Married Valerie Mendenhall 1968.

*Cohen, Valerie Patricia (Mendenhall).*  Ex-climber, ex-Park Service Ranger, watercolor artist and illustrator, environmental activist, Reno, Nevada.

*Dawson, Glen.*  Antiquarian bookseller, UCLA Ski Team, first ascents of Thunderbolt Peak and Mount Whitney's East Face and East Buttress.  Sierra Club Director 1937-1951 except for two years with the Tenth Mountain Division.  Married Mary Helen Johnson.  Lives in Pasadena, CA.

*Dawson, Muir.*  Brother and partner of Glen Dawson, champion skier, first ascent of Mount Whitney's East Buttress, married Agnes Cloud.

*Dawson, Mary Helen Johnson.*  Musician (Pasadena Philharmonic), helped edit *Mugelnoos* during WWII.

*Estes, Paul.*  Member of Rock Climbing Section.

*Fair, Agnes.*  Robert Brinton's first wife, returned to Alaska.

*Falconer, Phil.*  Accordionist from San Diego.

*Fuller, Homer.*  Member of UCLA's hockey team, good skier, worked for Associated Oil Co. in Los Angeles.  First ascent of Mount Whitney's East Buttress and Zion's East Temple.

*Gates, Howard S. (Gatesy).*  Hiked John Muir Trail 1933 via all the 14,000 foot summits.  Joined Ski Mountaineers 1936.  Nature photographer, led countless Angeles Chapter trips, largest financial contributor to ski huts.

*Gilbert, Wayland.*  Older than most Ski Mountaineers, donated mimeograph machine for Mugelnoos.

*Gorin, Jim.*  Noted one-legged rock-climber, taught rock-climbing.

*Gorin, Roy.*  Brother of Jim Gorin, taught rock-climbing, married DeDe Cartwright.

*Henderson, Randall.*  Founded *Desert Magazine* in 1937.  Publisher of *Calexico Chronicle*, author of books on exploring Southwest deserts, helped found Desert Protection League in 1954, Honorary Vice President of Sierra

Club, lives in Palm Desert.

*Henderson, Rand.* Son of Randall Henderson. Enlisted in the Marines at beginning of WWII, killed in action on Saipan, July 7, 1944.

*Harrer, Heinrich.* Austrian mountain-climber, first ascent of the Eiger in the Swiss Alps, 1939. Escaped from prison camp in 1944 and slipped into the forbidden city of Lhasa, tutored the Dalai Lama, wrote *Seven Years in Tibet.*

*Hennies, Walter.* Expert mechanic, retained a German accent, married Helen, retired to Visalia, CA.

*Ingwersen, Ray.* Accountant for Board of Equalization, retired to Joshua Tree.

*Jensen, Carl.* Medical doctor at Los Angeles General Hospital.

*Johnson, Arthur B. (Art).* First Chairman of Rock Climbing Section, conservation activist, Sierra Club Director 1951-1953.

*Jones, Richard M. (Jonesy).* Glen Dawson's best boyhood friend, worked for Dawson's father at Dawson's Book Shop. First ascent of Mount Whitney's East Face, lead first ascent of Mechanic's Route at Tahquitz, worked at North American Aviation during WWII, retired to Laguna Nigel, CA.

*Koster, Howard.* Worked for Los Angeles County Building Department, Chairman of Rock Climbing Section, first ascent of Mount Whitney's East Buttress.

*Mendenhall, Vivian Margaret.* PhD Zoology, Wildlife Biologist, U.S. Fish and Wildlife Service, Anchorage, AK.

*Merritt, Fuzz.* Pomona College football coach, placed first portable rope tow at Baldy Ski Hut.

*Merritt, Jack.* Son of Fuzz Merritt, member of Ski Mountaineers.

*Momyer, Joe.* Worked for San Bernardino Post Office, leader in protecting San Gorgonio Wilderness Area.

*Pratt, Chuck.* Yosemite first ascent routes include South Face of Mount Watkins, and the North America and Salathé Walls of El Capitan. Died 2000.

*Rice, Bill.* Joined Ski Mountaineers and Rock Climbing Sections 1935, PhD in History. Killed at age 27 with Dr. Clyde V. Nelson, Jr., Grand Teton, 1942.

*Rice, Sophie.* Sister of Bill Rice. Joined Rock Climbing Section 1937.

*Robbins, Royal.* Key player in Yosemite's "Golden Age"of climbing during the 1960s. First ascent of Northwest Face of Half Dome and of the three great faces on El Capitan. With wife, Liz Robbins, founded the Royal Robbins Company, which makes outdoor and travel clothing.

*Ruth descending below critical vertical pitch, Black Buttress, Strawberry Peak, June, 1940*

***Russell, Elizabeth*** (surnames Lewis, Sprang, King). Ruth Dyar's Cousin. Artist.

***Russell, Phoebe*** (surnames Finkleson, Sumner). Elizabeth Russell's sister.

***Sherrick, Mike.*** Hospital Clinical Engineering Technician, married Natalie Sherrick, lives in Sparks, NV.

***Smith, James N.*** ("Jim"). Discovered Tahquitz Rock as a climbing area. Electrical engineer from Cal Tech, worked for Vultee Aviation. Architect.

***Templeton, George.*** From Fontana, CA, joined Rock Climbing Section 1938, meteorologist for Air Corps during World War II, New York and Cal Tech.

***Wallace, Earl.*** Enthusiastic skier, older than most Ski Mountaineers.

***Wallace, Bill.*** Credit and office manager for Albers Brothers Milling Co.

***Wicks, Ren (Renny).*** Los Angeles area commerical artist, especially famed for his aeronautical illustrations. Ruth Mendenhall said that Wicks was "a frightfully good skier, formerly of the German Olympic team."

***Wicks, Tim.*** Renny Wicks' brother.

***Wilts, Chuck.*** Professor of Applied Physics and Electrical Physics, Cal Tech. Climbed the Finger Tip Traverse at Tahquitz with Glen Dawson, Chuck's first Tahquitz climb and Glen's last. Wrote *A Climber's Guide to Tahquitz Rock.*

***Wilts, Ellen Beaumont.*** First ascent routes in Yosemite (Traverses of Leaning Tower and Matthes Crest, Rixon's Pinnacle), Tahquitz (Orange Peel, Sling Swing Traverse, Lark and West Lark, Piton Pooper first free ascent), and several new routes in Canada's Gong Lake area. Lives in Pasadena, CA.

## APPENDIX C: CLIMBING EQUIPMENT

In the 1930s, climbers mail-ordered steel tools from Sporthaus Schuster in Munich. REI (Recreational Equipment, Incorporated) was established in Seattle in 1938 as a consumer cooperative to purchase equipment from Europe; REI began to sell Army Surplus equipment after World War II. Equipment was more widely available in American sporting goods stores by the early 1960s.

### ROPES

Francis Farquhar of the Sierra Club, and Robert L. M. Underhill of the Appalachian Mountain Club, instructed Club members in proper use of ropes in 1931. Thereafter, Sierra Club climbers taught safe belaying to countless people, and raised belay standards for technical climbing. In 1938, the Rock Climbing Section of the Sierra Club (Angeles Chapter) used funds from trail fees to purchase 440 feet of 7/16-inch manila hemp rope, the "best yachting line available," as well as 200 feet of 5/16-inch rope for rappelling (at that time, people never rappelled on their climbing ropes). At an official "rope-cutting party" in somebody's driveway, the long rope was cut into two 90-foot two-man ropes and two 130-foot three-man ropes. Each rope's middle was marked with paint. Anybody who ever climbed with manila ropes will not soon forget how they prickled the skin of one's waist, and how they tangled. In 1940, Ruth wrote, "We went off to the Washington Column, and climbed a few pitches, and then sat on the trunk of an ant-infested tree (an amazing number of ants live on that climb), and had a terrible tussle with our rappel rope which had (in the malicious way of ropes) tied itself into the most incomprehensible snarl of knots and twists, despite the careful way in which it had been coiled. Eventually the horrid thing was unkinked, and we roped down into the dusk." Ruth and John brought newspaper along on climbs, to protect the rappel rope from being cut by sharp edges of rock.

Nylon ropes were introduced in the United States in the 1940s by Richard Leonard. Stronger, stretchable Gold Line ropes (laid, twisted) were developed during World War II. Sheathed Perlon ropes came to the United States from Europe in the early 1960s.

Heat caused by friction in rappelling required a leather patch on pants and shoulder, although people without patches made do by stuffing extra clothes into their pants, and tying a knapsack over one shoulder. Sewing the leather patches onto pants tended to break sewing machine needles, so the task was usually finished by hand.

## PITONS

In 1938, the Rock Climbing Section possessed 20 pitons and 6 steel carabiners. Ruth's sisters gave her a piton hammer for Christmas, of which she said, "objectively speaking, it is not a dainty female gift from sister to sister–but it is lovely. It is such a gorgeous tool, indubitably handmade, and just fits me." Then she discovered how much hard work it was, to hammer a piton into a crack, or to remove one, while standing on the smallest of ledges.

Soft iron pitons imported from Germany became distorted through repeated use, and then were hammered flat again, "good as ever." In 1939, Howard Koster arranged for an ornamental ironworks company to manufacture pitons. Chrome-molybdenum steel pitons were first used by John Salathé in about 1948, and Chuck Wilts made the first knife blade pitons in the early to mid 1950s. Yvon Chouinard began forging chrome-moly pitons in 1957 (he went on to found the outdoor clothing company, Patagonia).

## SHOES

Ruth began rock-climbing with high topped, crepe soled girls' tennis shoes, which she bought for $1.80 a pair at the May Company department store. She discovered that they wore out after three climbs, while the men's shoes lasted much longer, but wouldn't fit her feet. German "Kluttershoe" replaced tennis shoes about 1956. Mixed climbing was done in leather boots that had Tricouni nails in their soles; unlike crepe soles, the nails grated horribly on the rock, but worked better than crampons when a climber frequently changed from snow to rock (John used to nail his own boots with Swiss edge nails). Lug-soled climbing boots were used for mixed rock, snow, and ice on high peaks, such as in Canada.

## SNOW AND ICE

Crampons, also called climbing irons, were fastened with webbing straps to boot soles for ice climbing. In 1939, Ruth borrowed a pair from Muir Dawson, and John sharpened their spikes on a hand-turned grindstone "till the sparks shot off the good steel of the Austrian crampons like Fourth of July sparklers." Long-handled ice axes were acquired from Europe. Short-handled axes became the norm in the late 1960s, although the Mendenhalls never used these.

Skiing in the early 20th Century was done with Nordic or "free heel" equipment (boot mounted to ski only at the toe), and that was what was used in the very first Winter Olympics in 1934. Alpine gear (boot mounted at both heel and toe) was not seen in the Olympics until 1936. Skis were long (measured from the floor, to the palm of one's up-stretched hand) and made of hickory; their tops were impregnated with hot linseed oil, their bottoms shellacked, then waxed with paraffin, hard wax, or klister. One could buy skis with metal edges, or else insert one's own stainless steel strips. For climbing up long mountain slopes, strips of sealskin or canvas were attached to the bottom surfaces. Loose leather ski boots were treated with grease, and required two or three pairs of socks to keep the feet warm.

Ruth encountered her first rope tows in 1947, at Norden Lodge near Donner Summit, which is west on present-day I-80 from Reno, Nevada. She reported that the tows were "terrible contraptions that are terrifying and exhausting. At least I found out that when one fell on them, nothing happened, nobody trampled one to death!"

## PACKS

Ruth and John made their own rucksacks out of heavy canvas, "at the expense of breaking several sewing machine needles," and attached the straps with hand-hammered rivets. Ruth repaired the "heavy smelly oiled canvas" knapsacks on her in-laws' Free treadle sewing machine. Backpacking loads were strapped to wooden Trapper Nelson pack boards, "tortuous for neck and shoulders." John was known to carry packs weighing more than 90 pounds (sixty percent of his body weight). In such circumstances, he added a tumpline across his forehead. Kelty's first lightweight pack frames came out in 1953. "Valerie had a new pack board–she has been hankering for one of these light aluminum Kelty frames that are so popular with backpackers now; and when she found out that her parents weren't planning to buy her one (they are very expensive), she went out and baby-sat afternoon after afternoon all summer, and saved up her allowance, until she had the $18 to buy herself one."

## TENTS

In 1942, Ruth sewed a tent. "As a tent, it is small; but as something to make, it is enormous! The idea is to have a tiny but very weather-proof tent to carry into the mountains with one. It seems much more three-dimensional than clothing, and so geometrical besides! John laid out the pattern on the 10 yards of cloth (which doesn't include the two floors, one waterproof and one percale)." It took her at least three months to make the tent. "Our tent poles, while doubtless the only ones of their kind in the world, are very efficient and wonderful now, and weigh almost nothing." Twenty-seven years later, that tent went to Bear Creek Spire: "We had brought our old tent which I made in Missouri in 1942, and which is really rotting to pieces, but we thought maybe it would last one more time."

## SLEEPING BAGS

Ruth sewed her own sleeping bag in 1938. Later, Army Surplus bags were available–the shafts of their feathers poked the sleeper awake all night, and the Army bags smelled oppressively of something like creosote (an odor which also pervaded the canvas covers, and the water inside, of Army surplus metal canteens). Eddie Bauer Company was founded in Seattle, producing the first down insulated garment in 1936; the company outfitted the Army Air Corp., and the 1953 American K-2 Himalayan expedition. Eddie Bauer's first mail order catalog came out in 1945. The Mendenhalls never owned down jackets, but did mail order down bags around 1958; Eddie Bauer sold square-ended bags with an optional hood that created a mummy-style closure for additional warmth, starting in 1958 at $36.95 plus $7.95 for the hood.

## CLOTHES

"It never rains at night in the Sierra Nevada," so goes the old saying. The saying is not perfectly true, and the weather on skiing trips, and in the Canadian Rockies, certainly required impermeable outer garments. In 1940, Ruth reported that waterproofing ski clothes turned her kitchen into a "most foul tropical hellhole.... The waterproofing element is Aridex, which we buy at Wallis-Rice in a fruit jar, a milky gummy stuff which is mixed up with one part Aridex to twenty parts water and a dash of vinegar. We don't see how waterproofing is soluble in water, but it is. I hung the garments up dripping sloppily on a line I draped about through the kitchen. Then I turned on the oven and two gas burners full blast."

Long underwear was made of wool: it itched and bit like red ants. Early in her career, Ruth carried flannel pajamas to wear while camping, though it was not always possible to change into them. "Never let it be said that I went to bed without my pajamas–I put them on top of all my other clothes. It is so sort of indelicate to go to bed with your clothes on, but it is easy to get dressed in the morning." Ruth sewed her own red plaid wool mountain shirts. "One has to have one, and my old one is just in shreds after about its seventh year, which is no wonder."

Female climbers in the Alps and the eastern United States wore skirts until the 1920s or even the 1930s (though Ruth always climbed in pants–even after a landlady evicted her for the immoral act of wearing coveralls for a hike in 1936). After World War II, climbers luxuriated in being able to buy Army Surplus parkas with fur around the hoods, and "GI ski pants that make such wonderful climbing pants because of the comfortable cut, tough cloth, and generous pockets." It must be recorded that Valerie Mendenhall, outfitted with GI pants as a teenager, found the "comfortable cut" and "generous pockets" a source of unspeakable embarrassment, and might well have preferred shorts, jeans, skirts, anything!

At age 4, Valerie "announced early in the morning, to my horror, that she was going to help me all day–I gave her some of our camp clothes to carry in from the garage. The next trip, she remarked, "I want to help you with something that doesn't smell. Everything left over from your trip smells."

## FOOD

Backpackers cooked on wood fires, whose smoke on a windy day made them "gag and weep," or, above timberline, on Sterno, a flammable hydrocarbon jelly packaged in a small can. A 2 1/2 ounce can burns for 45 minutes. The manufacturer sternly advises people not to drink their product. Sterno was a weak source of heat, and worked better if supplemented with dry pine needles. In 1938, Howard Koster got a "wonderful little Primus stove, a minute thing about 4 inches square and 6 inches high, operated on gasoline, which heats things in an instant." Cooking on a Primus stove on a very windy day might result in a "bitter struggle" and lukewarm food, but these little Swedish stoves are generally extremely efficient, durable, and cheap. The Primus company outfitted early polar expeditions. The technology for fueling camp stoves with bottled liquid propane existed in 1938, but it wasn't until the 1950s that Primus sold LP stoves (LP stoves still don't work well in cold conditions).

Some lightweight dried foods were available in grocery stores, such as powdered milk, packaged soup mixes, instant potatoes, vermicelli, and vegetable flakes. Ruth dehydrated food at home, such as fruit, and she parched rice so it would cook faster at altitude. (Raffi Bedayn was one of the first people to produce dehydrated food for backpackers.) Climbing breakfasts were hot or cold cereal with stewed fruit. Lunches included bread, cheese, sausage, raisins, nuts, the eternal supply of rye-crisp, lemon drops and chocolate. In addition to soup for dinner, and noodles or instant potato, there were cans of tuna or corned beef hash, and Jell-O or instant pudding mixes for dessert. Ruth's 1944 commissary for nine days in the Tetons weighed over 30 pounds (one and a half pounds per person, per day). Four climbers attempting Mount Robson in 1954 (an eight day trip) needed 70 pounds of food (a little over 2 pounds per person per day). Ruth wrote down every meal eaten during every mountain trip (and nearly every meal cooked at home), and saved some commissary plans.

## APPENDIX D:
## NOTABLE FIRST ASCENTS BY RUTH AND JOHN MENDENHALL

### SIERRA NEVADA AND EASTERN CALIFORNIA
Mount Sill, Swiss Arete (1938)
Whitney 3rd Needle (1939)
Temple Crag North Peak (1940)
Monument Peak (1940)
Mount Whitney, Southeast Buttress (1941)
Lower Cathedral Spire, Yosemite (1948)
Palisades Crest (routes, or entirely new?) (1954)
Williamson, North Face (1957)
Mt. Mendenhall (12,277-ft.) named for John Mendenhall

### SOUTHERN CALIFORNIA
Sierra Madre, Strawberry Peak (3+ routes) (1939)
Tahquitz, Traitor Horn (1st female?) (1939)
Tahquitz, Mummy Crack (1939)

### WYOMING
Tetons, Teewinot North Face (1944)

### CANADA
Mt. Confederation (1947)
Mt. Lowell North Peak (1948)
Aiguille Peak (1952)
Mt. Synge (1952)
Midway Peak (1952)
Mt. Palmer (1953)
Great Rock Tower (1953)
Mt. Temple Northwest Ridge (1957)

## APPENDIX E:
## HOW THIS BOOK WAS MADE

### LETTERS

Virginia Woolf (whose father was the noted British alpinist Leslie Stephen) was a "compulsive letter-writer," according to her editor; Woolf corresponded in order to ward off loneliness, to bind her friends to her, and to practice writing. Ruth Mendenhall, likewise, was a "compulsive" correspondent who wrote thousands and thousands of letters (with carbon copies) during her lifetime. I assume that she wrote in order to attach her parents and siblings to her, to give importance to her own days, to practice writing, and to create a record of mountain-climbs that she hoped would one day become a book.

Ruth's father encouraged her to write a climbing book as early as 1939, and doubtless that idea influenced the kind of letters she wrote: meticulously detailed, yet also personal and animated, in a way quite different from the formal, even stilted, style that Ruth adopted when writing for publication. I know Ruth would have thought it more than a bit unseemly–actually, downright unthinkable!–to print her own letters verbatim, as they appear in this book.

I discussed the tricky matter of editing one's mother's letters with the historian Richard White, who has written a book about his own mother. He says, "Your mother's letters are letters in the eighteenth century sense: they are a kind of public self-presentation, written with the knowledge, or at least the hope, that they would be read by people other than those to whom they are addressed. She puts in nothing that would subvert her own version of events. This can be purposeful, like a White House press briefing, or it can be because she sanitizes things not just for herself but for others. . . . You have memory (yours) subverting documents." Ruth was well aware of her own self-editing: "of course what I wrote to my parents was already censored to begin with."

–V.M.C.

# A BOOK NOT WRITTEN

Ruth began to reread her old letters late in life, with the intention of writing a book that would be both "a History of roped climbing" and "a personal climbing account ... edited, of course." She said she had "forgotten much of what is in these letters, yet they graphically remind me of some of it, and I believe the rest, so it is sort of like reading a series of novels in which I am the heroine. Naturally this is intriguing. Maybe it is more like having a sort of verbal journey back into the Past.... I really didn't remember I wrote all that. I also want my book to be entertaining and funny–few climbers seem to write in a way that the fun of it all comes through." She planned first to send an outline and sample chapters to Stackpole Books, as her contract required, but she never did.

Vivian says, "I did get the impression that after Daddy died, she lost heart in the project." I myself never heard about Ruth's book plans in the first place, and I don't know why she did not write it. I nearly didn't, either: for fourteen years after she died, I missed my mother too much to want to hear her written voice (moreover, I didn't want to know what my mother might have said about me, and I most certainly did not want to read about all that creepy rock-climbing!). At last, however, I decided that Ruth's lovely writing deserved to be published.

When Vivian and I were cleaning out our late mother's house in Seattle, we found stacks of manuscript boxes containing carbons of her life's letters. The fuzzy type is on both sides of translucent onionskin, much of it Depression or wartime paper that crumbles to the touch; the paper is beige, brown, or pink. Some of these pages were fourth or fifth carbons and can scarcely be read even with a magnifying glass; worse, Ruth used each sheet of carbon paper until it was limp as Kleenex and punched full of holes. Numerous marginalia are typed sideways, or added in pencil or fountain pen. She never owned an electric typewriter, and certainly not a computer.
–V.M.C.

*These original Mendenhall papers are housed at UCLA's Charles E. Young Research Library, Department of Special Collections, Sierra Club Angeles Chapter Records.*

# INDEX